The Union of 1707

New Dimensions

Edited by

Stewart J. Brown and Christopher A. Whatley

Edinburgh University Press for The Scottish Historical
Review Trust

© The Historical Review Trust, 2008

Edinburgh University Press Ltd
22 George Square, Edinburgh

Typeset in New Baskerville
by SR Nova Pvt Ltd, Bangalore, India, and
printed and bound in Great Britain by Page Bros, Norwich.

This issue was funded by the Scottish Historical Review Trust.

A CIP record for this book is available from the British Library

ISBN 978 0 7486 3802 4

CONTENTS

Preface

Notwithstanding the significance of the Union of 1707 for Scotland's history, and indeed for that of the United Kingdom, we became aware towards the end of 2005 that plans to mark the event were few in number and that, in the main, those planned looked to be low-key affairs. Perhaps this said something about the uncertainty at government level in Scotland and in London about how to handle an anniversary that might provoke unwanted reactions. Four years earlier, fingers had been burnt in the heat generated by the political posturing and attempts by the competing parties to make political capital from the four hundredth anniversary of the Union of the Crowns. The anniversary of the parliamentary Union might prove far more contentious. Was the parliamentary Union of 1707 to be celebrated as one of the building blocks of British-ness, or was it to be recalled and condemned as imposing a yoke from which the Scots should now break free? Not surprisingly, organisers of official events linked to 1707 tread warily in their anxiety not to offend present-day political sensitivities. Some publishers, to be sure, were less cautious, and vied to promote the distinctiveness of their authors' views on the Union, especially where these had a contemporary resonance. The media too sought to arouse interest in and stir public debate on the subject. But the overall response to the Union of 1707 seemed muted and guarded.

We were also concerned that the three hundredth anniversary of the Union might be something of a damp squib as far as the academic community was concerned, and that the questions of what actually happened in 1707, and why, might become incidental to the debates over the status and future of the Union in 2007. We were aware of the publishing plans of established historians whose views on the Union were already known, or were more or less predictable from articles and shorter pieces in which they had given notice of the positions they were likely to adopt – although in the event there have been some significant surprises in what has been a bumper period for the publication of Union-related work. What we envisaged in 2005 was a conference or symposium that would invite fresh thinking on 1707, and that would preferably – but not necessarily – be delivered by scholars who were at earlier stages of their careers.

The outline conference proposal was put to the Royal Society of Edinburgh. The subject, we believed, was sufficiently important to merit the attention of Scotland's national academy for the arts and sciences. Happily, the Royal Society took a similar view, and agreed to host and help support a one-day conference, to be held on 18 May 2007. (Our conference would, in the event, occur just two weeks after what turned out to be a momentous general election in Scotland, the result of which was a minority SNP administration.) The target audience for the conference was to be not only Fellows of the Royal Society of Edinburgh and interested members of the public, but also academics from the Scottish universities and, in particular, postgraduate students and others who might not have been familiar with the Royal Society and its activities. Generous financial support for the conference was also provided by the Faculty of Advocates, the Scottish Church History Society, and the University of Glasgow's Department of History. The conference attracted an audience of over a hundred.

The day's proceedings were opened with an overview provided by Professor T. Christopher Smout, FRSE, Historiographer-Royal, who has long had an interest in the Union, and written sagely about it. The conference was concluded by Professor Colin Kidd, FRSE, of the University of Glasgow, who offered his reflections on the legacy of the Union. During the day, eight papers were delivered, each of them stimulating lively discussion. Seven of the papers were then extensively re-written, to incorporate revisions and refinements, and the revised versions appear here. The one paper that was not revised for publication in this volume was that given by Kathrin Zickermann, a postgraduate research student at the University of St Andrews. Her paper, 'Scotland's Trade and Political Relations with Northern Germany', was drawn from the work being undertaken for her doctoral degree, the regulations for which precluded publication at this point.

This volume offers new interpretations of the Union of 1707, devoting attention to vital contextual issues, including European diplomacy, education, law, ideas of nationhood, public opinion, religion, and imperial trade. The book opens with an introductory chapter by Christopher Whatley, who provides a brief account of the issues that shaped the Union debates and indicates how the chapters in the volume contribute to our understanding of the broader context of the Union. In chapter 2, Christopher Storrs considers the European context, and in particular shows how the diplomacy and military movements of the War of Spanish Succession played a crucial role in shaping the parliamentary Union. Richard Saville turns in chapter 3 to the broader intellectual and cultural background of Scotland, giving particular attention to Scottish Calvinism and its influence in defining the Scottish institutions in education and the law that would be preserved by the Union settlement. In chapter 4, Clare Jackson analyses, from the perspective of political theory, the different conceptions of Scottish nationhood and identity that informed the Scottish debates over the Union, and demonstrates, in the process, the vital role of ideas in the making of the Union. Karin Bowie considers, in chapter 5, the enduring question of the extent to which Scottish politicians were 'managed' in order to achieve the Union. She demonstrates that while management was important, the political 'managers' were also profoundly influenced by the lively public debates surrounding the Union debates, and that Scottish public opinion did shape, in important ways, the Union settlement. Derek Patrick explores the theme of religion in chapter 6 – discussing the role of the national Church of Scotland in the Union debates and assessing the extent of the Church's influence in shaping Scottish opinion. Finally, in chapter 7, Andrew Mackillop investigates the imperial context, and provides fresh insights into the way in which the East Indies trade affected the Union negotiations. In doing so, he calls for a fundamental reinterpretation of the nature of the British empire that was formed in 1707.

The publication of this volume has been assisted by *The Scottish Historical Review* Trust. At an early stage in the planning process the Trustees had agreed to publish under the auspices of the *Scottish Historical Review* a volume that would be devoted to the Union of 1707. For this, we are enormously grateful.

Stewart J. Brown, FRSE, Professor of Ecclesiastical History, University of Edinburgh

Colin Kidd, FRSE, Professor of Modern History, University of Glasgow

Christopher A. Whatley, FRSE, Professor of Scottish History, University of Dundee

June 2008

The Royal Society of Edinburgh, Scotland's National Academy, is Scottish Charity No. SC000470.

Contributors

Dr Karin Bowie, Lecturer, Scottish History, University of Glasgow. Dr Bowie's main publication to date is *Scottish Public Opinion and the Anglo-Scottish Union, 1699–1707*, Royal Historical Society (Boydell Press, 2007), which is drawn from her University of Glasgow PhD thesis (2004). She has also published several papers in the field of public opinion and popular politics.

Stewart J. Brown, Professor of Ecclesiastical History, University of Edinburgh. His most recent book is *Providence and Empire: Religion, Politics and Society in the United Kingdom, 1815–1914* (Longmans, 2008). Amongst his previous books are *Enlightenment, Reawakening and Revolution, 1660–1815: The Cambridge History of Christianity, Volume VII* (Cambridge University Press, 2006), which he co-edited, and *The National Churches of England, Ireland and Scotland, 1801–1846* (Oxford University Press, 2001).

Dr Clare Jackson, Lecturer, History, Trinity Hall, University of Cambridge. Dr Jackson's first book-length publication was *Restoration Scotland, 1660–1690: Royalist Politics, Religion and Ideas*, Royal Historical Society (Boydell Press, 2003), and she is also the author of articles on aspects of the history of ideas, mainly in seventeenth century Scotland. She is currently co-editor of the *Historical Journal*, and is working on a biography of Sir George Mackenzie of Rosehaugh (1636–1691).

Dr Andrew Mackillop, Lecturer, Department of History, University of Aberdeen. Dr Mackillop's main publications include, *'More Fruitful than the Soil': Army, Empire and the Scottish Highlands, 1715–1815* (Tuckwell Press, 2000), and other articles and chapters on aspects of the history of the Scots and empire. His *The Scots, the Irish and British Imperialism in Asia, 1695 to 1813* (Manchester University Press), is forthcoming.

Dr Derek J. Patrick, Lecturer, Scottish History, School of Humanities, University of Dundee. Dr Patrick was research assistant on *The Scots and the Union* project, and prior to that worked on the University of St Andrews' Scottish Parliament project. He has published a number of articles and contributed chapters on later seventeenth and early eighteenth century politics in Scotland. He is currently completing a book, *Scotland under William and Mary*, for John Donald; this is based on his St Andrews' PhD thesis.

Dr Richard J. Saville, Coutts & Co, London. Dr Saville was formerly a Lecturer in Economic and Social History at the University of St Andrews. He is the author of *Bank of Scotland: A History, 1695–1995*

(Edinburgh University Press, 1996). Prior to that he published a number of papers and books, including *The Economic Development of Modern Scotland, 1950–1980* (John Donald, 1985), of which he was also the editor.

Dr Christopher Storrs, Reader, History, School of Humanities, University of Dundee. Dr Storrs' main publications are in the fields of early modern state formation, international relations and war; they include, *War, Diplomacy and the Rise of Savoy, 1690–1720* (Cambridge University Press, 1999), and *The Resilience of the Spanish Monarchy, 1665–1700* (Oxford University Press, 2006). He is currently working on a study of the re-emergence of Spain as a great power in the first half of the eighteenth century.

Christopher A. Whatley, Professor of Scottish History, Head of the College of Arts and Social Sciences, and Vice-Principal, University of Dundee. Professor Whatley's most recent substantial publication is *The Scots and the Union* (Edinburgh University Press, 2006, 2007). Amongst his previous books are *Scottish Society, 1707–1830: Beyond Jacobitism, towards Industrialisation* (Manchester University Press, 2000), and *The Industrial Revolution in Scotland* (Cambridge University Press, 1997).

The Scottish Historical Review, Volume LXXXVII: 2008 (Supplement), 1–30
DOI: 10.3366/E0036924108000450

CHRISTOPHER A. WHATLEY

Chapter 1
The Issues Facing Scotland in 1707

The focus of all of the papers presented at the Royal Society of Edinburgh's symposium was the British incorporating union of 1707, now just over three centuries old. In different ways, each paper, now re-written and edited as a chapter for this volume, offers a fresh perspective on this momentous event in Scotland's – and Britain's – history. The main purpose of this introduction is to outline the historical and historiographical contexts in which these new contributions can be located. By so doing, their significance will be better appreciated. What follows is by no means comprehensive;[1] but then, neither was the Royal Society of Edinburgh's symposium.

There was, for example, no presentation at the conference dealing directly with the economic impact of the Union, although in his powerfully argued chapter in this volume Andrew Mackillop contends that the Scots could have done better from union had the interest of the English East India Company in maintaining its monopoly been less influential. Richard Saville, in a chapter which identifies some of the key characteristics of religious training and schooling in pre-1707 Scotland, argues that these laid the basis of the hard-driving entrepreneurial culture that was necessary for the economic transformation of the eighteenth century. Saville has emphasised elsewhere the importance of events prior to 1707 – not the least being the Revolution of 1688–89 – in creating the conditions for Scotland's later economic success.[2] Readers in search of fuller treatment of the economic role of the Union, however, will have to search beyond this volume.[3] What is not in doubt, however, is that whatever the condition of Scotland's economy pre-1707 – and there are very different views on this – the Scots benefited enormously

---

[1] Often overlooked, but a fine, detailed account, is J. Mackinnon, *The Union of England and Scotland: A Study of International History* (London, 1896); more recent are, W. Ferguson, *Scotland's Relations with England: A Survey to 1707* (Edinburgh, 1977), and P. W. J. Riley, *The Union of England and Scotland* (Manchester, 1978).

[2] R. Saville, 'Scottish modernisation prior to the Industrial Revolution, 1688–1763', in T. M. Devine and J. R. Young (eds), *Eighteenth Century Scotland: New Perspectives* (East Linton, 1999), 6–23.

[3] See C. A. Whatley, 'Economic causes and consequences of the Union of 1707: A survey', *SHR*, 68 (1989),150–81, and the same author's *Scottish Society 1707–1830: Beyond Jacobitism, Towards Industrialisation* (Manchester, 2000), 48–95; for an examination of the economic effects of union in the long-run, C. H. Lee, *Scotland and the United Kingdom: The Economy and the Union in the Twentieth Century* (Manchester, 1995); for an up-to-date review of the immediate impact of 1707 on the economy, refer to T. M. Devine, 'The modern economy: Scotland and the Act of Union', in T. M. Devine, C. H. Lee and G. C. Peden (eds), *The Transformation of Scotland: The Economy Since 1700* (Edinburgh, 2005), 13–33.

from the Union, at home and especially overseas, where the gains attributable to Scotland's inclusion with the British Atlantic empire were immense.[4] India too proved to be a rich hunting ground for the Scots. Scots entrepreneurs and others – including doctors, army officers, and civil servants – strove hard and sacrificed much to obtain these benefits, which were by no means guaranteed.

There are other lacunae, including alternatives to an incorporating union, several of which had been advocated at various stages during the seventeenth century,[5] although Clare Jackson's chapter does capture something of the 'sheer diversity' of national visions that were articulated in the immediate pre-Union years. Also missing in the conference and from this volume is a look back – other than cursorily – at the Union of the Crowns of 1603 and its role in the making of the Union of 1707. That the status and operation of the regal union and the challenges posed by multiple kingship are essential elements in meaningful explanations for the Union of 1707 emerged during open discussion at the RSE symposium. In many respects, and certainly in the rhetoric used by Queen Anne and some of her ministers, (partial) incorporation was a further and perhaps the culminating stage in a *process* begun much earlier. As Roger Mason has very recently reminded us, the idea of Britain and interest in – even enthusiasm for – unionism, predate 1603, and are to be found in the writings of John Mair (*c*.1465–1550), John Knox, and the Presbyterian unionist David Hume of Godscroft.[6] By the end of the seventeenth century however, the Union of the Crowns was an arrangement that appeared to be at risk.

Mutual dislike between the Scots and the English was, to be sure, nothing new, and it had intensified in the years following 1603, not least as English ire was roused by the sight of Scots on the make, at court, in marriage and in the country at large. Moreover, differences between the two national Churches had early on posed a threat to James VI's union, although James was prudent enough to step back from his insistence that the Scots adopt the Five Articles of Perth (1618) – which, amongst other things, would have introduced the Anglican practice of kneeling during communion, a practice that was anathema to Scottish Presbyterians, and one that would come to the forefront again in the debates over incorporating union.[7] A forceful critique of the Union of

[4] See, for example, D. J. Hamilton, *Scotland, the Caribbean and the Atlantic World, 1750–1820* (Manchester, 2005), and T. M. Devine, 'Scottish elites and the Indian Empire, 1700–1815', in T. C. Smout (ed.), *Anglo-Scottish Relations From 1603 to 1900* (Oxford, 2005), 213–29.

[5] See in particular the chapters by David Stevenson and John Robertson in R. Mason (ed.), *Scotland and England, 1286–1815* (Edinburgh, 1987).

[6] R. A. Mason, 'Posing the East Lothian question', *History Scotland*, 8 (2008), 40–8; see too the same author's 'Scotland, Elizabethan England and the idea of union', *Transactions of the Royal Historical Society*, 14 (2004), 292–3.

[7] J. Wormald, 'O brave new world? The Union of England and Scotland in 1603', in Smout, *Anglo-Scottish Relations*, 13–36; L. A. M. Stewart, 'The political repercussions

Crowns emerged in Scotland by the turn of the eighteenth century. The substance of this attack was that the regal union was no longer serving Scottish interests, and was also eroding the Scots' sovereignty. For its harshest critics, it was a millstone round Scotland's neck.[8]

The road to 1707, therefore, was strewn with obstacles, even if for rulers of the two kingdoms and their advisers, such a course on occasion seemed highly desirable. Yet the outcome was by no means inevitable.

I

Anglo-Scottish relations deteriorated from verbal skirmishing almost to the point of open conflict in 1704 and 1705. This had in large part been precipitated when the Scottish Parliament passed the Act of Security in 1703 (ratified in 1704), a measure that defied Westminster's Act of Settlement of 1701, and asserted Scotland's right to nominate a Protestant successor to Queen Anne, who might be different from England's preference, unless Scotland's grievances were dealt with. The significance of the act and its content – a 'Scottish Magna Carta' that in the eyes of some contemporaries expressed the soul of the nation – is highlighted in Clare Jackson's chapter. Its clause announcing the raising of a militia in Scotland was interpreted in England as a threat of war – and gleefully seized upon by some Jacobites in Scotland as an invitation not only to arm, but also to fight.

From 1689, initially due to fears south of the border of an alliance between Scottish and Irish Jacobites, English naval vessels had been in the practice of interfering with, attacking, and sometimes seizing Scottish merchant shipping on the high seas and even within Scottish coastal waters. Having said this, Scottish seafarers were not immune from the temptations of the gains to be had from privateering, especially when opportunities for legitimate seafaring were restricted.[9] Nevertheless, with Anglo-Scottish tensions rising generally, and English maritime interests riding high (and at the expense of Scotland's) after the Revolution, the harassment of Scottish shipping continued into the early 1700s.[10] The reaction in Scotland was a further surge of anger directed towards England that manifested itself in the seizure of the English East Indiaman, the *Worcester*, and the subsequent trial and hanging of her captain and a couple of crewmen, with the executions watched by a massive, blood-thirsty crowd on Leith sands. Resentment in Scotland over the perceived inclination of London-based monarchs

---

[7] (*Continued*) of the Five Articles of Perth: A reassessment of James VI and I's religious policies in Scotland', *Sixteenth Century Journal*, 38 (2007), 1014.

[8] The matter is fully explored in K. Bowie, *Scottish Public Opinion and the Anglo-Scottish Union, 1699–1707* (Woodbridge, 2007); see too C. Kidd, 'Eighteenth-century Scotland and the three unions', in Smout (ed.), *Anglo-Scottish Relations*, 172–3.

[9] J. Ford, 'The law of the sea and the two unions', in Smout (ed.), *Anglo-Scottish Relations*, 134–5; for post-Union privateering and piracy, see E. J. Graham, *Seawolves: Pirates & the Scots* (Edinburgh, 2005).

[10] E. J. Graham, 'In defence of the Scottish maritime interest, 1681–1713', *SHR*, 71 (1992), 88–109.

to favour English interests had already reached new heights five years earlier, when it became apparent that the Company of Scotland's Darien venture had ended in defeat.[11] Although a complex of factors, some of which were self-inflicted, were responsible for this outcome, such was the depth of disappointment in Scotland that, as Karin Bowie's chapter reveals, it was relatively easy for the emerging country opposition to whip up latent anti-English sentiment and foist the blame on London – and King William – for their failure to support the Scottish company.[12] Given the success of this campaign, which aroused patriotic sentiment on the basis of real constitutional and economic grievances at social levels below the shire and burgh elites, there was an element of wishful thinking in the preamble to the act that instigated negotiations for union in 1702. The opening words declared that the aim of the negotiations was to 'compleat and confirm for ever' the 'love and friendship' that existed between the subjects of the two nations. That no agreement was reached seems hardly surprising.

Nevertheless, the deteriorating relations between the two countries caused cooler heads to look again at union as a means of settling and better securing the succession, and creating a framework in which the economic and other concessions demanded by the Scots could be granted.[13] Those concerned were encouraged by Queen Anne, prime mover and centrepiece in the sequence of events that would result in a union which would incorporate the venerable parliaments of England and Scotland into a single, Protestant, state. But to make clear to the Scottish Parliament that a resolution on the question of the succession should be sought sooner rather than later, the queen's ministers struck hard, by exposing the Scots to what has been described as 'open economic blackmail', that is, the Alien Act of 1705.[14]

Although previous unsuccessful attempts at closer union in the seventeenth century have received scholarly investigation, these probably deserve more attention than they have been accorded in recent writing on the Union of 1707. They were certainly an issue in 1706–7 for some politicians, several of whom were also well-informed about recent European experiences of union, as the work of Colin Kidd, John Robertson and others has made clear.[15] Union happened not in

---

[11] A. Forrester, *The Man Who Saw the Future* (New York, 2004), 281–6.

[12] *A Selection From the Papers of the Earls of Marchmont In the Possession of The Right Honorable Sir George Henry Rose. llustrative of Events From 1685 to 1750*, 3 vols. (London, 1831), III, 178–89.

[13] C. A. Whatley, *The Scots and the Union*, 2nd edn. (Edinburgh, 2007), 214–18.

[14] B. Lenman, *An Economic History of Modern Scotland* (London, 1977), 54.

[15] For example, see J. Robertson (ed.), *A Union for Empire: Political Thought and the Union of 1707* (Cambridge, 1995), in which volume appears C. Kidd, 'Religious realignment between the Restoration and the Union', 145–68; see too J. Robertson (ed.), *Andrew Fletcher: Political Works* (Cambridge, 1997), and for a telling case study, C. Jackson, 'Revolution principles, *ius naturae* and *ius gentium* in early-Enlightenment Scotland: the contribution of Sir Francis Grant, Lord Cullen (*c*.1660–1726)', in T. J. Hochstrasser and P. Schroder (eds), *Early Modern Natural Law Theories: Contexts and Strategies in the Early Enlightenment* (Dordrecht, 2003), 107–40.

an intellectual waste-land, but in a rich soil of political thought and constitutional theorising, which on key issues provided the parameters for debate and also, for several politicians, rationales for their respective positions.

At the start of the final session of the pre-Union Scottish Parliament, the principal leader of the opposition coalition, the duke of Hamilton, demanded that in light of the concern of previous generations of Scottish members of Parliament for 'the interest of their Country', records 'relative to treaties in former times may be laid before us'. Hamilton's reasoning conveniently overlooked the fact that it was largely English disinterest that had killed earlier initiatives (although the Scots had usually sought some sort of confederal settlement as opposed to the full union to which they had been forcibly subjected by Cromwell in 1654).[16] But Hamilton's request was reasonably made, even if it was also a delaying tactic. He was supported by Andrew Fletcher of Saltoun, who countered the court's objection that Hamilton's overture was too general by asking for specific information on James VI's union proposals, as well as on other proposals from 1667, 1670 and 1702–3.[17]

The attempt in 1702–3 at closer union appears from recent research to have been of greater significance than previously recognised in determining the character and shape of the 1707 settlement. Although there was less enthusiasm for union on the English commissioners' side, there appears to have been an honest exchange of views and positions, and when the two countries' representatives actually met, the minutes suggest that real negotiations took place. Twelve of the Scottish union commissioners in 1702–3 returned to London in the same capacity in 1706. However, as will be seen, they had learned important lessons from what had been, for some of them, a cathartic experience.[18] A number of the meetings had had to be abandoned as there had not been a quorum of members, on all but one occasion because of the failure of enough English commissioners to turn up. Their Scottish counterparts were left twiddling their thumbs – over the entire Christmas period in 1702 – and not surprisingly they were increasingly irritated at such offhand treatment. The dislike, contempt even, of English Tories for the Scots was palpable, as was their growing disinterest in the whole union enterprise, to the extent that the queen was forced to reduce the quorum from thirteen to seven. The second stumbling block was the unwillingness of the English side to concede anything to the Scots over the future of the Company of Scotland. The Scottish commissioners, led by the duke of Queensberry, had dug in their heels on the matter of compensation 'at the Publick expense' for the Company of Scotland. If that company were to be debarred from trading in the East Indies, in the

---

[16] See, for example, J. Morrill, 'The English, the Scots, and the dilemmas of union, 1638–1654', in Smout (ed.), *Anglo-Scottish Union*, 57–74.

[17] National Archives of Scotland [NAS], Hamilton MSS, GD 406/M9/266, Minute of Parliamentary Speeches, Oct. 1706–Jan. 1707, 12 Oct. 1706.

[18] Whatley, *Scots and the Union*, 214–15, 238.

interest of preserving the privileges of the English East India Company, the stockholders should be adequately compensated. Notwithstanding the retreat from Darien in 1700, the Company's commercial ambitions had survived more or less intact – and ships were sent on missions to Africa and the Far East; two such vessels, the *Speedwell* and the *Speedy Return*, had been part of the Darien expedition.[19] The Scottish Company's future was thus a major issue for both sides, and became the rock upon which the negotiations finally foundered. As noted already, the collapse of Darien had galvanised the parliamentary opposition – in the shape of the country party – together with public opinion, from 1699. And as Andrew Mackillop's chapter in this volume demonstrates, the company's supporters continued to be active on its behalf right up to the end of 1706.

Much of the rest of what had been agreed in London in 1702–3 would form the basis of the twenty-five articles of the 1707 union. There would be one monarch – after Anne's death to be drawn from the Protestant House of Hanover, commencing with the Electress Sophia, grand-daughter of James VI. There would be a single parliament serving the two nations that were to become the united Kingdom of Great Britain, and a free communication of trade and repeal of the Navigation Acts which would no longer debar the Scots. Neither country would be burdened with the other's debts, while the Scots would benefit from tax concessions until their economic circumstances improved; they would receive the Equivalent (see below), and support for certain Scottish industries – the argument being that such was the scale and impact of the losses incurred by the Company of Scotland's failings, that investors in Scotland had become risk-averse.[20]

II

In the years immediately preceding the Union in 1707 Scotland was a troubled nation, and a nation in trouble – although not without the capacity to trouble others. Internally the country was divided by deep fissures created by religious conflict and dynastic contest.[21] Linked were issues of governance – including the role of the Scottish estates, or Parliament – and attitudes to monarchical absolutism. The immediate cause of these divisions was the Revolution of 1688–89, when the Roman Catholic Stuart King James VII had been replaced on the thrones of both England and Scotland by the Low Countries' Protestant prince, William of Orange, and his wife, Mary. Presbyterianism had been re-established within the Church of Scotland in 1690, thereby returning

[19] Graham, *Seawolves*, 143–52; D. Watt, *The Price of Scotland: Darien, Union and the Wealth of Nations* (Edinburgh, 2007), 207–14.

[20] T. Thomson (ed.), *Acts of the Parliaments of Scotland* (1824), XI, Proceedings of the Commissioners Appointed to Treat For An Union Betwixt the Kingdoms of Scotland and England, 145–61.

[21] T. Harris, *Revolution: The Great Crisis of the British Monarchy, 1685–1720* (London, 2007), 409–21.

Scotland to its late sixteenth-century Melvillian inheritance. Yet neither of these arrangements was accepted by the nation as a whole, and certainly not by the supporters of James – now labelled by his enemies as the 'pretended monarch' or the 'pretender' – or by adherents of Episcopalianism.[22] More often than not, the two oppositional interests overlapped. William's death in 1702 did little to narrow the confessional and dynastic divide. His successor, the heirless Anne, was a Stuart, and looked more kindly on the Scots Episcopalians than William's Scottish ministers had done. But she was determinedly anti-Catholic, and insisted that her successor should be the aforementioned Hanoverian, Sophia, as determined by Westminster's Act of Succession of 1701, which had been passed following the death of Anne's last surviving child, the duke of Gloucester, in 1700.

Ultimately, most supporters of the Revolution settlement in Scotland allied themselves with Anne and her policies at home and abroad. They had done so nervously at first, fearing, as hinted above, for the security of the Presbyterian Kirk under Anne's policy of toleration towards Episcopacy. Anne, however, had fewer Scottish friends than William – she dropped his key adviser, the Rev William Carstares – and English influence over Scottish affairs increased further. The Jacobites, or cavaliers, were considerably stronger in the Scottish Parliament after the general election of 1702–3 than they had been under William.[23] They devoted themselves to blocking virtually every proposal relating to a succession that was designed to cast them into a dynastic wilderness. They played very cleverly the nationalist card, and conflated their dynastic self-interest with that of the nation – a strategy that allied them with the country party. This 'marriage of convenience' is explored in Karin Bowie's chapter, while Clare Jackson's chapter reveals the extent to which all sides claimed to represent the nation's interest. For posterity, the master of this political sleight of hand was the Jacobite, George Lockhart of Carnwath, whose detestation of the Revolution, the house of Hanover and the Union was of unparalleled intensity.[24] Historians have too often drawn uncritically on Lockhart's immensely readable interpretations of events. These were published in 1714, under the title *Memoirs Concerning the Affairs of Scotland from Queen Anne's Accession, to the Commencement of the Union of the Two Kingdoms of Scotland and England, in May 1707*. Publication – effected by his enemies – was intended in part to embarrass Lockhart by exposing his views to public

[22] A. Raffe, 'Episcopalian polemic, the London printing press and Anglo-Scottish divergence in the 1690s', *Journal of Scottish Historical Studies*, 26 (2006), 23–41.

[23] K. M. Brown, 'Party, politics and Parliament: Scotland's last election and its aftermath, 1702–3', in K. M. Brown and A. J. Mann (eds), *Parliament and Politics in Scotland, 1567–1707* (Edinburgh, 2005), 245.

[24] D. Szechi, *George Lockhart of Carnwath, 1689–1727: A Study in Jacobitism* (East Linton, 2002), 173–4.

scrutiny and possible legal action.[25] In fact the *Memoirs* are a skilfully written piece of political propaganda. But they are one man's deeply-coloured views of events – many of which were and can be contested. Lockhart's contemporary critics have largely been ignored by successive generations of writers on the Union, not a few of whom have drawn too literally on Lockhart's interpretations of events. The sound of grinding axes has accompanied studies of the Union for the best part of three hundred years.

Nevertheless, in seeking to understand the reasons for the Union, we ignore this political, ideological and confessional divide at our peril. To portray the Union as a measure over which most Scots were united in opposition against a single-minded attempt on the part of England to impose it by fair means or foul, is profoundly misleading. By and large, other than for a number of Jacobites, what was at issue was not whether Scotland's closest ally should be England, or even whether there should be a union, but rather the form a re-negotiated union should take. Proposals were aired in Scotland for unions with Holland and France, but such proposals found little support, either from the intended partners or from within Scotland.[26] It was with England that the future lay. What was at issue for the majority of Lowland Scots (whose opinions we can infer from the evidence surviving from 1706–7) were Scotland's sovereignty and nationhood within the British state, not Scotland's independence. This is not to deny the voices of the Jacobites and others in Parliament who spoke out against incorporation, or the sincerity of those who withdrew to engage in extra-parliamentary protest. But in this last respect they carried little weight in the country. The Jacobite movement came into its own after 1707, and exhibited its tenaciousness particularly in the north-east, the Highlands and the islands of the west. It did so through its capacity to act as a rallying point for Scots who felt betrayed by the Union and by successive Westminster ministries, and as a powerful if particular, classically-inspired form of patriotic sentiment.[27]

A major contrary strand in the tangle of factors that led to incorporating union in 1707 was what might be termed Presbyterian memory. By this is meant the searing experiences endured by many Scottish Presbyterians under the later Stuarts – a period that encompassed the so-called 'Killing Times' of the late 1670s and 1680s, and culminated in the atrocities of the Highland Host. The scale and severity of the suffering of Covenanters may have been exaggerated

---

[25] C. A. Whatley and D. J. Patrick, 'Contesting interpretations of the Union of 1707: The abuse and use of George Lockhart of Carnwath's *Memoirs*', *Journal of Scottish Historical Studies*, 27 (2007), 24–7.

[26] A. I. Macinnes, *Union and Empire. The Making of the United Kingdom in 1707* (Cambridge, 2007), 238–9.

[27] This argument is detailed by A. I. Macinnes, 'Jacobitism in Scotland: episodic cause or national movement?', *SHR*, 86 (Oct. 2007), 225–52; see too Szechi, *George Lockhart*, 197–211, for compelling insights into the mindset of one prominent Scottish Jacobite.

by subsequent generations of Whig commentators, especially those who
were less cautious than their herald, Robert Wodrow.[28] But for numerous
Scots who lived through the later Stuart years, the hardships and
constraints on their liberties were real enough, as was their detestation
of 'tyrannical monarchy', and informed their political beliefs and
practice.

The Restoration under Charles II had re-established crown control
over the Church of Scotland, and 1662 saw the return of Episcopacy
and patronage.[29] Over two hundred and fifty ministers were ejected
from their former charges. Many of them subsequently held illegal
conventicles and preached against the subordination of Parliament to
the royal prerogative, and against the suppression of Presbyterianism
– as their Covenanting predecessors had done thirty years previously
under Charles I. Attempted risings, as at Bothwell Brig in 1679, were
crushed, and many thousands of Presbyterians found themselves on the
receiving end of government-backed persecution. Several prominent
protesters were executed. Large numbers lost their livelihoods, and
were banished to the colonies, others were driven from their tenancies,
while many estates were forfeited. Not a few were subjected to brutal
punishments designed to extract confessions from those suspected of
acting against the state. These included judicial torture, by the use of
thumbscrews, introduced by the privy council expressly for this purpose,
and bone-crushing iron boots.[30] Imprisonment was commonplace, not
un-frequently on the bleak Bass Rock, purchased by the Scottish
secretary of state, the earl of Lauderdale, as a secure sea-ringed prison
for incarcerating the Stuart state's political and religious enemies.
Several hundred were forced to flee into exile, sometimes with their
entire families, most commonly to the Low Countries, as the recent
work of Ginny Gardiner has shown.[31] There the rebels met, caballed
and campaigned, by sending inflammatory literature back to Scotland.
And, in 1685, they dispatched an army of insurgents led by Archibald
Campbell, 9th earl of Argyll, which was subsequently crushed. Argyll
was beheaded. Although James introduced limited toleration for his
Scottish Presbyterian subjects in 1687, it was too late for him to
recover the ground his open association with and preference for Roman
Catholics like the earl of Perth had lost him. The king's fate was
sealed with the birth of his son – James Francis Edward – in June 1688,
an event that threatened to make permanent what had rapidly and

[28] C. Jackson, *Restoration Scotland, 1660–1690: Royalist Politics, Religion and Ideas*
(Woodbridge, 2003), 1–4.
[29] K. M. Brown, *Kingdom or Province? Scotland and the Regal Union, 1603–1715*
(Basingstoke, 1992), 148–50.
[30] See C. Jackson, 'Judicial torture, the liberties of the subject, and Anglo-Scottish
relations, 1660–1690', in Smout (ed.), *Anglo-Scottish Relations*, 75–101.
[31] G. Gardner, *The Scottish Exile Community in the Netherlands, 1660–1690* (East Linton,
2004), 9–28; 178–206.

perhaps unexpectedly become a deeply unpopular regime.[32] Although some émigrés had returned from the Netherlands, reassured by James's indulgences, many others remained to join forces with William of Orange, in some instances forming regiments in his service. It was men of this ilk who comprised the backbone of the Revolution of 1688–9 in Scotland. For such individuals and their families the Revolution was truly 'Glorious'.[33] They determined never again to be subject to the arbitrary power of Catholic-sponsoring monarchs who ruled by divine right, and disdained parliament. To this end they fashioned the Claim of Right, which, along with the 'Grievances', formed the political and religious manifesto of Scottish supporters of the Revolution. As enunciated in the Claim of Right, its promoters were committed to restoring Presbyterianism in Scotland, and to securing the Presbyterian Church from its Catholic enemies at home and abroad, as well as from the Episcopalians within the national Church.[34]

Overlooked and certainly underplayed until recently have been the direct links between the Revolution and the Union. Early in 1689 the convention of estates in Scotland had urged their new king, William, to forge what they called an 'entire' or incorporating union with England, including the formation of a single British Parliament. Indeed, such was the commitment of convention members to the proposal, and so confident were they that the king would respond favourably, that commissioners were appointed to treat for such a union. Amongst their number were three men who would serve again as commissioners not only in the abortive negotiations for union in 1702–3, but also in 1706: Adam Cockburn of Ormiston, James Ogilvie (first earl of Seafield from 1701), and John Dalrymple (first earl of Stair, 1704). These individuals steadfastly and actively supported union. Seafield, close to the queen from the start of her reign, played a prominent part in the 1702–3 deliberations. The importance of Stair's role is reflected in Lockhart's bile-laced depiction of him as 'the Origine and Principal Instrument of all the Misfortunes, that befell either the King [James] or Kingdom of Scotland [as defined by Lockhart]'. Lockhart condemned Stair as being the man who had carried 'underhand' the Revolution in Scotland, and who was at the 'Bottom of the Union', and 'so . . . may be stiled the Judas of his Country'.[35] Several reasons were offered in support of closer union with England in 1689, a step which at this stage was supported even by men who would later turn against it. (One of these individuals was Fletcher of Saltoun, who saw economic advantages for Scotland in such

---

[32] D. J. Patrick, 'Restoration to Revolution, 1660–1690', in Bob Harris and A. R. Macdonald (eds), *Scotland: The Making and Unmaking of the Nation, c.1100–1707* (Dundee, 2007), 63–7; Harris, *Revolution*, 153–81.

[33] See Rev R. Wodrow, *The History of the Sufferings of the Church of Scotland from the Restoration to the Revolution*, 4 vols. (Glasgow, 1828).

[34] See Harris, *Revolution*, 391–409.

[35] [G. Lockhart], *Memoirs Concerning the Affairs of Scotland From Queen Anne's Accession to the Throne to the Commencement of the Union of the Two Kingdoms England and Scotland* (London, 1714), 95–6.

an arrangement, although experience of government under William meant that, before long, his concern to limit the powers of the crown would take precedence in his radical but unwaveringly patriotic political agenda.[36]) The peoples of the two nations inhabited the same land mass and, the Gaels excepted, spoke the same language. More importantly, it was argued, once bound by closer union the Protestant peoples of the British Isles would be better able to resist France's Louis XIV and other sworn enemies of the new constitutional settlements in England and Scotland.

The idea of Great Britain as a Protestant bulwark against the Church of Rome and the Roman Catholic nations of Europe was nothing new: it had also been the bedrock of belief for sixteenth-century advocates of union, including James Henrison and John Knox. For their late seventeenth-century successors, it was through union that the gains of the Revolution would be better secured.[37] Almost certainly it was these last-named considerations that explain Cockburn's commitment: for not only was he a 'zealous Revolutioner', but he was also, at least in Lockhart's eyes, a 'bigotted' Presbyterian. The role of former émigrés and supporters of the Revolution in the making of the Union is a theme to which we will return below. What should be noted here is that the Revolution world-view remained constant up to and beyond 1707, but those who held it were not alone in advocating British unity – although not necessarily incorporating union – to maintain the balance of power in Europe and as a means of countering what many Presbyterians believed was a plot to restore Roman Catholicism across the globe.[38]

Scotland faced other domestic troubles in the reign of William – and Mary, until her death in 1694 – and during the early 1700s under Anne. The country struggled to recover from two hammer blows that had hit hard during the 1690s, a decade during which Scottish manufacturers and traders overseas had had to struggle against tariff walls erected by rival powers.[39] Adding to the country's woes was the ongoing war. With a pitifully small royal navy to protect them, and periodic English interference with Scottish shipping, Scottish traders were also at the mercy of French privateers, although as noted earlier, the Scots were not solely victims when it came to plundering on the high seas.[40]

The first blow was a debilitating period of falling crop yields, harvest failures, dearth and famine. In the two most difficult years the

---

[36] T. C. Smout, 'The Road to Union', in G. Holmes (ed.), *Britain after the Glorious Revolution* (London, 1969), 183–4; J. Robertson (ed.), *Andrew Fletcher: Political Works* (Cambridge, 1997), xvi.

[37] Mason, 'Posing the East Lothian question', 42–3; NAS, GD3/10/3/10, and National Library of Scotland [NLS], MS 7026.

[38] See, for example, George Ridpath's *The Great Reasons and Interests consider'd, anent the Spanish Monarchy* (1701), and *A Discourse upon the Union of Scotland and England* (Edinburgh, 1702).

[39] T. C. Smout, *Scottish Trade on the Eve of the Union, 1660–1707* (Edinburgh and London, 1963), 239–56.

[40] E. J. Graham, *A Maritime History of Scotland, 1650–1750* (East Linton, 2002), 77–80, 89–92.

equivalent of the entire revenues of the Scottish state may have been spent on importing grain, if the higher estimates of expenditure are to be believed[41] Faint reverberations from the famine years were still being felt as the debate in the Scottish Parliament over union got under way in the autumn of 1706. Rents in places were still in arrears in 1707. Some, regardless of their political persuasion, or position on union, were convinced that the situation was deteriorating. A widespread complaint, even amongst MPs – some of whom were finding it difficult to travel to Edinburgh – was that specie, or coin, was in desperately short supply.[42] This had resulted from money haemorrhaging from Scotland, to pay for grain in the late 1690s, and also for imports of the higher quality manufactured and exotic goods that were sought by more prosperous Scots but which could not be obtained at home. In short, there was a serious and unrelenting balance of payments deficit.[43] The bottom of the economic trough had probably been reached in 1703–4, with signs of recovery from this date onwards. Nevertheless, as late as February 1706 the Council of Trade, established the previous year to identify ways of 'Improving and Advancing the Trade of the Nation', issued a proclamation prohibiting any further out-payments in gold or silver.

Although frowned upon, this activity was to the advantage of individual Scots, and contributed positively to the country's *invisible* trade balance.[44] We should be wary of falling into the trap of believing that pre-Union Scotland was suffering from unrelieved economic depression. There was an active but illicit or 'black' economy conducted behind the barriers imposed by the English Navigation Acts. Substantial material benefits accrued to enterprising Scottish merchants and other participants – not least those who sought and realised the opportunities for gain overseas by operating, for example, through the Dutch East India Company.[45] Trade in several of the burghs of barony was reasonably buoyant and personal mercantile fortunes were being amassed through a range of entrepreneurial routes and connections.[46] Even in some of the royal burghs (Glasgow and Perth for example) rebuilding was taking place, while in the countryside much house-construction was under way, and with it a great deal

---

[41] M. Flinn (ed.), *Scottish Population History from the 17th Century to the 1930s* (Cambridge, 1977), 167; for a recent assessment which argues for a lower figure, see K. J. Cullen, 'Famine in Scotland in the 1690s: Causes and Consequences', unpublished Ph.D. thesis (University of Dundee, 2004), 125–41.

[42] Whatley, *Scots and the Union*, 184–223.

[43] R. Saville, *Bank of Scotland: A History, 1695–1995* (Edinburgh, 1996), 59–64.

[44] *Edinburgh Courant*, 16 Nov. 1705, 22 Feb. 1706; Saville, *Bank*, 66–7.

[45] S. Murdoch, 'The good, the bad and the anonymous: a preliminary survey of Scots in the Dutch East Indies, 1612–1707', *Northern Scotland*, 22 (2002), 63–76.

[46] A. I. Macinnes, *Clanship, Commerce and the House of Stuart, 1603–1788* (East Linton, 1996), 142–58, 172–3; S. Murdoch, *Network North: Scottish Kin, Commercial and Covert Associations in Northern Europe, 1603–1746* (Leiden, 2006), 242–4. For the most recent discussion of mercantile activity in relation to the Union, see Macinnes, *Union and Empire*, Part III.

of conspicuous consumption.[47] (This though was part of the *nation*'s economic problem.) Major domestic building projects undertaken by the more successful traders, lairds and aristocrats serve further to undermine overly pessimistic assessments of Scotland's economic condition in the pre-Union decades which fail to reflect the much more complex reality. Pockets of affluence were to be found in the ragged cloak of *relative* decline. It was this issue that exercised the minds of those both for and against incorporation in the years preceding 1707. For collectively, all the endeavour reported above was insufficient to alter the view of most observers that Scotland was a 'poor sinking nation'; nor was it strongly or widely enough based to have a noticeable impact on labouring peoples' wage levels, which remained flat.[48] The bold suggestion made recently that recovery was under way by 1702[49], is based on fragmentary evidence, depends on ruling as inadmissible that which shows anything to the contrary, and overlooks a raft of economic data and contemporary political economic analysis that points to a prolonged period of domestic economic depression that only began to lift in the 1730s and 1740s.[50]

The Scottish administrative machine was in a penurious condition, unable to pay the salaries of its employees – government ministers, the civil establishment and the forces – which in not a few cases were many years in arrears, stretching back in some instances to the beginning of William and Mary's reign.[51] In the opinion of the only modern writer to have investigated the pre-Union Scottish government's finances in depth, an independent Scottish state was no longer viable.[52] This is a conclusion that would be reached, reluctantly, by a number of Scots who genuinely believed they had their nation's interests at heart at the turn of the eighteenth century, and the years that followed. Alternatives to closer partnership with England were proposed by some of those hostile to incorporation, often with a stern moralising cast.[53] The problem was that measures designed to reduce imports of luxuries, for example, had been tried, and had failed, as had most efforts to establish new manufacturing industries. But to be fair, the promises of the unionists had not been put to the test, and in the short-term they were found to be

[47] For a fascinating case study, see M. Clough, *Two Houses: New Tarbat, Easter Ross, Royston House, Edinburgh* (Aberdeen, 1990); more generally, see M. Glendinning, R. MacInnes and A. Mackechnie, *A History of Scottish Architecture* (Edinburgh, 1996), 71–89.

[48] For a concise, balanced discussion, see Saville, *Bank of Scotland*, 59–73.

[49] I. A. Macinnes, 'The Treaty of Union: made in England', in T. M. Devine (ed.), *Scotland and the Union, 1707–2007* (Edinburgh, 2008), 65–7; Neil Davidson alleges that it is nationalist historians, in need of 'positive historical myths' to sustain their cause, who tend to deny the extent of Scottish 'backwardness' prior to the Union: N. Davidson, *Discovering the Scottish Revolution, 1692–1746* (London, 2003), 3.

[50] Whatley, *Scottish Society*, 39–61.

[51] J. S. Shaw, *The Political History of Eighteenth-Century Scotland* (Basingstoke, 1999), 11–14.

[52] A. L. Murray, 'Administration and the law', in T. I. Rae (ed.), *The Union of 1707: Its Impact on Scotland* (Glasgow, 1974), 34.

[53] Smout, *Scottish Trade*, 268.

hollow. On the monopoly of the East India Company, and opportunities for Scottish involvement in it post-1707, as Andrew Mackillop argues in his chapter, unionist prospectuses lacked substance and may even have been deliberately misleading.

The second substantial reverse was the financial and psychological damage that resulted from the bursting of the ambitious Company of Scotland's bubble and the cruel flights of Scots' colonists from Darien in 1699 and 1700. Darien was where this ambitious joint-stock company had attempted to establish its colony of New Caledonia – from whence the settlers would sell textiles, exploit slave labour to mine for silver and gold and, by straddling the isthmus of Panama, become the world's *entrepot*, connecting the Atlantic west with the far east. Darien was to be the means by which Scotland's fortunes would be restored, and enhance the nation's reputation by handling a large segment of global commerce.[54] The near manic enthusiasm with which news of the formation of the Company of Scotland had been welcomed was a measure of how desperate the Scots were for commercial success; its subsequent failure at Darien demonstrated that at a time of major inter-state rivalry and dynastic confrontation, the Scots as a nation-state were unlikely to achieve their economic goals independently.

But opinion was divided as to the causes of the setbacks, and over what action to take. For the country's more zealous Presbyterians, this and other disasters (such as the great fire that swept through central Edinburgh in 1700) provided unambiguous evidence that the Scottish people had been diverted from the path of righteousness; these were punishments meted out by a God angered at his chosen people's descent into sinfulness. Others looked to temporal causes and, as noted above, blamed King William and England for withdrawing support from the Company, and the colonists at Darien, at crucial moments. Not all contemporaries were convinced, however, and even a patriot like Fletcher had his doubts, seeing Spain as the culprit.[55] He was probably right. In his recent investigation of the Darien venture and its finances, Douglas Watt has revealed that the directors of the Company encouraged the belief that King William and English interests had led to the loss of the colony in order to deflect attention from their own shortcomings, including their foolhardiness in imaging the Scots could succeed in a location and climate so unsuitable for settlement, and in a region of such strategic importance to the Spanish.[56] This point is emphasised and elaborated upon in Christopher Storrs' chapter, which underlines the fact that Spain was far from being the spent force that the Company of Scotland's directors assumed it to be. Nevertheless, as noted earlier, it was the directors' interpretation of events that united the disparate elements forming the nascent patriotic country party.

[54] D. Armitage, 'The Scottish vision of empire: intellectual origins of the Darien venture', in Robertson (ed.), *Union for Empire*, 108–9.
[55] Whatley, *Scots and the Union*, 175.
[56] Watt, *Price of Scotland*, 143.

Others, far less numerous, looked to some sort of union, perhaps a union of trade with England, as a way forward. Such an arrangement had been long sought by the Scots, and at the end of 1699 union was being openly talked about in London as a recipe for relieving Anglo-Scottish tensions, apparently with the king's concurrence.[57] What the Darien episode had brought to the forefront of Scottish political consciousness was that the composite monarchy inaugurated by the regal union of 1603 was no longer working in Scotland's interests, and needed radical revision. Perhaps, even, closer union.[58]

At the beginning of the eighteenth century there were external threats to Scottish stability, and prosperity, not only from England and Spain but also from France. After a brief interlude from 1697, war with France was renewed in 1702, in the so-called War of the Spanish Succession, of which the alliances, diplomacy and campaigns provided the European tapestry into which the threads of the story of the British Union of 1707 were woven. As Storrs reminds us, the same conflagration was also the catalyst for a series of shifts in the relations between the states of Europe. These included new unions, such as that enforced by Austrian conquest in the case of Naples – a union that also took place in 1707 – and substantial territorial gains and losses.[59] Ranged against England and her allies were the formidable forces led by the Roman Catholic King Louis XIV of France, who aspired to European hegemony.[60] As in the previous decade, the capacity of a united Britain to counter French ambitions, including its hold over trade in the Mediterranean and elsewhere, was a key consideration that had led William Seton of Pitmedden, younger, to advocate incorporating union even before the hostilities commenced (and some years prior to the award of the £100 pension that allegedly brought him round to the union cause).[61] Of acute interest to the nations of the British Isles was one of the factors that had triggered the conflict, Louis XIV's reneging on the 1697 Treaty of Ryswick by recognising James VIII, son of the deposed King James, as the rightful king of Scotland, England and Ireland. Scotland, as we have observed, was divided. To varying degrees, Scottish Presbyterians, who, as we have seen, concerned themselves with the future of Protestantism in Europe as well as in Britain, and who wished therefore to maintain the Revolution settlement, welcomed the war. Those who imagined that men cut from this cloth might have done otherwise, wrote one English commentator three years later (in an essay advocating union with Scotland), were wholly mistaken: 'the Disagreement between French Popery and Scotch Presbytery is

[57] Whatley, *Scots and the Union*, 174.

[58] Davidson, *Discovering the Scottish Revolution*, 103.

[59] See J. Robertson, *The Case for Enlightenment. Scotland and Naples 1680–1760* (Cambridge, 2005).

[60] For English responses, see S. Pincus, 'The English debate over universal monarchy', in Robertson (ed.), *Union for Empire*, 37–62.

[61] W. Seton of Pitmedden, *The Interest of Scotland in Three Essays* (London, 1702), 58–9.

such... [that] you must conclude all the World a Bedlam before they be United.'[62]

However, there was resentment over the war on the grounds that it had been declared without consulting the Scottish Parliament, thus breaching the terms of the 1696 Act of Security. There were objections too to the additional burden of taxation that the conflict would impose upon a nation already protesting its impoverishment. The Jacobites of course made hay with all of this, opposed as they were to a war against the alliance led by Louis XIV, who had made available his royal palace at St Germain near Paris for the displaced King James and his family, their associates, agents and spies.[63]

The attachment of the Scots to Anne warmed as news of British military victories percolated northwards, first with the success of Marlborough's land forces in 1704 at Blenheim, and then in 1706 at Ramilles. It was no coincidence that when the commissioners who had thrashed out the terms of union with their English counterparts in the spring of 1706 returned to Edinburgh, they carried with them a freshly painted portrait of the queen which they had commissioned from Sir Godfrey Kneller, the leading portraitist of the day. They had done their monarch's business, and it was her cause they served. Many thousands of Scots were in royal service in the army, and almost certainly thought of themselves as British soldiers.[64] In the case of the sizeable number of officers who were also members of the Scottish Parliament, there was a palpable attachment to a united British kingdom – which would reveal itself in solid pro-union voting behaviour in Edinburgh in 1706–7.[65] Allied to this, there was a commitment, especially at elite level, to the idea – if loosely imagined – of Britain, and of Scots as Britons.[66] Self-identification of this sort, however, did not necessarily equate with support for incorporation. With such an outcome looking likely by November 1706, Fletcher was prepared to accept the term Great Britain to describe the new political entity, but urged that the terms 'English' and 'Scotch' should both be abandoned in favour of 'Great Brittains', fearing that otherwise the term Scot would be lost and replaced by that of Englishman. By this time Fletcher had more or less given up on his proposals for a pan-European confederation of small city states, or indeed his vain hope that the king of Prussia might be offered the Scottish crown. Other alternatives to incorporating union with England were floated – although it was a federal treaty that was advocated most powerfully and which was favoured in the country.

---

[62] *Edinburgh Courant*, 19 Dec. 1705.

[63] See J. Callow, *King in Exile. James II: Warrior, King & Saint* (Stroud, 2004).

[64] S. Murdoch, 'James VI and the formation of a Scottish-British military identity', in S. Murdoch and A. Mackillop (eds), *Fighting for Identity: Scottish Military Experience, c.1550–1900* (Leiden, 2002).

[65] K. M. Brown, 'From Scottish lords to British officers: state building, elite integration, and the army in the seventeenth century', in N. Macdougall (ed.), *Scotland and War, AD 79–1918* (Edinburgh, 1991), 152.

[66] Whatley, *Scots and the Union*, 84–9.

The Jacobites' preference was to wait until Queen Anne's death and then negotiate better terms with England, failing which, they argued, the Scots could unite with Holland or, preferably, France.[67] For reasons outlined already, support for this option was thin on the ground.

What all this reveals is that there were several crucial, often interconnected issues facing Scotland in the years immediately prior to the Act of Union. They included the future of the regal union with a neighbour that looked first to its own interests. There was the succession to Anne and related questions of Scottish sovereignty, including the Scots' right to declare war and peace. Also influencing thought and behaviour was the Claim of Right which, amongst other things, placed strict limits on the powers of the monarch; linked to this was the inheritance and integrity of the Revolution.[68] Religion – rejected by some historians in the second half of the twentieth century as a cloak of convenience – was fundamental, as Derek Patrick's chapter in this volume makes clear. There was amongst Presbyterians deep-seated anxiety about the future, faced as they were by an active and regionally strong Episcopalian body within Scotland, and the resurgent Roman Catholic Church without. Securing the Revolution on the ground was a drawn-out process that would take decades to complete.[69] Some, mainly moderates, looked outwards and to the place of Protestantism in Europe and even beyond. But there were other Presbyterians, generally the more zealous, whose focus was Scotland and their locus mainly among the United Societies of the south-west. They sought to return the Kirk to Covenanting principles; for them, the Church was to be subservient neither to king nor state.[70]

On top of all this were widespread worries over the economy. For its laggard condition much blame was directed towards the country's aristocrats and leading landowners, with their attachment on their estates to 'feudalism', and the rack-renting of tenants who had little security and therefore no motive for improvement.[71] A related question was how the Scots in an era of muscular mercantilism could achieve material success and the cultural and political ambitions that would follow – not just for individuals, but collectively, as leading citizens of a respected nation state. Amongst the political elite were those whose ambitions could not be satisfied in Scotland; a united kingdom, with a London legislature, was more likely to provide opportunities for strutting on the European stage. For all of the ambition and energy displayed by the Scottish Parliament after the Revolution, there was a

[67] Robertson (ed.), *Andrew Fletcher*, p.xxvii; J. Stephen, *Scottish Presbyterians and the Act of Union* (Edinburgh, 2007), 186–7.

[68] R. Mitchison, *Lordship to Patronage: Scotland, 1603–1745* (London, 1983), 117–18; Ferguson, *Scotland's Relations*, 197–8.

[69] I. D. Whyte, 'Ministers and society in Scotland, 1560-*c*.1800', in C. MacLean and K. Veitch (eds), *Scottish Life and Society: Religion* (Edinburgh, 2006), 439–41.

[70] Stephen, *Scottish Presbyterians*, 4–6.

[71] Kidd, 'Eighteenth-century Scotland and the three unions', in Smout (ed.), *Anglo-Scottish Relations*, 182–3.

perception in some quarters that in important respects it was phantom-like, unable to defend the nation's sovereign interest, and incapable of effectively promoting Scotland's agriculture, commercial needs, or manufacturing.[72] Laws were passed, orders given and proclamations made, but much less of substance was achieved than anticipated.[73] All of these issues were the subject of intense debate in the first years of the eighteenth century, with arguments exploding into the 'pamphlet war' of 1705–6. In their various ways these were the factors that shaped the views of Scottish politicians as they deliberated upon the nation's future from the spring of 1706 into the first weeks of 1707.

III

The portrayal of the Union as the outcome of an uneven contest between an all-conquering England on the one side and a poor defenceless Scotland, united in opposition, on the other is less persuasive now than it may have been ten years ago.[74] The notion of a Scotland betrayed by politicians who were bullied and bribed into an arrangement against their will or better judgement has been subject to close scrutiny, and has also been found wanting.[75] Government ministers and officers of state campaigned to capture minds (capturing hearts was a step too far) by persuasive argument. It is clear too that there was a view south of the border that any new constitutional arrangement should be negotiated – a *modus operandi* fixed upon in the previous century – rather than imposed arbitrarily. There were even Englishmen who argued that if the Scots were less than willing to accede to union, they should be left alone rather than be dragged to the altar against their wishes.

This is not to say that England was uninterested in Scotland. Far from it: that England was a key determinant in the making of the Union has long been recognised.[76] The later seventeenth century and the opening years of the eighteenth century were troubled and insecure times for England too.[77] The English military-fiscal state was in the ascendant, but its accomplishment was some way off. The eyes first of William and then of Anne and her chief ministers had been drawn – somewhat reluctantly – to Scotland by a number of developments that might have been damaging to English ambitions. These included the Scots' commercial aspirations, their stance over Darien and their growing

---

[72] C. A. Whatley, 'Taking stock: Scotland at the end of the seventeenth century', in Smout (ed.), *Anglo-Scottish Relations*, 123; Jackson, 'Revolution principles', 122.

[73] Whatley, *Scottish Society*, 23–41; Davidson, *Discovering the Scottish Revolution*, 82–3.

[74] See, for example, I. MacLean and A. McMillan, *State of the Union: Unionism and the Alternatives in the United Kingdom since 1707* (Oxford, 2005).

[75] This position, however, has been re-iterated by P. H. Scott, *The Union of 1707: Why and How?* (Edinburgh, 2006).

[76] See, for example, R. Lodge, 'The English standpoint (II)', in P. Hume Brown (ed.), *The Union of 1707* (Glasgow, 1907), 170.

[77] See J. Hoppit, *A Land of Liberty? England 1689–1727* (Oxford, 2000).

intransigence over the succession. In addition, as noted above, the general election of 1702–3 had produced a more voluble parliament in Scotland with a stronger opposition. Members were more than willing to speak their mind and vote accordingly – by resisting supply, for instance – and proposals were made and measures were passed that threatened to undermine the regal union. The Act of Security and the Act anent Peace and War were the most alarming of these, but there were other attempts to impose limitations upon the crown.[78] Another looming cloud – arising in part from the Scots' outrage in the wake of their withdrawal from Darien – was the possibility that the Jacobites might seize power in Scotland, forge an alliance with France, and threaten England's northern border at a time when British forces were concentrated in the main theatres of war on the European continent. The prospect of the armed Scots marching south caused considerable consternation in England, especially in the northern counties.

Arousing concern in mercantile circles was the success that certainly some Scottish merchants and settlers were enjoying in the Caribbean and elsewhere, notwithstanding the stricter enforcement of the Navigation Acts.[79] There were reasons to bring the Scots to heel. Other considerations that may have attracted England to union were the manpower requirements of the British forces when global war was depleting traditional sources of recruits, and the demands of the colonies. In both respects, physically able, Protestant Scots fitted the bill admirably.[80] But if containing the Scots and harnessing Scottish resources were considerations for England, such objectives were not necessarily to be achieved through union. English Tories looked askance at the prospect of a closer relationship, dominated as Scottish society was (in the eyes of Englishmen who had been fed with a decade and a half's Episcopalian propagandising), by fanatical, ranting Presbyterians, unforgiving in their belief in predestination.[81] It was Whigs who were keener, seeing in incorporating union a vehicle for entrenching their authority at Westminster, provided Scottish Whigs retained the upper hand and were able to send reinforcements south from 1707.[82]

There is no doubt that from 1703, as the war in Europe intensified, Anne and her advisers were doubly determined that the Scots should agree to the Hanoverian succession. In the background were recollections of the Cromwellian occupation, with the prospect of a re-run kept warm by occasional hints from Godolphin.[83] If such a course of action was unlikely, what is less clear is whether incorporation

[78] Robertson (ed.), *Andrew Fletcher*, 129–73.

[79] Macinnes, 'Treaty of Union', 62–3.

[80] Macinnes, *Union and Empire*, 189–97.

[81] Raffe, 'Episcopalian polemic', 29–36.

[82] C. A. Whatley, *Bought and Sold for English Gold? Explaining the Union of 1707* (East Linton, 2001), 51–2, 69–71; see too Davidson, *Discovering the Scottish Revolution*, 104–8.

[83] J. Robertson, 'An elusive sovereignty. the course of the Union debate in Scotland, 1698–1707', in Robertson (ed.), *Union for Empire*, 204, 211.

on terms that would be acceptable to the Scots was to be the means of achieving court goals. As has been seen, the 1702–3 negotiations, instigated by King William and encouraged by Queen Anne, had collapsed. Although there seems little reason to question Anne's continuing enthusiasm for union, John Clerk, younger, who was in Parliament from 1703, was convinced that union was only resorted to by English ministers after it had become apparent that the Scottish Parliament was dragging its heels over the succession – by demanding greater parliamentary control of patronage, limitations on the power of the crown, and a commercial treaty. This interpretation is close to that offered by Karin Bowie, who has added a new layer of interpretation to the apparently chaotic behaviour of the estates during 1704 and 1705, behaviour which has been portrayed as an intense, and unseemly, scramble for power by the main competing factions.[84] Nevertheless, to focus Scottish minds, Westminster had passed the Alien Act, which, if implemented, would have, amongst other things, crippled Scotland's economy: some fifty per cent of Scottish visible exports including the key commodities of linen and black cattle were sold in England.[85] For inviting this measure (and the Union) Clerk was inclined to blame the Jacobites, whose tails were up during what were the feistiest days of the pre-Union Scottish Parliament, from 1703 through to the end of 1705.[86] Yet the Alien Act had not insisted on union; the Scots' agreement to the Hanoverian succession alone might have satisfied.[87] If the Scots were to insist on concessions, however, incorporation was to be vehicle by which these would be forthcoming.

Amongst the thirty-one Scottish commissioners appointed by the queen to meet with their English counterparts to negotiate a treaty, were those men who had learned hard lessons during the failed negotiations of 1702–3. Accordingly, as they returned south on a similar mission in March 1706, there was in some men's minds a determination that they would not be humiliated a second time; this was most notable in one of the staunchest defenders of Scottish interests both pre- and post-Union, Sir David Dalrymple.[88] Missing from reports of the commissioners' business in the historical literature (which is heavily dependent upon Lockhart's account) is also the clear sense of purpose of at least some of their number. They were to represent the views of the Scottish Parliament, dig in their heels and ensure that they extracted from England the concessions Scots had been demanding since 1702, and earlier. To dismiss them out of hand as yes-men would be seriously to misrepresent the evidence, which has too rarely been brought to light.[89]

---

[84] Riley, *Union of England and Scotland*, xvi, 57; MacLean and McMillan, *State of the Union*, 23.

[85] Smout, *Scottish Trade*, 238.

[86] NAS, GD 18/6080, Sir John Clerk's annotated copy of Lockhart's *Memoirs*, 120.

[87] NAS, GD1/1158/3, Godolphin to the duke of Argyll, 17 July 1705.

[88] See E. Cruickshanks, S. Handley and D. W. Hayton (eds), *The History of Parliament: The House of Commons 1690–1715*, 5 vols. (Cambridge, 2002), III, 824–34.

[89] Whatley, *Scots and the Union*, 233–42.

IV

How were the union-related issues outlined above reflected in the Scottish Parliament during the fateful months from October 1706 to January 1707? The 227 or so members divided themselves into three main groupings, or proto-parties, although within these semi-formal associations there were various alliances and factions. One was Andrew Fletcher of Saltoun's fifteen-strong band of constitutional reformers who were part of the country-cavalier opposition of eighty-plus members. This fragile coalition was led by two rivals, James, fourth duke of Hamilton, and the duke of Atholl. The cavalier wing comprised the Jacobites, whose leaders included the earl of Home, who died before the union votes took place, and the earls of Errol and Marischal.[90]

The country-cavalier alliance's stance was pro-Darien, and anti-incorporation, although most of the coalition's Presbyterian adherents were favourably inclined towards Hanover and had no serious objections to a treaty with England, or even a negotiated federal union. Hamilton – and John Hamilton, lord Belhaven – had even been willing to work actively for such an arrangement provided the duke was appropriately rewarded. It was to 'an entire and complete' union that they were implacably opposed.[91] Hence it was the country party that mobilised opposition to the measure outside Parliament, and that led the resistance to the court party's proposals within. The party appealed to Scottish national sentiment, and there is no doubting the power of what seems to have been a revived sense of nationhood in pre-Union Scotland, even if, as Clare Jackson explains in her chapter, it was a difficult concept to pin down. What was not much contested was Scotland's existence as an independent nation, a sentiment captured in many of the petitions presented to the Scottish Parliament in the winter of 1706–7. These rejected incorporation on several counts, including, expressly, the Scots' valiant defence for 2,000 years of their sovereignty and independence, which were not to be bartered at any cost. The similarity of the language used in more than half of the addresses, however, points to a single origin – the well-organised country party. In fact, most of the addresses came from territories associated with the party's leading figures.[92] Appeals to Scottish patriotism were also heard in a number of the speeches delivered by opposition speakers in Parliament during the last quarter of 1706. Several drew deep from the well of Scottish history, and mythology. They sought inspiration in the heroism of Wallace and Bruce – the cult of the former having been revived in the 1690s — although few found as much succour directly from Scottish history as did the duke of Atholl. On 4 November 1706

[90] Essential reading on the political groupings in the Union Parliament, and their voting patterns, is A. I. Macinnes, 'Influencing the vote: The Scottish Estates and the Treaty of Union, 1706–7', *History Microcomputer Review*, 6 (1990), 11–25.
[91] *Selection From the Papers of the Earls of Marchmont*, III, 435–8.
[92] Bowie, *Scottish Public Opinion*, 120–1.

he concluded a powerful oration adapted from the 1320 Declaration of Arbroath, by declaring that so long as there were 100 Scots men alive 'we will not enter into a treaty so dishonourable and entirely subversive of us as this is'. The effect this had on Atholl's listeners is unknown. Others, like Fletcher, looked to antiquity as a guide, and also to contemporary Europe, advocating the model of the United Provinces rather than incorporation, which they viewed as 'the best handle ever... for oppression and slavery', and likely to draw people, trade and wealth away from Scotland to London.[93]

But many of the objections to the union proposals, expressed in signed addresses and parliamentary speeches, were about bread and butter issues. There is little evidence that they were fed by the rampant Anglophobia that could be heard on the streets of Edinburgh. However, even those sympathetic to union had reservations about the trustworthiness of the English, and at the very least could be profoundly irritated by the arrogance and offhand manner of those English ministers with whom they had to deal. (Countering this to some degree, however, is the evidence for cultural convergence, certainly at elite level, with shared interests in literature, law, history, philosophy, medicine, science and other subjects; indeed, Roger Emerson is persuaded that common values and attitudes were a pre-condition of union.[94] This is not to be confused with Anglicisation, which was confined to a small minority. The Gaelic and vernacular verse traditions remained strong, and became channels for patriotism after 1707, while Scottish and Dutch universities continued to be preferred to those of England.[95]) Several speakers raised the question of the security and status of the Church of Scotland, even after Parliament passed the Act of Security on 12 November confirming its position as Scotland's national Church, unalterable after the Union. For the Revolution-supporting, Presbyterian judge and learned tract-writer, Sir Francis Grant, a positive attraction of the Union was that it enshrined Protestantism as a fundamental element of the constitution; in this regard, he argued, the treaty was unique.[96] Nevertheless, as Derek Patrick emphasises in his chapter, there was deep-seated anxiety within and about the Kirk, outside Parliament as well as inside. Patrick follows Jeffrey Stephen in countering the frequently-repeated claim that the act for securing the Church of Scotland was a 'master stroke' on the part of the court, designed simply to placate those within the Kirk who feared that union would put the Scottish Presbyterian Church at the mercy of the Anglican

---

[93] NAS, GD 406/M9/266, ff.31, 35.

[94] R. L. Emerson, 'Scottish cultural change, 1660–1710, and the Union of 1707', in Robertson (ed.), *Union for Empire*, 121–44.

[95] R. Crawford, *Scotland's Books: The Penguin History of Scottish Literature* (London, 2007), 207–14, 224–7, 237–40; K. M. Brown, 'The origins of a British aristocracy: integration and its limitations before the treaty of union', in S. G. Ellis and S. Barber (eds), *Conquest and Union: Fashioning a British State, 1485–1725* (London, 1995), 222–49.

[96] Jackson, 'Revolution principles', 115–16.

majority at Westminster.[97] It was more than this, according to Patrick, who reveals how the opposition country coalition leaders strove to exploit the Kirk issue for their own ends. Voting patterns reflect the real concern in the Scottish estates for Presbyterianism after the Union, so much so that even some members of the country opposition voted with the court party for the measure. Even so, this was not enough to quell the fears of every parliamentary Presbyterian, or of those in the country, notably in the south-west, where Covenanting fundamentalists of the United Societies continued to oppose the Union long after 1707. Men and women of this persuasion felt that only after securing a separate Scottish Parliament – and ridding the nation of its uncovenanted queen – would Presbyterianism be safe. They railed too against being exposed to the Anglicans' 'popish' practices, which included kneeling before the altar while taking the strongly-resisted sacramental test. They objected too at the prospect of Scotsmen participating in a House of Lords contaminated by the presence of bishops.

Within and outside Parliament, as the terms of the proposed union were subjected to close scrutiny, fears deepened over its economic implications. The anticipated 'Insupportable burden of Taxation' was a matter of acute concern in the burghs, several of which argued that this far outweighed any advantages that might accrue from freer trade. This is reflected in Belhaven's well-known speech – evidently more effective in its published form outside Parliament Close than in the chamber itself – in which he envisioned his poor countrymen, the 'poor industrious tradesman... drinking water instead of ale, eating his saltless pottage'. The price of salt, and the ability of Scottish salt manufacturers and colliery proprietors to compete if they were subject to English levels of taxation after 1707, were matters that roused passions and produced much lobbying on the part of the groups concerned.[98] There were other doubts about the advantages of free trade, including recognition of Scotland's 'supply-side' weaknesses. It was alleged that the main benefits would accrue to England, whose manufacturers and merchants would increase their exports of high-value goods into Scotland, taking in return Scotland's lower-grade products like coarse linen and unfattened cattle. Such anxieties go a long way toward explaining why, despite a massive majority of votes in favour of the fourth article that established full freedom of trade and navigation (154 votes to 19), there was so much heated debate about other economic issues, and several closer votes where the producers of vulnerable Scottish commodities were at risk.[99] However, there is fairly compelling evidence to support the proposition that, by and large, contemporaries who were most familiar with Scotland's economy and financial situation were pro-union. It is surely significant that of

[97] Stephen, *Scottish Presbyterians*, 72.
[98] C. A. Whatley, 'Salt, coal and the Union of 1707: a revision article', *SHR*, 66 (April 1987), 26–45.
[99] Whatley, *Bought and Sold*, 72–7; Macinnes, 'Studying the Scottish estates', 16.

the members of the two commissions established by the pre-Union
Scottish Parliament to investigate and deal with Scotland's financial
and economic weaknesses, substantial majorities voted for union.[100]
Amongst the sixteen members of the 1705 Council of Trade who
voted for incorporation were John Clerk, Sir Patrick Johnston (who
represented Edinburgh), and the Clyde merchant Sir James Smollett
of Stainflett and Bonhill. They were joined by prominent economic
modernisers, who included directors of the Bank of Scotland such as
David, third earl of Leven, and leading Company of Scotland investors.
Some parliamentarians – Clerk, for example – regretted profoundly the
loss of Scotland's sovereignty, but felt that a parliament that was unable
to implement its own economic legislation was a sacrifice worth making
in return for the promise of material gain and the greater influence
Scots would have at Westminster.[101]

Free trade was a long-standing Scottish demand, not only of
commercial traffic over the border and coastwise with England, but
also *legal* access to the plantations in the West Indies, and around
the Chesapeake. This was notwithstanding the undeniable successes
of several Scottish merchant entrepreneurs in circumventing the
Navigation Acts and exploiting loopholes and exemptions in the
system.[102] Sometimes overlooked but worth emphasising too is the fact
that trade by sea was to be protected; even before the articles had
been approved in Edinburgh, Scottish merchants were able, courtesy
of their sovereign, to call on the Royal Navy to escort their vessels in
the Baltic, the North Sea and the English Channel.[103] The importance
to the Scots of maintaining established commercial linkages should not
be forgotten.

A major grievance, which was also felt in some royal burghs (which
were each represented by a separate commissioner in the Scottish
Parliament, where a total of seventy-seven burgh members sat), was the
proposed allocation of MPs from Scotland who would sit in the House
of Commons. The number was to be forty-five. But as was pointed
out by the earl of Kincardine in a penetrating attack on 29 October,
this was only one more than the number of English MPs representing
Cornwall. Even Old Sarum, he went on, 'where there is not one house,

---

[100] Whatley, *Scots and the Union*, 197, 302, 381–2.

[101] Whatley, 'Taking stock: Scotland at the end of the seventeenth century', 122–5.

[102] Macinnes, 'Treaty of Union', 56–9; it is paradoxical that Scottish economic success in
the immediate post-Union decades appears to have owed much to the Scots' capacity
(as re-exporters of commodities such as tobacco, sugar and rice) to use to their own
advantage a tax regime that acted as a barrier to domestic economic endeavour;
the scale of smuggling – notably in tea – also increased, to the extent that it has
been described as the 'third pillar of Scottish commercial activity in the eighteenth
century': P. R. Rossner, *Scottish Trade in the Wake of the Union, 1700–1760* (Stuttgart,
2008), 40–1, 105–7, 175–85.

[103] Whatley, *Scots and the Union*, 258; London Scots trading legitimately – and illicitly
– with England's American and Caribbean colonies had long benefited from the
protection of Royal Navy convoys: Macinnes, 'Treaty of Union', 59.

but a shepherd's coalhouse' sent two members to Westminster. But forty-five was more than the Scots had called for in 1689, and seven more than the thirty-eight originally proposed by the English negotiators. In addition, for a few Scots, what mattered more was that by moving from Scotland's unicameral parliament where the nobility dominated, to Westminster with its two chambers, 'Courtiers would no longer be a Grievance to the Nation', especially as the number of peers from Scotland was set at sixteen. By this means the grip of feudalism would be weakened and, with commercial expansion, agriculture would flourish, and tenants would be relieved of rack-renting and secured by longer leases.[104] In fact it would be another four decades – in 1747 – that the heritable jurisdictions were abolished.[105]

However, and notwithstanding the force of some of its supporters' arguments, the opposition could only muster between 80 and 90 votes. The court or government party could raise around 10 to 12 more, but a secure majority depended upon a third grouping. This was the new party, better-known as the *squadrone volante*, an alliance of some 25 members that had been formed following the general election in 1702–3.

It has been argued that only through a combination of highly effective parliamentary management techniques – which included gifts of government posts and promises of promotions and pensions, along with other forms of bribery – was the court able to steer the twenty-five articles of the Act of Union through the Edinburgh Parliament. More recently, other historians have supplemented this argument by reference to English bullying – in the shape of a threat to invade Scotland if the Scots failed to accept incorporation.[106] Both of these factors played their part, but the importance of the first can be exaggerated, and without account being taken of countervailing evidence, appears as caricature. Supporters of the Union exploited the opportunity the parliamentary situation opened up for them to make demands upon the court (not unusually for monies owed), and several were rewarded, but others also benefited from the court's largesse in 1706 and 1707.[107] That the nobility, the largest of the three estates in the unicameral Scottish Parliament, tended to vote more strongly for the Union than the others, may be indicative of the influence of the London court. However, there were majorities in favour in all three of the estates, albeit a bare majority from the burghs, whose representatives – as with the shire members – were elected, and may have felt more keenly the anti-Union sentiment of their constituencies.[108]

[104] Seton of Pitmedden, *Interest of Scotland*, 57–8.

[105] For an intriguing analysis of the demise of feudalism in Scotland and the emergence of capitalism see Davidson, *Discovering the Scottish Revolution*.

[106] J. R. Young, 'The Parliamentary incorporating union of 1707: political management, anti-unionism and foreign policy', in Devine and Young (eds), *Eighteenth-Century Scotland*, 39–46.

[107] Shaw, *Political History*, 15–17.

[108] MacLean and McMillan, *State of the Union*, 30–2.

English troops were stationed on the border and others were mustered in the north of Ireland – but they would have been mobilised at the request of ministers in Scotland, and welcomed by many Scots Presbyterians if they had been called on, as seemed likely at one stage, to crush a Jacobite-led insurrection in Edinburgh. On the undesirability of popular action in the form of mobbing and rioting against the union proposals all parties – apart from a handful of extreme Presbyterians, Fletcher and some Jacobites – were firmly at one.[109] Too easily dismissed is the real concern – alluded to earlier – that existed in England's northern counties over the possibility of a Scottish incursion; indeed, to minimise such a possibility, insisted Daniel Defoe, was a powerful reason for the English to support union. In fact there are more persuasive explanations for how ministers managed to garner enough support to secure what was a series of majority votes on the articles. Some of these are outlined in Karin Bowie's chapter. Another, introduced earlier, was political ideology.

Reference has been made to the Presbyterian memory and its impact on the Revolution of 1688–89 in Scotland. This catalyst for political action contributed significantly to the support for union both within the court party and the *squadrone volante*. In addition to the names of prominent pro-Unionists already mentioned – those whose politics had been informed by their personal experience of later Stuart rule – there were individuals such as the aforementioned earl of Leven (son of the exiled 1st earl of Melville), who had served William in a military capacity prior to the Revolution, was a leading court politician, and, by the time of the Union, held offices as commander-in-chief of the army in Scotland and governor of Edinburgh castle.[110] Not dissimilar was John Campbell, 2nd duke of Argyll, a senior military figure in the British army whose hard bargaining with Queen Anne in return for political service in the Union Parliament has attracted the attention of disapproving historians who have been inclined to write him off as a venal careerist in the court interest.[111] Yet Argyll had lost his grandfather and his great-grandfather on the scaffold in 1661 and 1685 respectively, both men having taken up arms against Stuart absolutism. Although the 9th earl's motives in leading the 1685 rebellion were mixed, his standard declared that he was 'For God and Religion against Poperie, Tyrrany, Arbirtrary Government and Erastianisme', and at his death he was treated by onlookers as a something of a protestant martyr.[112] For all his personal failings and self-serving demands, the 2nd duke's

[109] Whatley, *Scots and the Union*, 54–5, 277–81.
[110] Saville, *Bank of Scotland*, 827.
[111] Most recently by Macinnes, *Union and Empire*, 292–3, but see too P. H. Scott, *Andrew Fletcher and the Treaty of Union* (Edinburgh,1992), 123–4.
[112] Harris, *Revolution*, 77, 87.

Presbyterianism and Revolution pedigree were beyond question. Nor was his commitment – at this stage – to union.[113]

Indeed, of those members of Parliament in 1706–7 who had first entered Parliament either at the Revolution, or during King William's reign, almost two-thirds were pro-Union. As noted earlier, two of the three men in the Union Parliament who were most influential in mobilising support for incorporation, the earls of Stair and Seafield, had been union commissioners in 1689, 1702–3 and 1706. Thus, these two, and the third man in this category, the lord justice clerk Adam Cockburn, were no last-minute converts. Rather, an 'entire' union was something to which they had periodically and publicly demonstrated their commitment for almost two decades. With some justification, Stair, his son was convinced, gave his life for the Union, his health having been 'ruined by his continual attendance and application' in parliament.[114]

Of the 25 *squadrone* adherents, some 14 had been in exile. One of these was the earnestly Presbyterian Patrick Hume, elevated by William to the earldom of Marchmont. Despite having fallen out of favour under Queen Anne, Marchmont – who in 1688 had tried from Utrecht to persuade his co-religionists in Scotland to reject any compromise with King James, who 'had sucked in hatred, chiefly against Presbyterians, with his milk' – was steadfast in his allegiance to the Hanoverian succession.[115] He was also an ardent proponent of union from at least 1699 and probably earlier. Marchmont carried with him the votes of his two sons (also émigrés), and two sons-in-law, one of whom was George Baillie of Jerviswood, another émigré. Jerviswood had witnessed the public execution of his father, one of the Rye House plotters.[116] It was Marchmont who opened the debate in Parliament on the articles. In short men like these (from both the court party and the *squadrone*) were on what contemporaries called a 'Revolution foot'. Their enemies, such as Lockhart of Carnwath, were less flattering, terming several of them 'rotten fanaticks', but what Lockhart meant when he used pejorative terms of this kind was that they were implacable enemies of the male Stuart line, and of Roman Catholicism.

The other issue that galvanised the *squadrone* was the economy. Although not particularly enthusiastic about the union proposals, the earl of Roxburghe, the party's main spokesman in Parliament, observed on 2 November that whilst he had heard many 'fine' speeches against a union, none had offered a 'remedy ... for our present ill circumstances'. Consequently, he declared, 'I knou no way but this

---

[113] Whatley, *Scots and the Union*, 226–8; A. Campbell of Airds, *A History of Clan Campbell, Volume 3: From Restoration to the Present Day* (Edinburgh, 2004), 94–123.

[114] Whatley, *Scots and the Union*, 312.

[115] *A Selection of Papers From the Earls of Marchmont*, III, 78–9.

[116] D. J. Patrick and C. A. Whatley, 'Persistence, principle and patriotism in the making of the Union of 1707: the Revolution, Scottish Parliament and the *squadrone volante*', *History*, 92 (2007), 182; Davidson, *Discovering the Scottish Revolution*, 103.

union'.[117] This was simply a shorter, sharper and more eloquent way of encapsulating the prognosis of John Clerk and others. Another factor drawing the *squadrone* towards union was that, unlike 1702–3, it had become clear by 1706 that England was prepared to compensate the Scots for the Company of Scotland's losses to the tune of £219,000. This was a component of what was called the Equivalent, a sum of just under £400,000 sterling–in today's money something over £55 million–which also included a transfer of funds to the Scots for assuming a proportion of England's national debt, compensation for the calling in of the Scottish currency and its re-issue in sterling, and support for certain Scottish industries. In addition, long-overdue salaries for state service were to be paid, in many cases to those who had no influence in Parliament, although the union commissioners, who were to be rewarded for their services, did.[118] The many thousands of company investors, who ranged from the great nobility to ordinary people in the burghs, were to get their money back, with interest at five per cent per annum. The settlement has been described by Douglas Watt as 'an unusual departure in corporate history; a shareholder bail-out with cash provided by a foreign government', although there were those–particularly within the company – who reckoned that the Scots should have had more.[119] There were those in Scotland, although not many, who saw a future for the company after 1707. The Equivalent was attacked at the time by Lockhart and other opponents of the Union as a national bribe, a charge which still resonates. In addition, there is now also a question mark over the extent to which England's concession of the Equivalent should be regarded as a negotiating success, a victory for members of the Scottish Parliament who had held out for just such a payment from London throughout the preceding four years in return for abandoning part of the Scots' imperial dream. Certainly, larger sums do appear to have been floated in discussions south of the border prior to 1706–7.[120] Whether these might have been brought to the table had the Scots' commissioners pressed harder in the spring of 1706 is hard to tell. What is undeniable, however, is that in England there was a view that far too much had been conceded.[121]

For Parliament as a whole, the lure of the Equivalent appears to have been less potent than has sometimes been assumed. Other than a handful of individuals, Darien subscribers who were also members of Parliament showed little inclination to change sides on this basis. Those who held Darien stock and voted in favour of the Union, would, it seems, have done so anyway – although their support was

---

[117] NAS, GD 406/M9/266, fo.33.
[118] Shaw, *Political History*, 11–14.
[119] Watt, *Price of Scotland*, 230–1.
[120] Macinnes, 'Treaty of Union', 67–9; *Union and Empire*, 278–83.
[121] A. Murdoch, 'The legacy of Unionism in eighteenth-century Scotland', in Devine (ed.), *Scotland and the Union*, 79.

particularly robust.[122] Qualifying this, however, is the evidence that non-stockholders were more likely to support union than to oppose it. This is not to say that the indirect effects of Darien on politics in Scotland were anything other than profound; the shadow of the broken Company of Scotland loomed large over the entire decade that culminated in incorporation.[123]

In one respect the Equivalent was critical. That *squadrone* adherents included Revolution men and supporters of the Hanoverian succession has been established, but amongst their number too were individuals who had been directors of or investors in the Company of Scotland. These included Jerviswood, Marchmont and John Hay, second marquess of Tweeddale, but also another Borders' member of Parliament, William Bennet of Grubbet. An army officer, and a staunch supporter of William and the house of Hanover, Bennet had lost his son on the sea journey to Darien, as well as the money he had invested. Revealingly, on 13 April 1706, after hearing rumours of what the union commissioners then meeting at London might have obtained, Bennet wrote to a fellow *squadrone* member, William Nisbet of Dirleton: '... I think a fair bargain, with our neighbour nation, the best handle to give us peace, and save us from anarchy and confusion ... if we are now to have compensation, for what we have suffer'd from our neighbours, in the matter or Darien and the like, and the advantages of their trade, and plantations' would be 'full union'.[124] Thus early, therefore, it appeared that the party's multiple interests – which included a marked patriotic dimension – had been safeguarded, all in all a successful outcome for Whigs like Bennet and his allies. Significant though satisfaction with what sums the Equivalent would return to Darien investors was for the *squadrone*,[125] its importance as a determinant of the voting behaviour can be over-stated. Neither Roxburghe nor the duke of Montrose, another notable associate, had any claim on the bounty it brought.[126]

Perhaps of greater moment in ensuring that parliamentary support for the articles remained solid, and that protests outside were contained, was the preparedness of court politicians to accept or add amendments to the articles where these had been the focus of particularly sharp criticism or complaint. The outcome was a treaty which dealt *at least in part* with the main issues that concerned Scots in the early eighteenth century. The much-maligned commissioners who negotiated the broad terms of the Union in the spring and early summer of 1706 were convinced that they had secured within the articles what they termed the 'fundamentals' of Scottish civil society – primarily the legal system,

[122] Shaw, *Political History*, 4–5.

[123] See J. R. Young, 'The Scottish Parliament and the politics of empire: Parliament and the Darien project, 1695–1707', *Parliaments, Estates & Representation*, 27 (November 2007), 175–90.

[124] Whatley, *Scots and the Union*, 249–50.

[125] Young, 'Scottish Parliament and the politics of empire', 187–8.

[126] Shaw, *Political History*, 13.

the courts and the privileges of the convention of royal burghs. In this respect, there may have been more force than is immediately apparent in Sir Francis Grant's argument that the most important elements of Scottish sovereignty had been preserved within the union. Lawyers in Scotland had long determined that the legal system should remain separate, whatever the form of union, and it is significant that the profession was strongly-represented (not least by Sir Hew Dalrymple, Lord President of the Court of Session) amongst the membership of the union commissioners in 1706.[127] Under pressure, as has been noted, the court had ensured that the Church of Scotland was protected by a separate act. Further prudent concessions by ministers over the winter of 1706–7 took the sting out of the tails of their critics, and so made 'incorporation' more palatable. The final outcome was far from being the 'full' union that some had sought and many had resisted.

Reservations and fears, sometimes reflected in petitions sent to Parliament, meant that amendments to the articles were demanded, and conceded, in order to protect industries that might suffer from English competition – malt, coal and salt for example – and to lighten the burden of taxation on a population whose earnings were significantly lower than those of England.[128]

Possibly the issue that most exercised the hearts and minds of people outside Parliament Close was the fate following union of the 'visible mark' of Scotland's nationhood and sovereignty, the honours of Scotland – the ancient crown, and the sword and sceptre of state, which even Cromwell's army of occupation had been unable to locate and seize. Late in 1706, in Edinburgh, fears were fanned by country party politicians that the regalia were to be sent to England and melted down and lost forever, an outcome represented as deeply humiliating, as it would have symbolised conquest by Scotland's ancient foe. Consequently, ministers agreed to add a clause to the twenty-fourth article to the effect that the regalia as well as the public records of Scotland should remain in Scotland 'in all Time coming, notwithstanding of the Union'.[129] This of course was no substitute for real sovereignty, but the undertaking was important, and helped to sustain the Scots' sense of and belief in the continued existence of their nationhood within the British state. It was one of a number of features of the union settlement that ensured that incorporation was not the subjugating experience for Scotland that many had feared.

[127] Ford, 'Law of the sea', 137; Whatley, *Scots and the Union*, 237.

[128] Whatley, 'Salt, coal and the Union of 1707', 29–31, 37–41; Whatley, 'Economic causes and consequences', 158–65.

[129] *Papers Relative to the Regalia of Scotland*, Bannatyne Club (Edinburgh, 1929), 45–6.

The Scottish Historical Review, Volume LXXXVII: 2008 (Supplement), 31–44
DOI: 10.3366/E0036924108000462

CHRISTOPHER STORRS

Chapter 2
The Union of 1707 and the War of
the Spanish Succession

I

The Union of 1707 is too often thought of in narrowly British,
even – quite understandably in Scotland – in almost exclusively Scottish
terms. In fact, however, there was an important European dimension to
this major reconfiguration of the political structure of Britain, and it is
this European context which will be the subject of this chapter. More
specifically, the chapter will look at the Union in the context of the War
of the Spanish Succession (1701–1713/14), one of the great European
conflicts, and comparable in its impact on the first half of the eighteenth
century to that of the First World War on the first half of the twentieth.[1]
British contemporaries were well aware of the larger context of the
war: for one English politician, the successful conclusion of the Union
negotiations in 1706 ranked with the allied victories outside Turin in
Italy, and at Ramillies in Flanders, as among the great allied successes
of that year.[2] This chapter will seek to demonstrate that the War of the
Spanish Succession played a crucial part in determining the timing,
the mode and aspects of the implementation of the Union, as well as
defining some of the benefits it brought to the Scots. That the conflict
provided the crucial context or occasion for this decisive event is hardly
a novel insight;[3] nevertheless, the point bears reiteration and its various
aspects merit fuller exploration.

On the face of it, the War of the Spanish Succession was not about
essential Scottish interests.[4] The war was occasioned by the death

---

[1] I refer here primarily to the determination of many political leaders in the generation
after 1713 to avoid another war on the scale of that of the Spanish Succession,
and which led to a policy towards Spain in particular which in some respects pre-
figured 'appeasement'; those leaders included James Stanhope, who served in Spain
itself during the conflict and who was made a prisoner of war from 1710, see
Oxford Dictionary of National Biography, 60 vols. (Oxford, 2004) [henceforth *DNB*],
'James Stanhope'. The broader 'cultural' impact of the war in Britain, Scotland and
elsewhere, and the parallel with that of the First World War, remains to be explored.

[2] G. Holmes, *British Politics in the Age of* Anne, 2nd edn. (London, 1987), 85.

[3] It was treated most recently in J. Robertson, 'Union, state and empire', in L. Stone, ed.,
An Imperial State at War: Britain from 1689 to 1815 (London, 1994), 224–57, which in
some respects complements the present paper but which also has different concerns.

[4] The War of the Spanish Succession has, not surprisingly, generated a vast bibliography
regarding its origins, its course and its conclusion. The best brief account of the
international background is in D. McKay and H. M. Scott, *The Rise of the Great Powers
1648–1815* (London, 1983), 54–66. On the origins, see G. Clark, 'From the Nine

without heirs in 1700 of the last Spanish Habsburg monarch, Charles, or Carlos II. The two main contenders for what was still a vast and wealthy Spanish empire were the grandson of Louis XIV of France, the Bourbon Philip of Anjou, and the Austrian Habsburg, the future Holy Roman Emperor Charles VI. William III of England (who was William II of Scotland) and Louis XIV had sought, by means of two Partition Treaties (1698, 1700) to divide up the Spanish empire between the rival pretenders to the Spanish crown and thus prevent a war, but when Carlos II left his entire inheritance in his will to Philip of Anjou – stipulating that if Philip refused the whole should then pass to the Austrian Habsburg claimant – Louis XIV opted to accept the will rather than implement his prior agreements with William. The war effectively began in 1701 with England, Austria and the Dutch Republic ranged in the so-called 'Grand Alliance' against Bourbon France and Spain. The main area of fighting was Flanders and the Rhine – the scene of Marlborough's victories at Blenheim, Ramillies, Oudenarde and Malplaquet – but other major theatres included Piedmont in northern Italy and, of course, Spain itself, which developed into a considerable sideshow. Surprisingly, perhaps, there was relatively little fighting outside Europe.[5] The war was brought to a close after more than a decade of conflict by the peace of Utrecht, concluded in 1713, and by that of Baden and Rastatt, in 1714.

II

The decades around the turn of the seventeenth and eighteenth centuries – in effect between the outbreak of the Nine Years War (or War of the League of Augsburg) in 1688 and the treaty of Vienna of 1725 which put a temporary end to the hostility between the main rivals for the Spanish crown, Philip V of Spain and the Holy Roman Emperor Charles VI – were a period of remarkable state formation, or reconfiguration, in Europe. The Union of England and Scotland

[4] (*Continued*) Years War to the War of the Spanish Succession', in *The New Cambridge Modern History* [henceforth *NCMH*], vol. 6: *The Rise of Great Britain and Russia 1688–1725*, ed. J. S. Bromley (Cambridge, 1971), 381–409. As for the fighting, there is no good, simple, modern survey, but see (from a largely) French perspective, J. A. Lynn, *The Wars of Louis XIV 1667–1714* (London, 2002), 266–360, A. J. Veenendaal, 'The War of the Spanish Succession in Europe' *NCMH*, vol. 6, 410–45, and the older but still immensely useful, G. M. Trevelyan, *England under Queen Anne, vol. 1: Blenheim* (London, 1930), vol. 2: *Ramillies and the Union with Scotland* (London, 1932) and vol. 3: *The Peace and the Protestant Succession* (London, 1933). For the peace settlement(s) of 1713–14, see H. G. Pitt, 'The Pacification of Utrecht', *NCMH*, vol. 6, 446–79, and A.D. MacLachlan, 'The Road to peace 1710–1713', in *Britain after the Glorious Revolution 1689–1714*, ed. G. Holmes (London, 1969), 197–215.

[5] There was some, however: see C. T. Atkinson, 'Queen Anne's War in the West Indies Part 1. Jamaica', *Journal of the Society for Army Historical Research* [henceforth *JSAHR*], 24 (1946), 100–09'; C. T. Atkinson, 'Queen Anne's War in the West Indies Part II. The Windward sphere', *JSAHR*, 24 (1946), 183–97, and, for the abortive Quebec exhibition of 1711, W. T. Morgan, 'The South Sea Company and the Canadian expedition in the reign of Queen Anne', *Hispanic American Historical Review*, 8 (1928), 143–66.

should not be viewed in isolation. Spain, for example, lost its non-Spanish European territories. In Italy, the duchy of Milan fell to the allies following their victory at Turin in 1706, and passed to the Austrian Habsburg Emperor, Joseph I. The kingdom of Naples was conquered by Joseph's forces in 1707.[6] Flanders fell to the allies in the wake of Ramillies, and – following an abortive attempt to appoint Marlborough as interim governor – was jointly governed by the English and Dutch until it was formally handed over to Charles VI in 1716.[7] The island realm of Sardinia, which surrendered to the English admiral, Sir John Leake, after a bombardment in the summer of 1708, also passed to the Austrian Habsburgs.[8] Sicily was never conquered by the allies but the British government demanded that Philip V cede it to the Duke of Savoy as part of the price of peace in 1713.[9] Gibraltar, on the mainland, was seized by the allies in 1704, was held thereafter by the English and was not returned at the peace.[10] Finally, Menorca was another of Leake's conquests in 1708.[11] Besides these territorial changes, inside the peninsula the relationship between the territories of the Crown of Aragon (i.e. Aragon, Catalonia and Valencia) and the kingdom of Castile was transformed to such an extent that for many historians 'modern' Spain was finally created.[12] In Italy, the Savoyard state, too, was transformed: as a member of the victorious Grand Alliance, the Duke of Savoy received in 1713 the island realm of Sicily (which was effectively in the gift of the British government), although he was later obliged to exchange it for the poorer island kingdom of Sardinia in 1720.[13] Austria, another victorious ally, secured (as has already been indicated) Flanders, Milan, and Naples, becoming the dominant power in Italy. In central and eastern Europe, from 1697 the electorate of Saxony entered into a *de facto* union with Poland-Lithuania.[14] As for northern Europe, the collapse of the Swedish empire was accompanied by the loss of various territories to its neighbours, the chief beneficiary

[6] C. Ingrao, *In Quest and Crisis: Emperor Joseph I and the Habsburg Monarchy* (W. Lafayette, 1979), p. 79ff; M. Hochedlinger, *Austria's Wars of Emergence: War, State and Society in the Habsburg Monarchy 1683–1797* (Harlow, 2003), 176ff; Trevelyan, *Ramillies*, p. 313.

[7] Trevelyan, *Ramillies*, 142ff; A. J. Veenendaal, *Het Engels-Nederlands Condominium in de Zuidelijke Nederlanden tijdens de Spaanse Successieoorlog* (Utrecht, 1945); Ingrao, *In Quest and Crisis*, 161ff.

[8] Trevelyan, *Ramillies*, 399; *DNB*, 'Sir John Leake'.

[9] D. McKay, 'Bolingbroke, Oxford and the defence of the Utrecht settlement in southern Europe', *English Historical Review*, 96 (1971), 264–84; C. Storrs, *War, Diplomacy and the Rise of Savoy, 1690–1720* (Cambridge, 1999), 4.

[10] Trevelyan, *Blenheim*, 420ff; *Ramillies*, 48ff.

[11] Trevelyan, *Ramillies*, 397–402.

[12] There is a substantial literature on this in Spanish, but see, in English, H. Kamen, *The War of Succession in Spain 1700–1715* (London, 1969), 309–60, and J. Lynch, *Bourbon Spain 1700–1808* (Oxford, 1988), 22–66.

[13] Storrs, *War, Diplomacy and the Rise of Savoy*, 4–5.

[14] J. Gierowski and A. Kaminski, 'The Eclipse of Poland', *NCMH*, vol. 6, 681–715; N. Davies, *God's Playground. A History of Poland, 1: The Origins to 1795* (Oxford, 1981), 492ff.

being Peter the Great's Russia.[15] More examples could be given, but the point is clear enough: the Union of England and Scotland occurred in a Europe in which some existing states were being dismantled, and others constructed. It was an era of political upheaval.

III

The examples of state formation just cited represented or offered models of reconfiguration, or union, through military conquest and forcible incorporation – which were very different from that adopted by England and Scotland. They were also associated with – and a consequence of – war. Of the three main routes to union – conquest, inheritance or marriage, and negotiation – the first was certainly more common than the last.[16] In the following pages, I will demonstrate that the War of the Spanish Succession helped to bring about the Union of England and Scotland, and also to ensure that the mode of Union was very different from most of the examples cited above.

The timing of the Act of Union was influenced by the war in various ways. Firstly, there was the looming prospect – following the passage by the Scottish Parliament of the Act of Security – that England and Scotland might have different monarchs following the death of Queen Anne, due to Scotland's refusal to follow England in determining that the Crown should pass to the House of Hanover should Anne (as seemed likely) die without issue.[17] There was the possibility that Scotland might be neutral – or worse, that it might be ruled by a Jacobite client of Louis XIV, the main continental backer of the Jacobite cause from 1689[18] – while England was at war with France. Secondly, the progress of the war ruled out foreign intervention to prevent union. In 1703–4, apparently, Louis XIV promised the Scots Jacobites military aid once French arms were successful in Germany. However, this intervention – if it was ever seriously meant – was knocked on the head by Marlborough's victory at Blenheim, which deprived the Bourbon powers of their only German ally, the Elector of Bavaria, and put France on the back foot. A few years later, in 1706, Marlborough's victory at Ramillies and that of Prince Eugene of Savoy outside Turin brought the collapse of the Bourbons in Flanders and Italy. This in turn both enhanced the (military) prestige of the Allies and rendered Louis XIV unable to intervene in Britain to obstruct the Union.

---

[15] R. M. Hatton, 'Charles XII and the Great Northern War', *NCMH*, vol. 6, 648–80; M. S. Anderson, 'Russia under Peter the Great and the changed relations of East and West', *NCMH*, vol. 6, 716–40; L. Hughes, *Russia in the Age of Peter the Great* (New Haven and London, 1998), 26–62; S. Dixon, *The Modernisation of Russia 1676–1825* (Cambridge, 1999), 27–56.

[16] M. Greengrass, *Conquest and coalescence: The Shaping of the State in Early Modern Europe* (London, 1991), 7ff.

[17] Trevelyan, *Ramillies*, 255ff.

[18] C. Nordmann, 'Louis XIV and the Jacobites', *Louis XIV and Europe*, ed. R. M. Hatton (London, 1976), 82–111; D. Szechi, *The Jacobites: Britain and Europe 1688–1788* (Manchester, 1994), 41ff; Trevelyan, *Ramillies*, 358–9.

That the Union of England and Scotland was not achieved by conquest as in so many of the examples cited earlier also owed a great deal to the war. For one thing, despite the allied victories, Queen Anne and her ministers could not afford to withdraw from Flanders and Spain troops for the purpose of military action against Scotland. The diversion of large numbers of troops to deal with the threat posed by James II in Ireland between 1689 and 1691 had demonstrated the dangers of such a distraction from the war in Europe.[19] During the War of the Spanish Succession, and despite the hiring of troops from foreign princes – above all in Germany – large numbers of men were still needed in both Flanders and Spain.[20] France in 1706 had suffered a succession of defeats but was fighting on, and the Allies still needed to secure Flanders. In addition, English ministers were planning a decisive blow against French sea-power in the Mediterranean for 1707, by means of an attack on the great naval base at Toulon.[21] In such circumstances, to deploy troops in and against Scotland unless absolutely necessary would be highly risky.

But the use of force against Scotland was not necessary because many Scots supported England's stance in the War of the Spanish Succession, and for various reasons. Firstly, the Scots were defending their Protestant religion against the threat from a militant Roman Catholic France and the advancing Counter-Reformation. We tend to think of the Counter-Reformation, that is, the reform, renewal and reinvigoration of Roman Catholic Christendom, as something defined by the Council of Trent (1545–63), by the [Spanish] Inquisition and by the Society of Jesus (the Jesuits) – and as something that was largely over by about 1600.[22] Nothing could be further from the truth. In many respects the Counter-Reformation was only really getting going, and recovering lost ground, *from* 1600. And crucial to the success of the Counter-Reformation in much of Europe was the role of the state. In France, where the Huguenots had seemed in the 1560s to be on the verge of seizing control of the state, the Reformed Church was in retreat a century later. Forcible conversions by Louis XIV's troops – the so-called 'dragonnades' – were followed in 1685 by the French monarch's revocation of the Edict of Nantes of 1598 which had promised a degree of religious toleration.[23] Many Huguenots preferred to flee France, with a few settling in Scotland, the majority of these

[19] Lynn, *Wars of Louis XIV*, 203–4; S. B. Baxter, *William III* (Harlow, 1966), 258ff.

[20] J. Brewer, *The Sinews of Power, War, Money and the English State 1688–1783* (London, 1989); on the financial aspects, D. W. Jones, *War and Economy in the Age of William III and Marlborough* (Oxford, 1987), and P. G. M. Dickson, *The Financial Revolution in England 1688–1756* (London, 1967), 100.

[21] Trevelyan, *Ramillies*, 179, 312–13.

[22] R. Birely, *The Refashioning of Catholicism 1450–1700: a Reassessment of the Counter Reformation* (Basingstoke, 1999), *passim*; R. Po-Chia-Hsia, *The World of Catholic Renewal 1540–1770*, 2nd ed. (Cambridge, 2005), *passim*.

[23] R. L. McCullough, *Coercion, Conversion and Counterinsurgency in Louis XIV's France* (Leiden, 2007), 125ff.

in Edinburgh.[24] Louis was not only keen to extirpate Protestantism in his own state: he also obliged the Duke of Savoy to seek to extirpate the Protestant Vaudois, or Waldensians, from neighbouring Piedmont from 1685.[25] More examples could be cited from other parts of Europe but these are sufficient to demonstrate that the Scots and the English were entirely justified in worrying in 1700 about the threat posed to their religion by an aggressive, crusading Catholicism spearheaded by the 'Sun King'. These fears and the supposed existence of thousands of resentful Huguenots in southern France ready to take up arms – a view given some credibility by the outbreak of the so-called Camisards revolt in 1703[26] – helped shape Allied strategy in the War of the Spanish Succession: the English and Dutch certainly hoped to land Protestant forces in France which might trigger or sustain such a revolt by their co-religionists, but were never able to realise this ambition,[27] mirroring the disappointment of France which hoped to foment Jacobite revolt in Britain.[28] Once again, this was a crucial part of the context of Union.

It was not simply that Louis XIV was the champion of a resurgent Catholicism. His style of rule, what historians call 'absolutism' – according to which the king approximated to a modern all-powerful ruler, largely by-passing representative institutions and imposing his will by means of a centralised bureaucracy whose local agents, the intendants, could also call on an expanding royal army to enforce the king's will[29] – was also unattractive. In recent decades, historians have questioned the reality of this traditional image of monarchical absolutism.[30] This revisionism is salutary, not least because many of the very negative contemporary depictions of Louis as tyrant and despot were created as part of the anti-French propaganda campaign mounted during both the Nine Years War and the War of the Spanish Succession.[31] It has also been suggested that war – and above all the War of the Spanish Succession – put such strain on Louis'

[24] D. Dobson, *Huguenot and Scots Links 1575–1775* (Baltimore, 2005), 'Introduction'. I thank Dr. Derek Patrick of the University of Dundee for this reference.

[25] G. Symcox, *Victor Amadeus II: Absolutism in the Savoyard State 1675–1730* (London, 1983), 92ff; Storrs, *War, Diplomacy and the Rise of Savoy*, 293ff.

[26] McCullough, *Coercion, Conversion*, 181ff.

[27] In 1706, typically, an expedition was planned under the leadership of earl Rivers, whose objective was to land a force of more than 11,000 men in south-west France which should ignite Protestant rebellion in the Midi, but this expedition was ultimately diverted to Spain. Trevelyan, *Ramillies*, 314–15, and *DNB*, 'Richard Savage, fourth earl Rivers'.

[28] The observations of the French commander, the Duke of Berwick, in Trevelyan, *Ramillies*, 170. Berwick, illegitimate son of James II and VII, was a leading figure in the Jacobite movement between 1701 and his death in 1736. See *DNB*, 'James Fitzjames, Duke of Berwick'. There is a pressing need for a full, modern study of Berwick.

[29] D. Ogg, *Louis XIV* (Oxford, 1967), 56ff.

[30] R. Mettam, 'France', in *Absolutism in Seventeenth Century Europe*, ed. J. Miller (London, 1990), 43–68; W. Beik, *Absolutism and Society in Seventeenth Century France: State Power and Provincial Aristocracy in Languedoc* (Cambridge, 1985), *passim*; N. Henshall, *The Myth of Absolutism* (London, 1995), 43–68.

[31] P. Burke, *The Fabrication of Louis XIV* (New Haven, 1994), *passim*.

regime that in some respects the royal state faltered.[32] However, even if we accept the revisionist portrayal of Louis XIV's reign, we should not ignore the views of those contemporaries for whom the French monarch's authority and effective power were greater than that of his own predecessors and of many contemporary monarchs, and for whom the 'Sun King's' style of government was both alien and deeply unattractive, just as James II and VII's putative absolutism had been to many in England and Scotland before 1688.[33] In this respect, the War of the Spanish Succession was a clash of political ideologies and regimes. It was a struggle between the revolutionary regime established in England and Scotland in the wake of the revolutions of 1688–89 and a French-style absolutism. Indeed, England could be said to have been pursuing a distinctive 'Revolutionary' foreign policy after 1688, and well into the War of the Spanish Succession and beyond, not simply in terms of defending the achievement of 1688–89 but also in encouraging, *ancien régime* style, representative institutions: in Flanders, in Spain, in France. It was hoped that the revival of these representative assemblies would put a restraint on Louis XIV's ability to find funds for and thus to wage aggressive war abroad, including in and against Scotland.[34]

Not surprisingly, then, many in England and Scotland worried about the supposed aspirations of Louis XIV, the most powerful sovereign in western Europe to what the age called 'universal monarchy'.[35] A generation or so ago, the Sun King was regarded by historians as little more than a naked aggressor, who aimed to be the 'dictator' of Europe.[36] Once again, however, in recent decades revisionist historians have questioned this view, suggesting instead that Louis's foreign policy was in fact largely defensive and driven by anxiety about France's vulnerability.[37] But in this instance, too, we should not forget the views of those contemporaries, including many Scots, for whom Louis's actions – and not least Louis's recognition of the Old Pretender as king of England in September 1701 on the death of James II and

---

[32] D. Dee, 'Wartime government in Franche Comte and the demodernisation of the French State, 1704–1715', *French Historical Studies*, 30 (2007), 21–7.

[33] J. R. Western, *Monarchy and Revolution: The English State in the 1680s* (London, 1972), *passim*; J. R. Jones, *The Revolution of 1688* (London, 1972), *passim*.

[34] In 1706, in order to encourage Brabant (Flanders) to adhere to the allies, Marlborough promised that the Austrian Habsburgs would abide by the so-called *Joyeuse Entrée*, a sort of constitutional guarantee dating from the fourteenth century. Trevelyan, *Ramillies*, 142ff. Similarly, earl Rivers' abortive expedition to Guienne (above) was expected to proclaim the restoration not only of the Edict of Nantes but also of the States General. Trevelyan, *Ramillies*, 314. Subsequently, in 1713, the British government insisted that Philip V renounce his claims on the French throne before the Castilian Cortes, which had not met for more than fifty years and which was rarely assembled in the eighteenth century. J. L. Castellano, *Las Cortes y su Diputacion 1621–1789* (Madriod, 1990), 141ff.

[35] On this term, part of the common currency of the political culture of the age as far as international relations was concerned c. 1700. Robertson, 'Union, state and empire', 228–9, 240.

[36] Ogg, *Louis XIV*, 44ff.

[37] McKay and Scott, *Rise of Great Powers*, 16–17.

VII[38] – were interpreted as a threat to their liberties, their faith and their independence.[39]

The war also impacted, finally, upon the immediate implementation of the Union: some of the money promised as part of the so-called 'equivalent' was – initially at least – paid in Treasury Bills rather than cash.[40] This reflected not so much bad faith on the part of London as the fact that, like the Nine Years War, the War of the Spanish Succession presented a serious challenge to the finances of the English and new British state, as it did to all the participants. One consequence was an astonishing increase in the national debt in the short and long terms;[41] another was a serious shortage of specie in London,[42] where ministers found it very difficult to meet all their obligations.[43]

IV

That many Scots shared the concerns just discussed (and that there were issues of principle at stake for many Scots in 1706–07 as much as the lure of access to larger markets) is suggested by their participation as front-line troops in both the Nine Years War and the War of the Spanish Succession.[44] Indeed, it is arguable that a common British army was emerging before the union of the parliaments.[45] The military (and naval) commitment implied by participation in these conflicts was partly met by the use of continental allies, but it also necessitated an increase in the size of the armies of both William and Anne,[46] and Scots contributed to that expansion. Of course, we must be cautious about the commitment to – even awareness of – the big political or religious issues on the part of the rank and file, many of whom were *de facto* conscripts, although we should also beware of underestimating their political awareness, or their commitment to an ideal.[47] Many of the

---

[38] Trevelyan, *Blenheim*, 158–9. The hostile Grand Alliance had been concluded just days earlier.

[39] For a recent restatement of this older view, see H. Hasquin, *Louis XIV face à l'Europe du Nord: L'absolutisme vaincu par les libertés* (Bruxelles, 2005). See also J. F. Bosher, 'The Franco-Catholic danger 1660–1715', *History*, 79 (1994).

[40] D. Watt, *The Price of Scotland. Darien, Union and the Wealth of Nations* (Edinburgh, 2006), 240–1.

[41] Brewer, *Sinews of Power*, 114; Dickson, *Financial Revolution*, 100.

[42] P. G. M. Dickson and J. Sperling, 'War finance 1689–1714', *NCMH*, vol. 6, 284–315.

[43] For the difficulties faced by others to whom Queen Anne had financial obligations, including her subsidy-receiving allies, one of whom was the Duke of Savoy, see Storrs, *War, Diplomacy and the Rise of Savoy*, p. 114.

[44] For the second of these conflicts, see S. H. F. Johnston, 'The Scots army in the reign of Anne', *Transactions of the Royal Historical Society*, 5th ser., 3 (1953), 1–21.

[45] J. Goodare, *State and Society in Early Modern Scotland* (Oxford, 1998), 324, makes a similar point but on rather different grounds.

[46] For the War of the Spanish Succession, see R. E. Scouller, The *Armies of Queen Anne* (Oxford, 1966); G. Davies, 'Recruiting in the reign of Queen Anne', *JSAHR*, 28 (1950), 146–91, and I. F. Burton, 'The Supply of infantry for the War in the Peninsula, 1703–1707', *Bulletin of the Institute of Historical Research*, 28 (1955), 35–62.

[47] CF. K. Bowie, *Scottish Public Opinion and the Anglo-Scottish Union, 1699–1707* (London, 2007), *passim*.

men who served in the Cameronian regiment, which was raised in 1689 by the earl of Angus, and which fought in Flanders in the Nine Years War[48] and War of the Spanish Succession, were probably fighting for their faith: this is certainly true of captain John Blackader whose diaries are a valuable source for the War of the Spanish Succession.[49] The many other regiments raised in these decades offered similar opportunities to men of faith and principle.[50] Numerous other Scots served in this emerging 'British' army. It was an attractive career for younger sons in noble families: Lord John Hay, younger son of the second marquis of Tweeddale, became lieutenant colonel of the Scots dragoons in 1694, and colonel (by purchase) in 1704. He and his regiment distinguished themselves in the Blenheim campaign and again, at Ramillies, in 1706. Hay's death later that year was – according to Marlborough – 'regretted through the whole army', suggesting that by serving together in a common cause some English and Scots developed a greater appreciation of and respect for each other *before* the Union.[51] Another younger son, Lord Mark Kerr, served in Flanders in the Nine Years War and in Spain in the War of the Spanish Succession.[52] Yet another cadet of a noble house, George Hamilton, later earl of Orkney, played a distinguished military role in both wars.[53] So, too, did the sons of the third earl of Balcarres, Colin and Alexander Lindsay.[54] But it was not only younger sons who were participating. The Duke of Argyll, Scotland's premier aristocrat, fought at Ramillies and Oudenard and secured the command-in-chief (1711–12) of the British forces in Spain.[55] Similarly, the future second earl of Stair had established a distinguished military record in the service of William III and Anne well before 1707.[56] Scots were serving at all levels, even the very highest, in this emerging 'British' army,[57] their service involving long periods of

[48] S. F. H. Johnston, 'A Scots chaplain in Flanders, 1691–97', *JSAHR*, 27 (1949), 3–10, quotes extensively from the letters of Alexander Shields, chaplain to Angus' regiment. Among many noteworthy observations is the fact that other Scots regiments in William III's army, notably those of a different religious persuasion, barracked the regiment in camp.

[49] *The Life and Diaries of Lieut. Col. John Blackadder*, ed. A. Chrichton (1824); *DNB*, 'John Blackader'. Trevelyan, *Ramillies*, 135n., notes that Blackader had no love for the English.

[50] For the forces raised by David Melville, third earl of Leven, during and after the Revolution of 1688–89, and their service in Flanders in the Nine Years War, see *DNB*, 'David Melville, third earl of Leven'; H. Maxwell, *The Lowland Scots Regiments: Their Origin, Character and Services previous to the Great War of 1914* (Glasgow, 1918).

[51] *DNB*, 'Lord John Hay'.

[52] *DNB*, 'Robert Kerr, first marquess of Lothian'.

[53] *DNB*, 'George Hamilton, first earl of Orkney'.

[54] *DNB*, Colin, Lindsay, third earl of Balcarres'. Another of the earl's sons served in the navy, suggesting the same was happening in the other fighting arm of the incipient British state.

[55] *DNB*, 'John Campbell second duke of Argyll and duke of Greenwich'.

[56] *DNB*, 'John Dalrymple, second earl of Stair'.

[57] K. Brown, 'From Scottish lords to British officers: state building, elite integration and the army in the seventeenth century', in *Scotland and War, AD 79–1918*, ed. N. Macdougall (Edinburgh, 1991), 133–69.

absence.[58] Many of those who defended the revolution settlement in the field in this way also voted for Union.[59]

V

Contemporaries also tended to see the Union very much in terms of current events, and not least of the War of the Spanish Succession. Unfortunately, this is a statement easier to make than to prove, not least because hardly any research has been done on foreign reactions to the Union. There are references to the Union in the correspondence of Dutch leaders – notably the Grand Pensionary, Anthonie Heinsius – and diplomats, but they do not amount to very much. What there is, as with references to Scotland in the Dutch correspondence in 1688–89, is overwhelmingly about the relevance of the Union for Scotland's contribution to the war effort.[60]

The same is true of the reaction in London of the representative of one of Queen Anne's allies, her cousin, Victor Amadeus II, Duke of Savoy.[61] The duke's territories offered the Grand Alliance a route into France from Italy, through the Alpine passages. He depended enormously upon the support of his more powerful allies, and particularly England, which not only paid a subsidy but also effectively gave him troops.[62] Clearly, Victor Amadeus had to be alert to anything which might affect England's ability to support the war in Europe and his minister in London, count Briancon (or Brianzone) therefore monitored the progress of the Union negotiations. On 23 January 1705, Briancon reported a proposal of the House of Lords to fortify various places along the border with Scotland, and to 'discipline' the militia there, ready for any confrontation between the two realms over the succession; he also noted its rejection by the Commons, on the grounds that to do so might give the 'ill intentioned' in Scotland an opportunity to foment disturbances which would then necessitate the re-location of troops being used so effectively against the common enemy, Louis XIV

---

[58] The extent to which – particularly among the elite – military service (and service of the state more generally) meant the absence of Scots noblemen, thus allowing their female relations greater 'space' and a greater voice (not least in the run-up to the Union) is an issue which has yet to be properly addressed but which is currently being investigated by Nicola Cowmeadow at the University of Dundee.

[59] C. A. Whatley with D. J. Patrick, *The Scots and the Union* (Edinburgh, 2006), 302, where further examples are given.

[60] I owe this information to David Onnekink, whose help I am delighted to acknowledge. William III's Dutch favourite, the earl of Portland, who took an interest in Scottish affairs, favoured union, D. Onnekink, *The Anglo-Dutch Favourite: The Career of Hans Willem Bentinck, 1st Earl of Portland (1649–1709)* (Aldershot, 2007), 254.

[61] It is noteworthy that there was virtually no diplomatic presence in the Scottish capital, Edinburgh.

[62] Storrs, *War, Diplomacy and the Rise of Savoy*, 106ff., 54ff. The Duke's sons, by virtue of his marriage, also had a claim on the English succession, a claim which had been set aside (in favour of the house of Hanover) in 1701, prompting a formal protest by the Duke's minister in London; *ibid.*, 152.

and the Bourbons.[63] More than a year later, on 30 April 1706, Briancon mentioned the first conferences between the English and Scottish commissioners negotiating the Union, although he gave no details.[64] In the summer, on 6 August 1706, Briancon was able to report not only that the queen had received the draft treaty of union but also attached a copy of the [25] articles.[65] On 3 December 1706, Briancon wrote that the Scottish Parliament had agreed to an Act of Succession in favour of the House of Hanover, noting that the majority had been fifty-four, and that this encouraged a belief that the other articles of Union would also be approved.[66] On 11 February 1707 Briancon reported that Queen Anne had appeared before the English Parliament to report that the Scottish Parliament had passed the Act of Union, and to request the English body to conclude rapidly a business so advantageous to the nation, and one which – the crucial point for Briancon and his master – would greatly increase its power. Briancon again expressed confidence that the matter would be concluded speedily, not least because the opposition was too weak.[67] Finally, on 17 March 1707, Briancon noted the Queen's visit to Parliament the previous day to give the royal assent to the Act of Union, which now – he declared – was concluded happily to general content and equal advantage to this nation. We may not entirely agree with Briancon on the extent of satisfaction with the Union,[68] given that he was largely restricted to London. In addition, other aspects of the war – including allied strategy, Victor Amadeus' subsidy, and his territorial ambitions – merited full discussion in the Savoyard minister's despatches to Turin.[69] However, he clearly recognised that the Union was worthy of comment and, equally clearly, he saw its significance in terms of England's (and Scotland's) power and importance in Europe.

The same must also be said of Queen Anne's foreign enemies, that is, the Bourbon powers (above all Louis XIV) and apparently the Pope, Clement XI. Louis XIV made every effort within his power to foment opposition to the Union before 1707. Unable to send troops, he instead channelled funds towards the opposition to Union in the Scottish Parliament (including some money made available by the papal Curia).[70] It is worth observing then, given the way Scottish supporters of the Union have been charged with accepting money to vote through the Union – in effect, selling their country – that, had the Union failed, those responsible might well have incurred the accusation that they

[63] Count Briancon to Duke of Savoy, 23 Jan. 1705, London, Archivio di Stato. Torino [AST], Lettere Ministri [LM], Inghilterra, mazzo 12.

[64] Briancon to Duke of Savoy, 30 Apr. 1706, London, AST, LM Inghilterra, mazzo 13.

[65] Briancon to Duke of Savoy, 6 Aug. 1706, London, AST, LM Inghilterra, mazzo 13.

[66] Briancon to Duke of Savoy, 3 Dec. 1706, London, AST, LM Inghilterra, mazzo 13.

[67] Briancon to Duke of Savoy, 11 Feb. 1707, London, AST, LM Inghilterra, mazzo 14.

[68] Briancon to Duke of Savoy, 17 Mar. 1707, London, AST, LM Inghilterra, mazzo 14.

[69] Much of the correspondence is printed in *Le Campagne di Guerra in Piemonte (1703–1708) e l'assedio di Torino (1706)* ed. C. Contessa et al. 10 vols. (Turin, 1908–33), vol. 5.

[70] Trevelyan, *Ramillies*, 358.

had been 'bought and sold', but for French and papal gold.[71] The success of the Union did not deter Louis from seeking to undermine and overthrow a development which clearly enhanced the strength of the state which was emerging as the paymaster of the coalition which was gradually reining in France, by encouraging and exploiting Jacobite – and other – discontent in Scotland (and thus perhaps weaken the British military effort in the Low Countries). In 1708, buoyed up by the failure of the allied attempt on Toulon in 1707,[72] and with few other strategic options that year,[73] Louis backed a Jacobite attempt in 1708.[74] Despite its failure, French and – particularly after 1713 when Britain and France temporarily drew together – Spanish) ministers continued to target Scotland and the Union.[75]

VI

Finally, some questions suggest themselves regarding the short-term domestic impact of the Union in creating a common political culture in the two kingdoms, as measured by attitudes to the War of the Spanish Succession. Historians of England have long been aware of the way a general enthusiasm for war against France (and Spain) developed in England between 1700 and 1702 largely on the basis of the errors of Louis XIV – in, for example, acknowledging the Old Pretender as King of England (and Scotland) on the death of James II and VII in 1701.[76] But the war was in some respects a Whig affair in an England which was seriously divided along party lines in these decades, and in which the war, and how it was fought and paid for, were divisive issues.[77] Increasingly, as the war went on and victory continued to elude the allies (despite Marlborough's victories), English opinion turned against the war. In October 1710, the General Election witnessed a landslide in favour of the Tories.[78] The new government then proceeded to negotiate what was to all intents and purposes a separate peace – that of Utrecht – with Louis XIV (and Philip V) largely at the expense of their

[71] It must, however, be admitted that this is a difficult matter to penetrate, and that it needs much fuller investigation, drawing above all on the French and Vatican archives.

[72] Trevelyan, *Ramillies*, 324ff.

[73] D. Szechi, *George Lockhart of Carnwath 1689–1727: A Study in Jacobitism* (East Linton, 2002), 69–70.

[74] Trevelyan, *Ramillies*, 359ff; Szechi, *Jacobites*, 41ff.

[75] C. Storrs, 'Foreign penetration of the Spanish Empire 1660–1714: Sweden, Scotland and England', in *Shaping the Stuart World, 1603–1714. The Atlantic Connection*, ed. A. I. Macinnes and A. H. Williamson (Leiden, 2006), 337–65. In 1725, intercepted letters apparently revealed a plot to land arms in the Highlands in preparation for a venture on behalf of the Old Pretender; one English minister believed that only Spain could fund such an attempt. Townshend to Newcastle, Oct. 1725, in W. Coxe, *Memoirs... of Sir Robert Walpole*, 3 vols. (London, 1798), 2, 480ff.

[76] Trevelyan, *Blenheim*, 159.

[77] G. Holmes and W. A. Speck, *The Divided Society: Party Conflict in England 1694–1716* (London, 1967), 91ff; Holmes, *British Politics*, 71ff.

[78] G. Holmes, *The Making of a Great Power. Late Stuart and Early Georgian Britain 1660–1722* (Harlow, 1993), 423.

allies.[79] To cement support at home for their policy of disengagement abroad, the Tories undertook a major propaganda campaign aimed at depicting the allies as selfishly exploiting England and its resources for their own ends, a campaign brilliantly promoted by Jonathan Swift's pamphlet *The Conduct of the Allies*.[80] The questions here are: how far did this war weariness extend to Scotland, and to what extent did the two countries share in a desire to bring it to a close? One means of answering this question might be to look at the General Election in Scotland in 1710, another might be to identify the extent of the sale, readership and response to Swift's and similar pamphlets in Scotland.

Another issue meriting attention is contemporary Scottish perceptions of Catalonia. In 1705, as England's commitment to the war in Spain expanded, Queen Anne's government promised – in the so-called Pact of Genoa – to back a Catalan revolt against Philip V.[81] And for the next five years, Anne's ministers did support the Catalans. However, the Tory government's abandonment of its allies between 1710 and 1714 also involved the sacrifice of the Catalans, in order to secure from Philip V Gibraltar, Port Mahon and the asiento, i.e. the lucrative contract to supply African slaves to the Spanish colonists in the Americas.[82] This betrayal caused a political storm at home,[83] although the affair has been largely ignored by British historians of the domestic politics of Queen Anne's reign. How far did the treatment of the Catalans exercise Scots in these years?[84] And how far did Scots see parallels between their own union with England and the forcible incorporation of Catalonia (and indeed the rest of the Crown of Aragon) into a largely Castilian Crown, including as it did the abolition of the various Corts or representative assemblies of Aragon?[85]

The War of the Spanish Succession also, finally, impacted upon the extent to which Scotland and its people were to benefit from the Union.[86] It is generally argued that the Union opened up remarkable new economic opportunities for Scots. While this may well have been the case, it might not have happened if the war had gone badly for the new polity. In addition, just how Scots' economic horizons broadened after 1707 needs further study, particularly concerning just how far economic privileges hitherto thought of as being confined to the English – or explicitly expressed as such in treaties – were now extended to subjects north of the border. In the spring of 1713, Queen Anne's

79 Pitt, 'Pacification of Utrecht', *passim*.
80 Trevelyan, *The Peace*, 121–2, 213–14; *DNB*, 'Jonathan Swift'.
81 Trevelyan, *Blenheim*, 200; *DNB*, 'Mitford Crowe', who negotiated the pact on behalf of Queen Anne.
82 Storrs, 'Foreign penetration', 360ff.
83 J. Albareda, *Felipe V y el triunfo del absolutismo. Cataluna en un conflicto europeo (1700–1714)* (Generalitat de Catalunya, 2002), 129ff.
84 Among the most important of these pamphlets was *The Case of the Catalans Consider'd* (London, 1714).
85 See the works referred to in note 12 above.
86 For what follows, see Storrs, 'Foreign penetration', 362–3.

ambassador in Paris, the Duke of Shrewsbury, observed that the trading privileges in the Spanish empire granted by the asiento agreement were confined to 'the English nation' whereas he took it for granted that all of the queen's subjects were included and thus that a different wording was needed. His comments had effect: the final trade treaty concluded at Utrecht in December 1713 spoke of the subjects of Great Britain. We still do not know enough about how existing treaties were reinterpreted to the advantage of Scots after 1707 or the extent to which Scots exploited the new economic concessions won in 1712–13, but at the least the War of the Spanish Succession expanded the possibilities of commercially minded Scots.

Much more could be said, exploring some of the issues articulated by John Robertson in his earlier attempt to set the Union in its broad international context, and more specifically against the background of the 'Great War' that was the War of the Spanish Succession. But the foregoing pages should have made clear that the Union cannot be understood, either in its timing, its manner, its execution or its consequences, without taking into account the War of the Spanish Succession. Equally, England's or Britain's success in what has been called the Second Hundred Years War against France between 1688 and 1815, and its emergence in the long eighteenth century as a major world power is incomprehensible if we fail to take into account the very successful and peaceful Union which removed a potentially serious threat to England's northern flank.

The Scottish Historical Review, Volume LXXXVII: 2008 (Supplement), 45–60
DOI: 10.3366/E0036924108000474

RICHARD SAVILLE

Chapter 3
Intellectual Capital in Pre-1707
Scotland[1]

By the seventeenth century, the extension of grammar schools and university education, coupled with the Calvinist theology, provided the Reformed Church of Scotland with an intellectual base well suited to theological and philosophical controversy. The improvement in methods of learning, persistent correction and criticism, and a rigorous logic inculcated the ability to establish where connections lay between Scripture and natural law, which enabled theologians and lawyers to cull hearsay and isolate pleading for particular interests. Severity of upbringing – a noteworthy feature of Scotland – inured the young to the long hours of study essential for success in disputation and intellectual progress. While these rigorous standards lent themselves to theology and philosophy, they also benefited the professions, by promoting the intellectual patience needed for understanding sequences, precedents and consequences as required for success in law, administration, medicine, banking and foreign trade. We see in this the rise of the Scottish administrator; the manager trained in the grammar schools, prepared to work long hours for low pay in business, trade and improved husbandry, and who after work would enlist in the civilian army of the Church and municipal government. The embrace of the intellect ensured that the deep roots nurtured by sixteenth-century theologians in business, trade and science assisted in the formation of the middling and upper ranks.[2]

In the early eighteenth century few believed that Scotland's middle and upper ranks possessed sufficient knowledge, resourcefulness, banking expertise, and legal acumen to enable the country to become

[1] Thanks are due to Paul Auerbach, Robin Pearson, Stana Nenadic, Jane Dawson, Isobel Long, Tracey Earl, Helen Redmond-Cooper and Seonaid McDonald.
[2] Questions of the intellect and the direction of Western societies in respect of human capital are central to understanding the advance of western Europe before industrialisation; A. Gershenkron, *Economic Backwardness in Historical Perspective* (Cambridge, Mass., 1962), chaps. 1, 2, 3; Karl Marx, *Grundrisse: Foundations of the Critique of Political Economy*, (ed.) trans. B. Fowkes (London, 1973), 459–71; W. Sombart, *Luxury and Capitalism*, ed. P. Siegelman, trans. W. Dittmar (Ann Arbor, Mich., 1967); Max Weber, *The Protestant Ethic and the Spirit of Capitalism*, ed. R. H. Tawney (London, 1930); W. Cunningham, *Growth of English Industry and Commerce in Modern Times*, 6th edn, 3 vols (Cambridge, 1919), ii, Pts. 1, 2, 3; W. Lipson, *The Economic History of England*, 3 vols (London, 1931), Pts. ii, iii; H. J. Habbakkuk & M. Postan (eds), *The Cambridge Economic History of Europe* (Cambridge, 1965), 6, 'The Industrial Revolutions and After', Pts. 1, 2.

a foremost manufacturing and trading nation.[3] Customs records and the Sound Toll registers showed a poor record relative to the rest of northern and western Europe. The dearth of the 1690s and the disaster of the Company of Scotland Trading to Africa and the Indies underlined the shortage of both internal and external capital. Certainly, while day-to-day horizons were dominated by suffering and want Scotland was hardly a candidate for sustained economic growth. Yet aspects of the country's affairs stand out as advanced, predominantly so in the church, family organisation, education, the legal profession, amongst landowners, and also in business, local politics, municipal governance, and the level of thought among the professional classes and officials. In the formation of the Bank of Scotland and Coutts & Co, one discerns an understanding of how money should be treated in a poor country with no meaningful supplies of gold and silver; and how, in respect of the national good, a banking network might help. Scots aired incisive views about how they might progress from 'suffering and want', especially on the organisation of government, property rights and the duties incumbent on legislators and judges in dealing with the relations between government and locality. Governance by the middle and upper ranks, in association with the church, was well thought out, and there were clear views of landholding and the social purposes attached to land. Farming and burgh households alike in the lowlands displayed a coherent economic and social perspective, with similar views on religious observance and church organisation, and on the value of schooling. Thus, in far-reaching respects Scottish history offered a mirror for those parts of Europe which, after Scotland, underwent industrialisation, although around 1707 this mirror was rather foggy.

The prime task of holding lowland Scotland together on social and economic issues fell to the Church of Scotland. Geographical obstacles to the country's unity were obvious to contemporaries; for months of the year much of Scotland was cut off from most of the rest. Bearing in mind the harsh environment and the isolation suffered by townsfolk and villagers during the dark months, the mindset of ministers was paramount: 'By character and education the minister was the leader of his parishioners. The sermon was their chief source of information and instruction on all matters of local, national, moral and spiritual concern. Nothing more interesting or exciting

---

[3] For the economic state of Scotland prior to the Union, see C. A. Whatley, *The Scots and the Union* (Edinburgh, 2006), chap 4; C. A. Whatley, *Scottish Society, 1707–1830: Beyond Jacobitism, towards Industrialisation* (Manchester, 2000), chap 1; R. Saville, *Bank of Scotland: A History, 1695–1995* (Edinburgh, 1996), Tables 4:1, 4:2; H. Hamilton, *An Economic History of Scotland in the Eighteenth Century* (Oxford, 1963), chap 1; B. Lenman, *An Economic History of Modern Scotland 1660–1976* (London, 1977), 45–52; R. H. Campbell, 'Stair's Scotland: the social and economic background', *The Juridical Review* NS, 26 (1981); C. A. Whatley, 'Taking Stock, Scotland at the end of the seventeenth century', *Proceedings of the British Academy*, 127 (Oxford, 2005).

than the sermon occurred to relieve the monotony of their weeks'.[4]
The church required exceptional local leadership and a political and
theological outlook which laid down both the individual's loyalty to
the community, and the standing of their locality with respect to
neighbouring valleys, burghs and the larger commonwealth. Not every
Scot was a theologian, although, as G. D. Henderson pointed out, and
most historians agree, 'practically everyone was interested in theology'.
As this was Scots Calvinism, questions of sovereignty, government,
politics and economic life were inseparable from theology. 'Mental
and spiritual nourishment came to [most people] almost entirely from
the pulpit, with its 'painful sermons, reverently prepared, strongly
biblical, strictly doctrinal, logical, systematic and comprehensive, with
the catechetical instruction begun in their childhood and revised before
each Communion, and the most popular of the metrical psalms printed
clear upon every memory'.

Calvinism appeals to people in adversity; it steadies households
facing economic and social crisis. Its discipline instilled in believers
the need for a life centred on devotion and duty; all had a moral
duty to follow God's instruction to work to the best of their ability, to
avoid giving offence or cause for reproach in personal behaviour, and
to practice prudence and frugal living.[5] Time must be used fruitfully, to
study Scripture, to work at one's lawful calling, whether as the servant to
the plough, the teacher or the magistrate. Frivolity, gambling and other
such activities as leave no tangible benefit to the commonweal are sins in
the eye of the Lord. You live off your own, not taking from neighbours
or family: 'in the sweat of thy brow shalt thou live'. Cain and Abel may
have been the heirs of the world, but they also had callings, 'the one
was a tiller of sheepe, the other a tiller of the ground'.[6] To those on
the margins of subsistence, who lived in the villages and burghs frozen
in winter and cold in spring, where a living had to be wrestled for – to
these people the ministers extolled the virtue, as well as the necessity,
of commitment to one's calling. Living thus, recourse to the poor box
was to be avoided: 'Even in paradise, God would not have man idle,

---

[4] G. D. Henderson, *Religious Life in Seventeenth-Century Scotland* (Cambridge, 1937),
219, 217.

[5] *The Westminster Confession of Faith, the Directory, the form of Presbyterial Government,
approved by the General Assembly of the Church of Scotland; with the Larger and Shorter
Catechisms, the Solemn League and National Covenant, and the form of kirk government;*
G. Marshall, *Presbyteries and Profits: Calvinsim and the Development of Capitalism in
Scotland, 1560–1707* (Oxford, 1980), 106, comment on the seventh commandment
in the Larger Catechism included as sins, immodest apparel, idleness, gluttony,
drunkenness, dancing and stage plays. J. Cunningham, *The Church History of Scotland*,
2nd edn, 2 vols (Edinburgh, 1882), vol 1, chap xiii; Henderson, *Religious Life*, 396–7;
R. H. Campbell, 'The Union and economic growth,' in T. I. Rae (ed.), *The Union of
1707, its Impact in Scotland* (Glasgow, 1978), 67–8.

[6] G. Marshall, *Presbyteries and Profits*, 78, 94–103; for biographies, *Dictionary of Scottish
Church History & Theology* (Edinburgh, 1993); Henderson, *Religious Life*, for works by
Scottish ministers.

though as yet there was no need to labour.'[7] As the marginal notes to the Geneva Bible explained, 'there the Lord God tooke the man, and put him into the garden of Eden, that he might dress it and keep it'.

Gordon Marshall's analysis of the Scottish sermons underlines the importance of instilling in the wider audience – potentially everyone within the commonwealth – the essentials of discipline and diligence at work.[8] Whether for the agricultural labourer, the workman with a trade or the professional, all must 'soberly follow the duties of [their] respective lawful callings without being cuttingly or cackingly careful, vexed or anxious, what be the success of them'. Guild rules and burgh by-laws must be observed, as must one's own conscience, which ought to develop in accordance with scriptural guidance. God sees every transgression of the Decalogue; sinners and mere pretended reformers will be punished. Moreover, the focus was on 'man's moderate, sober and bounded inclinations, desires and designs... covetousness and contentment are opposed... contentment is a mans silent reverencing of God's way with him, and restrains him from inordinate and preposterous pressing after more than he hath'.

The Decalogue provides the bedrock of all law, and obedience is thus critical for harmony in society.[9] Subsequent laws of the Old Testament were God's additional instructions for the needs of societies as economic functions developed. John Calvin, Ulrich Zwingli, John Knox, Samuel Rutherford, Johannes Althusius, all agreed that the declension of the Decalogue forms the legal structure of the commonwealth, and natural law formed in accordance with the Decalogue is written in God's path.[10]

---

7   *The [Geneva] Bible, that is, the Holy Scriptures contained in the Old and New Testament* (London, 1611/12), Genesis, chap 2, v 15, marginal notes; for Sir Herbert Grierson, *The English Bible* (London, 1943), 14, the Geneva version was the 'popular Bible' used by Shakespeare; the first of 120 editions was published in English from 1557 to 1560, with marginal notes critical of divine right of kings, absolutist politics, and Rome, to whom 'all the contents of the Apocalypse are interpreted as applying'. The marginal notes were extended for later editions, and form essential connections with political and religious works of the reformers; C. Hill, *The English Bible and the Seventeenth Century* (London, 1993), 60–2; L. E. Berry (ed.), *The Geneva Bible: a facsimile of the 1560 edition* (Madison, 1969), discusses later editions. The Authorised Version omitted the critical notes. A. W. Pollard (ed.), *Records of the English Bible: Documents relating to the Translation and Publication of the Bible in English, 1525–1611* (Oxford, 1911), 337/339.

8   Marshall, *Presbyteries and Profits*, 97.

9   J. Hastings, with J. A. Selbie, *Encyclopaedia of Religion and Ethics*, 12 vols (Edinburgh, 1911), iv, 'Decalogue'; W. Cunningham, *The Reformers and the Theology of the Reformation* (London, 1860) 32–33, 6th essay on John Calvin, 529–31.

10 Johannes Althusius, the elder of Emden, was the foremost theorist of devolved and federal government, where independent provinces and towns existed under a single sovereignty. His work on Calvinist political thought, *Politica Methodice Digesta of Johannes Althusius (Althaus)*, 3rd edn (1614), ed., C. J. Friedrich (Cambridge, Mass., 1932), xcv; F. S. Carney, (trans. and ed.), *The Politics of Johannes Althusius* (London, 1965), *Politica Methodice Digesta atque Exemplis sacris et profanis illustrata*, Preface to the 3rd edn. (1614), 8. Johannes Althusius placed the precepts of the Decalogue first in law, 'they infuse a vital spirit into the association [of people], and the symbiotic life that we teach, they carry a torch before the social life that we seek, and they prescribe and constitute a way, rule, guiding star, and boundary for human society'.

After biblical times, the laws of the ancient and medieval world could be divided into those designed by particular interests and tyrants, such as the Donation of Constantine and parts of the false decretals, and laws that were the outcome of progress, which followed Scripture and sound natural law.[11]

Imbued with this legal structure is the understanding that 'in living this life no man is self sufficient, or is adequately endowed by nature'. As Johannes Althusius explained, man requires 'mutual communication or common enterprise', and thus the needs of each and every [believer] are supplied, the self-sufficiency and mutuality of life and human society are achieved, and social life is established and conserved'.[12] The origin of the symbiosis, 'for the common advantage of the symbiotes individually and collectively', lies in the family and kinship networks, the association of workers and farmers for mutual benefit, the natural associations we read of in the Old Testament as making up the foundation of society. Later in time, as a natural outcome, come the public associations, the gatherings for public and political purposes which keep corporate books and pass laws appropriate to their work. Usually associated with towns and cities are the

> collegia of bakers, tailors, builders, merchants, coiners of money, as well as philosophers, theologians, government officials, and others that every city needs for the proper functioning of its social life. Some of these collegia are ecclesiastical and sacred... others are secular and profane, instituted for the sake of human things. [Such are] collegia of magistrates and judges, and those of various craftsmen, merchants and rural folk.

[10] (*Continued*) Of the Scottish theologians who appreciated Althusius, Samuel Rutherford stands out with *Lex, Rex: the Law and the Prince; A Dispute for the Just Prerogative of Kings and People* (1644), although every writer of note on theological politics, including the delegation to the Westminster Assembly, Johnston of Wariston, and even, in very different circumstances, Alexander Shields, *A Hind Let Loose, or an Historical Representation of the Testimonies of the Church of Scotland* (1687), refer to, or imply some reliance on, Johannes Althusius.

[11] Constantine the Great (*c*. 274–337 A.D.) donated civic and political powers to the bishop of Rome, Sylvester I (*c*. 314–35), and successors in perpetuity, over 'all the provinces, places and civitates' of the western empire; incorporated into the Decretals of Isidore Mercator, c. 850: which emphasised the rights of diocesan bishops, papal supremacy and subordinated temporal powers. The Donation was a vital administrative and political weapon in the hands of Christian Europe faced with the onslaught of the barbarians, accepted as law well into the seventeenth century, and as late as 1533 deemed heresy to dispute; Hastings, *Religion and Ethics*, iv, 79; Sir Thomas Craig, *The Jus Feudale*, 2 vols, ed. J. A. Clyde (Edinburgh, 1934), i, 34–5. Protestant theologians questioned the Donation, for which Meric Casaubon, *General Learning: a Seventeenth Century Treatise on the Formation of the General Scholar*, ed. R. Serjeantson, *Renaissance Studies*, no 2 (Arizona, 1999), 'The Acts of Sylvester and the Donation of Constantine', 38–44; '[Forgery and the Donation of Constantine]', 102–13; J. M. Levine, 'Reginald Pecock and Lorenzo Valla on the Donation of Constantine', *Studies in the Renaissance*, 20 (1974), 118–43.

[12] Carney, *Politics of Althusius* 12, 14, 33, 38; Althusius leans on Cicero, *The Republic*, i, 25, 'a political community is a gathering of men associated by a consensus as to the right and a sharing of what is useful'.

Together, these associations form the community, a coming together of diverse interests; and together, they forge a senate of the wise and learn to make laws which also accord with scripture and previous natural law, and they in turn devolve sovereignty upwards, if necessary to estates, as in the United Provinces, and to kings and princes.[13]

Thus, the successive layers of society owned the right to administer their own economic and political lives, to exercise the sovereignty pertaining to their station and to rebuff infringements upon their natural rights. To John Calvin the divine law of the Decalogue was to 'make explicit what reason did teach the natural man', so that man can commune with God's word and implement that word in everyday society.[14] Bad government should be upbraided and recalled:

> For though the correcting of unbridled government be the revengement of the Lord, let us not by and by think that it is committed to us to whom there is given no other commandement but to suffer and obey...
> I affirm that if they wink at kings wilfully raging over and trading down the poor commonalty, their dissembling is not without wicked breach of faith, because they deceitfully betray the liberty of the people, whereof they know themselves to be appointed protectors by the ordinance of God.[15]

In so doing, the failings of the church and crown were tackled by the positive instruction to magistrates and public bodies to witness, in public, and intervene against wrongdoing, including that by kings.

The foregoing discussion has highlighted three central tenets of Scottish Calvinism: first, the approach to work and living required of all believers; second, the political organisation of society and the modes of governance to be observed, including the autonomy for society's constituents; and third, the contingent sovereignty of kings and magistrates. All three were included in the deliberations around the Scottish National Covenant of 1638. The Covenant was subscribed by all layers of society: nobles, bourgeois, professionals, the universities, all the collegium of trades, royal burghs, judges and lawyers. Sovereignty was delegated from below, governed by Scripture and natural law and recallable at the will of the lower layers. In the form of sovereignty chosen by the Scots, 'neither any laws or lawful judicatories can be established' without the authority of Parliament, the devolved guardian of sovereignty. No magistrate, judge or king could set up law, or proclaim any change in law, without first coming to Parliament. Parliamentary Acts in favour of the reformed church, 'in her national, synodal assemblies, presbyteries, sessions, policy, discipline

[13] Johannes Althusius is clear that this is a writ from the Lord; also J. N. Figgis, *Studies of Political Thought from Gerson to Grotius, 1414–1625*, 2nd edn (Cambridge, 1923), 183, 206–13.

[14] Frederick, *Politica Methodice Digesta*, xi.

[15] John Calvin, *The Institution of the Christian Religion in Four Books*, trans. Thomas Norton, (Glasgow, 1762), chap xx, s. 31.

and jurisdiction thereof', remained sound law, for ever, and were to be observed when making new law.[16]

Acts and proclamations, canons civil or municipal made in prejudice of the true religion were annulled and rescinded. Magistrates were ordered, not merely empowered, to seize and punish all who rejected the reformed church. Attempts by the Crown or any other magistrate to undermine the autonomy of the economic and political lives of the people were outlawed. In particular any Crown pretension to pre-reformation church lands was prohibited 'by the fundamental laws, ancient privileges, offices, and liberties of this kingdom, not only the princely authority of his Majesty's royal descent hath been these many ages maintained, but also the people's security of their lands, livings, rights, offices, liberties, and dignities preserved'. When elders, legislators and judges acted in their respective jurisdictions, it must be for the well-being of all the community, to redress grievances, and to veto efforts to monopolise public goods. The Covenant rescinded all innovations in worship by James VI and Charles I, which 'sensibly lend to the re-establishing of the popish religion and tyranny, and to the subversion and ruin of the true reformed religion, and of our liberties, laws and estates'. Thus the Five Articles of Perth, with all rites, ceremonies and false doctrine, the high commission, the service book, government of the church by bishops, and the civil places and powers of clergymen were all declared unlawful.[17] In spite of the convulsions consequent on trusting Charles I and II, to the Rev. Alexander Shields the years 1638–1660 witnessed the advance of the true faith 'to the greatest hight of purity and power, that either this church or any other did ever arrive unto'.[18] This new 'hight of purity and power', derived from the stirring of decades, found roots in every lowland parish.

Calvinist theologians foresaw that compliance with God's word required that the people have mentors to guide them in society, in business, on the land, in the burghs or in the armed forces. On the doorstep, harmony and the virtues of prudence and frugality were inculcated through the work of the kirk elders, and, out on the farms and among the hills, by bands of believers acting together, guided by conscience and Scripture. In the higher levels of society, the basis of guidance was the same. Merchants and managers of companies worked together to enforce their procedures, and, if required, to arbitrate disputes. This understanding, and the working out of the Old Testament laws appropriate to a predominantly agricultural community,

---

[16] Hastings, *Religion and Ethics*, x, 244–71; W. L. Mathieson, *Politics and Religion: A Study in Scottish History from the Reformation to the Revolution*, 2 vols (Glasgow, 1902), i, chap xi.

[17] Charles I, 'Act anent the ratification of the Covenant', *The Acts of Parliament of Scotland* (House of Commons, 1817), v, 1625–1641 (11 June 1640), 292–8.

[18] Shields, *A Hind Let Loose*, 60; D. Stevenson, *The Scottish Revolution 1637–44. The Triumph of the Covenanters* (Newton Abbott, 1973); for an alternative view, see G. Donaldson, *Scotland: James V–James VII* (Edinburgh, 1978), 313–16.

should be understood as representing a real economic force, the instruments of God's will, carried right through early modern times and beyond. It was also a democratic force, extending across business, farmland and burgh, in everyday life of significance for the eighteenth century.

The education required for these social mentors could only be met by a new schooling system similar to those pioneered on the continent for the middle and upper ranks, one offering the chance to instil a common understanding of society, the church and the ancient world, imbued with the renaissance perspective on affairs essential for understanding current problems. The similarity to the educational philosophy of the Roman philosopher Quintilian is striking:[19] the 'formation of the orator', one steeped in history, literature and philosophy with a mastery of grammar and language, enabling advocacy on any question before the public offices. No longer were a thin layer of clerics and aristocrats able to preside over questions of the intellect.

All those expected to hold a station in society would attend school.[20] As Althusius explained, publicly funded 'schools provide for the conserving of true religion and the passing of it on to later generations, for informing the life and customs of citizens, and for acquiring knowledge of the liberal arts. Schools are to be opened in the cities and provinces of the commonwealth in order that professors and instructors of liberal arts may publicly teach, . . . so that good citizens may go forth as pious, manly, just and temperate persons'.[21] Scottish schools were to be overseen, by 'the ministers and elders, with the best learned in every town, [who] shall every quarter take examination how the youth hath profited'. Once started the process was a step towards change in economic and social life, though one that had to be argued for, against the pressure from households for forcing children into a narrow

[19] Quotations from Rev. John Selby Watson, *Quintilian's Institutes of Oratory or, Education of an Orator in Twelve Books* (London, 1903), vol i, Preface addressed to Marcellus Victorius, 4–5; Marcus Fabius Quintilianus, *Nouvelle Biographie Generale* (Paris, 1862), vol. 41, 361–6; for the strict interpretation of the 'orator or advocat', see Casaubon, *General Learning*, 127.

[20] By the Act of 1633 all the middle ranks, and families in trade, could expect access to schooling in the lowlands, borders and the north-east, and in the fringe of towns along the Highland line. James Grant, *The History of the Burgh and Parish Schools* (Glasgow, 1876) i, 63–5; D. Withrington, 'Schooling, literacy and society', in T. M. Devine and R. Mitchison (eds), *A Social History of Modern Scotland*, 3 vols (Edinburgh, 1988), vol. 1; D. Withrington, 'What was distinctive about the Scottish Enlightenment?' in J. Carter and J. Pittock (eds), *Aberdeen and the Enlightenment* (Aberdeen, 1987), chap 1; P. McNeill and H. MacQueen, *Atlas of Scottish History to 1707* (Edinburgh, 1996), 437–8; I. D. Whyte, *Scotland before the Industrial Revolution: An Economic and Social History c.1050–c.1750* (London, 1995), 240–3; J. Kerr, *Scottish Education: School and University from Early Times to 1908* (Cambridge, 1910); also, for the eighteenth century, see S. Nenadic, *Lairds and Luxury: The Highland Gentry in Eighteenth Century Scotland* (Edinburgh, 2007), chap 2; W. Ferguson, *Scotland, 1689 to the Present* (Edinburgh, 1968) chap 7; Aspects of the text on education below rest on P. Auerbach and R. Saville, 'Education and social capital in the development of Scotland to 1750', unpublished paper, Economic History Society Conference, 2006.

[21] Carney, *Politics of Althusius*, 71.

understanding of work and against the short-term horizons associated with ordinary people. The demands made by John Knox and the church must have rescued many of the deserving poor from a life of drudgery and enriched the young minds of the middling and upper ranks.[22]

What was the curriculum to consist of ?[23] The dominant influence was ancient Rome, which provided the intellectual sources of the Empire, administration, law, military glory and civic duty. Scots schoolmasters strived to find clearer methods of teaching Latin grammar, in which they displayed more enterprise than the English. School years were divided into layers, usually equivalent to a year; in 1573, Glasgow grammar school specified five such layers. The first two aimed for fluency in reading and writing in Latin, to be achieved through legions of exercises; pupils were also expected to discuss dialogues, including the epistles of Cicero and some adages by Erasmus. The third and fourth years included Cicero, Terence and Ovid; later came Virgil, Horace and Buchanan's Psalms, all designed to provide a thorough grounding in history and literature. Twice a week in the fourth year, around age thirteen, pupils considered a sentence 'having some wit or point, or an argument or narrative; those who can, turn the same into verse, heroic, elegiac or lyric; those who cannot write poetry [to] convert loose sentences into grammatical language and in writing themes'. Pupils unable to meet the demands of a course, through sickness or failure of their 'engine' to keep up, could expect to repeat the year. Children would converse in Latin, construct commentaries on the Latin authors, and write compositions in Latin. Their poetry was expected to be properly classical. Further, 'none of the Latin scholars shall speak English within or without school', and pupils were publicly whipped for transgression.[24] On leaving school they could write trade correspondence in Latin, which would be understood in every part of the Christian world. The legal systems of Europe were also open to them, and, if they were so inclined, they could continue studying the ancient learning of the Roman authors whose texts abounded with adages and homilies of use to an urban bourgeois.

Also using a classics-based syllabus, French provincial schools taught classes of two hours, three times a day, plus homework.[25] By contrast the Scots reformers realised that Scots children had greater stamina,

---

[22] John Knox, *The Book of Discipline*, in W. C. Dickenson (ed.), *John Knox's History of the Reformation in Scotland*, 2 vols (Edinburgh, 1949), ii, Appendix viii, 295–6.

[23] M. L. Clarke, 'Scotland from the sixteenth to the eighteenth century', *Classical Education in Britain, 1500–1900* (Cambridge, 1959), 134–7; George Chapman, *Advantages of a Classical Education: the Importance of Latin, in particular, and its Usefulness for the Attainment of the English Language* (Edinburgh, 1804); William Hamilton, 'Pillans on classical education', *Edinburgh Review*, 64 (October, 1836), 106–24; for English grammar schools, see F. Watson, *The English Grammar Schools to 1660: their Curriculum and Practice* (Cambridge, 1908), chap. xvi; G. Huppert, *Public Schools in Renaissance France* (Chicago, 1984), 53–4.

[24] Grant, *Burgh Schools*, i, 161, citing the case of Dundee grammar school. Compulsory use of Latin in conversation was normal in grammar schools.

[25] G. Huppert, *Public Schools in Renaissance France*, 41–3, 79–81.

and would last for nine and ten hours of direct teaching per day, for five and a half days a week. School would start between five and six a.m., and learning would continue until five and six pm: from darkness to darkness in the winter, light to light in summer.[26] Pupils carried away homework, on which testing would be carried out the next morning. Children benefited from the abolition of the pagan and catholic holidays; Christmas was abolished alongside witchcraft, Catholic ceremonies and hints of Arminianism: all were to be extirpated in order that God's work could be advanced. Harvest was the exception and for about eight weeks, children switched to the fields and the work of food processing. Schooling thus lasted for forty-four weeks a year, for five and a half days, which translates to fifty-five hours a week, plus homework. Leaving the latter aside, this still meant 2,420 hours a year for five or six years, from the age of nine or ten. The Sabbath was not a day of ease; pupils went to church to listen for two and three hours to the minister, and back to school to discuss Scripture, the older pupils talking it over in Latin. The Sabbath was a day of reflection, not one of idleness for untrained minds.

The few who entered university were also taught in Latin, so attention was paid to grammar, although the need for formal Latin tuition at university faded with the evolution of the grammar schools. By the second year of the university course, students encountered the use of the dialectic and other forms of criticism and ways of thought, followed by moral philosophy, mathematics, and natural philosophy (including hydraulics, geography and astronomy). Historical study based upon the Roman and Greek authorities continued the school tradition in the universities, and the development of historical writing in Scotland added to the growth of interest in the discipline.[27] All students attended church, and theological discussion was integral to college life; all universities offered training for the ministry.

This education enabled Scots to proceed to professional instruction before formal entry to business and the professions. The results were justification for the years of schooling and college although there is evidence that the fierce conflicts of mid-century, and the lack of money for books and manuscripts, diverted attention from some continental scientific developments. Ensconced in Calvinism was a rational and considered approach to theology: 'Calvinism embodied a strong intellectual element, appealing much more to the head than the heart. In the elaborating of its doctrines a rigorous logic had been pursued and this had been exploited by its seventeenth century scholastic exponents'.[28] As Professor J. K. Cameron underlined, 'an

---

[26]   Edinburgh grammar school hours were, 6–9, 10–12, and 1.30–6.00, or nine and a half hours, with closure by three on Saturday. Stirling (1613) taught for ten hours a day; Elgin (1649) also taught ten hours; and Jedburgh (1656) taught for nine hours a day.

[27]   W. Ferguson, *The Identity of the Scottish Nation: An Historic Quest* (Edinburgh, 1998), contains much of relevance on the reception of historical research in Scotland.

[28]   J. K. Cameron, 'Theological controversy: a factor in the origins of the Scottish Enlightenment', in R. H. Campbell and A. S. Skinner (eds), *The Origin and Nature of the Scottish Enlightenment* (Edinburgh, 1982), 118.

intellectual approach to religion had already become, amidst all the fanaticism of the seventeenth century politico-religious struggles, part of the Scottish scene'. After mid-century the new ideas of natural philosophy spread, and by the 1690s the work of Huygens and Newton were explained in lectures and their books appeared in the libraries; and gradually the Aristotelian system languished.[29] This new dawn of the Scottish intelligentsia was aided by the return of the exiles with their libraries. The arrival of continental and English ideas into the open air of the revolutionary settlement helped to embed the idea of intellectual curiosity and progress as normal in Scottish society.

As all professions drew on Scripture and ancient learning, all had common points of reference and a common purpose. The day-to-day work of school required all to tackle the syllabus, and as this discipline continued at university, so graduates also emerged with a common intellectual language. As the working life of professionals required exploration of past and present knowledge, the process of forming an individual's intellectual resources reinforced connections between the professions. Effectiveness, as we know, resides in nurturing the mind and is only appropriated by extensive study and working with one's peers. For early modern Scottish professionals, this nurturing included reflection on the day's labour before giving thanks to the Lord. The cohesion formed by this work ethic proved decisive for the revolutionary settlement, and remained so long into the eighteenth century.

In a formal sense Scots law was not part of the classical syllabus and university education. It was though, the ghost of Banquo, which appeared in Scripture and the classical curriculum, and then reappeared in political theory, philosophy and administration. Aspiring lawyers came to formal study with a truth about their world – that law touched every part of business and much of life, including kingship and estates, master and servant connections, matrimonial contracts, parent and child relations, wardship, land and property rights, succession, insolvency, business contracts, means of payment by coin and paper, arbitration and obligation.[30] Law involved all who owned and all who administered; all the above matters may be traced to Scripture, and to the subsequent laws in the Old Testament. After Scripture, though, Scots lawyers relied on manuscripts and law books detailing the Canon law and the *Curia Romana*, as well as reports of cases and statutes

---

[29] C. M. Shepherd, 'Newtonianism in Scottish universities in the seventeenth century', and R. G. Cant, 'Origins of the Enlightenment in Scotland: the universities', in Campbell and Skinner (eds), *Scottish Enlightenment*; H. F. Kearney, *Scholars and Gentlemen: Universities and Society in Pre-Industrial Britain, 1500–1700* (London, 1970), chap. ix; D. R. Kelley, 'History and the Encyclopedia', in D. R. Kelley and R. H. Popkin (eds.), *The Shapes of Knowledge from the Renaissance to the Enlightenment*, Archives internationales d'histoire des idees, 124, (Dordrecht, 1991), 11–15; N. W. Gilbert, *Renaissance Concepts of Method* (New York, 1960), chap. 10; R. W. Serjeantson, 'Testimony and proof in early-modern England', *Studies in History and Philosophy of Science*, 30, (1999), 224–7.

[30] J. S. Shaw, *The Management of Scottish Society 1707–1764, Power, Nobles, Lawyers, Edinburgh Agents and English Influences* (Edinburgh, 1983), chap. 2.

relevant to their specialisation. If Scots lawyers could not recite the ancient laws, there was something amiss with their memory. Canon Law and the *Curia Romana* rested upon the *jus divinum* from Scripture and the *traditio divina*, the spoken word of Jesus Christ passed on by the founding fathers. After these came the role of the bishops and papal supremacy over civilian authority, derived from the Romans. Even if the Donation of Constantine was mistaken, aspects of the *jus divinum* and *traditio divina* offered similar powers, extensively used in the legal apparatus of medieval Scotland.[31] To express this again, most canon law was written in the path of Scripture, assembled in the *jus canonicum*. No religious authority could reasonably be found for some intrusions, though, and sorting out which were acceptable, and which were not, became a necessity for the proper regulation of civil society as well as the church.

With the superiority of Gratian's *Decretum* (d. *c.* 1160), which codified 4,000 legal texts in a systematic fashion,[32] jurists were clear that continued work on the *jus canonicum* should be expressed in terms of precepts and laws of eternal validity on the one side, compared with variable elements of law which arose out of particular circumstances of time, place and person. When updating the law, jurists could thus examine 'secular legal sources, chiefly Roman law, Germanic law and customs, medieval town law and feudal custom', to ascertain whether new legal proposals had a scriptural origin, or reflected particular contexts.[33] The Canon Law and this legal procedure, together with the Scottish-Roman tradition, proved so efficacious for the law that Thomas Craig reminded readers of *Jus Feudale*,

> in Scotland notwithstanding that we have thrown off the papal yoke, the authority of the Canon law endures; so much so, that where it differs from the Civil law (and the differences are many and have been made the subject of several works, we follow the Canon law ... provided always that the rule of the Canon Law is consistent with the principles of sound religion.[34]

Sir David Dalrymple, Lord Hailes (1726–1792), confirmed 'the canon law is not the law of Scotland, but the law of Scotland contains much of the canon law. This is so certain that in many cases we

---

[31] Lord Cooper, 'From David I to Bruce, 1124–1329, The Scoto-Norman Law', *An Introduction to Scottish Legal History*, intro. Lord Normand, Stair Society, 20 (1958), 4–5, 9, 14–15.

[32] S. Kuttner, *Gratian and the Schools of Law 1140–1234* (London, 1983); A. Winroth, *The Making of Gratian's Decretum* (Cambridge, 2000), 1. For this work Dante awarded Gratian a place in paradise, and Gratian remains to this day, 'the only lawyer authoritively known' to reside there.

[33] 'Canon Law', E. R. A. Seligman (ed.), *Encyclopaedia of the Social* Sciences, 15 vols. (London, 1930–1935), iii, 182; O. J. Reichel, *A Complete Manual of Canon Law*, 2 vols. (London, 1896), vol. 2, 'Church Discipline'; R. H. Helmholz, *The Oxford History of the Laws of England*, vol. 1, *The Canon Law and Ecclesiastical Jurisdiction from 597 to the 1640s* (Oxford, 2004), 'Canonical sources and learning'.

[34] Craig, *Jus Feudale*, i, xxiii, 47–8.

determine according to the canon law without knowing it'.[35] This tradition was rational, written and progressed 'in orderly and logical steps from proposition to proposition'. With such a vast hinterland of learning, Scottish lawyers of these centuries stood in high esteem, their knowledge and discipline of mind enabled them to sort out the legal problems of their times, and also those of the subsequent industrialisation, both at home and in the Westminster courts.

Intellectual work is unceasing. All the professions noticed above encouraged research on ancient and medieval sources, and all consulted Parliament and the church for new positions in law. Thus parliamentary commissions in 1425, 1469, 1487, 1566, 1574, 1592, 1628 and 1649 undertook codification, and a variety of Practicks and 'notes on statutes and judicial decisions' also excised particular pleading where it was out of date.[36] Aside from the work on feudal law, and the new edition of the *Regiam Majestatem*, by Sir John Skene (1609), these Practicks rested on the Canon Law and the Romano-Scottish tradition.[37] Lord Stair's *Institutes of the Laws of Scotland* (1681), was the outstanding example of legal synthesis, motivated in part by the need to defend the Romano-Scottish tradition against the tyranny of kings, of which the reign of Charles II was the current instance. Practicks and statutes aimed for succinct legal prose which Scots lawyers, with their wide learning in the ancient and medieval sources, could amplify in decisions and re-direct and adjust to changing circumstances. To speed up the legal process, decisions originally reserved to Crown and Parliament were donated to the Session, to make 'sik actes, statutes and ordinancies as they sall thinke expedient'. Accepted as a true donation, the judges proceeded to declare acts on all manner of questions, and ensured that civil and criminal law would usually find remedies at home.[38] Scots law recognised the customs and by-laws of burghs and trades and the law merchant; and lawyers were familiar with Dutch and English law to ensure Scots could sail in the mainstream of industrial and trade laws as circumstances required.[39]

[35] M. C. Merson, W. D. H. Sellar and Lord Cooper, *The Scottish Legal Tradition*, Saltire Society, new edn. (Edinburgh, 1991), 43, 48; Lord Cooper, 'From David I to Bruce, 1124–1329', in *Scottish Legal History*, Stair Society, 20, (1958), 9, agrees, 'abundant evidence has survived of the detailed working of this Roman-Canonical procedure, which was carried to a high pitch of elaboration and refinement with the use of many ingenious expedients some of which survive in Scottish practice to the present day'; also, T. B. Smith, 'Scots law and Roman-Dutch law: a shared tradition', *The Juridical Review*, NS, 6 (1961).

[36] Craig, *Jus Feudale*, i, 88.

[37] Sir Thomas Hope, *Practicks* (covering the law into the 1630s); Sir James Balfour, *Practicks* (1469–1579), Sir Robert Spotiswoode, *Practicks* (1541–1637). Most collections were guides to particular aspects of the law and remained in manuscript. J. Irving Smith, 'The Transition to the Modern Law 1532–1660', *Scottish Legal History*, 20, (1958), 30–1; Lord Cooper, *Scottish Legal Tradition*, 48.

[38] Irving Smith, 'The transition to the modern law 1532–1660', *Scottish Legal History*, Stair Society, 20, (1958), 27–8; Lord Cooper, 'The central courts after 1532', *Scottish Legal History*, Stair Society, 20, (1958), 344–5; by 1837 the surviving record came to 1300 printed folio pages.

[39] Lord Cooper, *Scottish Legal Tradition*, 11.

Lawyers made efforts over the centuries to obtain judgement over land and to marginalise Crown interference. For this to be effective, it was necessary for the law to develop to the point where legal decisions were the dominant form of discussion in disputes; and this is in fact what happened. As Lord Cooper noted, 'in the seventeenth and eighteenth centuries, and even earlier, our classical system of conveyancing and heritable rights was worked out to the last detail with a rigorous logic and a felicitous ingenuity'.[40] Lawyers assembled written devices to render possessions unalienable and everlasting. Tailzies enabled an estate owner, when drawing up the order of inheritance, to insert fencing and blocking clauses to bar those in succession from altering the original succession, from selling any part of the land, or from taking on debt attached to the estate. Although the Session and Parliament could not secure lands from seizures by the Crown before the revolution, such behaviour persuaded heritors that their rights must be registered in permanent legal form, as a guarantee of ownership. By the 'Act concerning Tailzies' 1685 c.26,[41] entails were formed to stand up in the Court of Session, listed in a new Register of Tailzies, to be written into estate charters, precepts and instruments of sasine. The second innovation was the Register of Sasines, 1617, which superseded oral statements of possession, improved by the Court of Session and by Acts of 1693.[42]

These Acts followed the path of the Old Testament and the word of Jesus Christ. It fell to the elders of the church and judges to ensure that behaviour accorded with Scripture, and with natural law in the path of Scripture. Orderly production of man's worldly goods, and the absolute prohibition of damaging seizures of land, came high on the needs of society: ownership might be unequal, but owners should not have to suffer the jealousy of the powerful and the raging of kings.[43] In this work, the codification of the Scots feudal law was essential, allied to a clear view of the economic role of landowners and the duty of care by the sovereign power. Distinctive from English feudal law and mainstream Canon Law, it 'has been allowed to evolve without the intrusion of alien influence' from the twelfth century.[44] The feudal law and tailzies were connected to a gradual shift towards larger estates, and, with the revolution, ended up as a secure and transparent system of ownership. To William Robertson, the Scots feudal laws, with the development of the registers and entails, were integral to economic progress: in particular secure 'entails, endorsed as far as

---

[40] *Ibid.*, 23; N. Phillipson, 'Lawyers, landowners and the civic leadership of post-union Scotland', *The Juridical Review*, NS, 21 (1976).

[41] *APS*, ix, 477–8; Whilst tailzies were strengthened by this Act, James VII tacked on a final clause, 'that nothing in the Act shall prejudge his Majesty as to confiscations, or other fynes, as the punishment of crimes'.

[42] *APS*, ix, 271, c. 13 & c. 14.

[43] Sound property law was central to economic development; M. Dobb, *Studies in the Development of Capitalism*, rev. ed. (London, 1963), 177–8.

[44] Lord Cooper, *Scottish Legal Tradition*, 76; Craig, *Jus Feudale*, i, 99–100, puts the development of the Scots feudal law 'considerably earlier than the Conqueror's time'.

human ingenuity and invention can reach that end', rendered the possessions of landowners 'unalienable and everlasting'. As they had full power to add to the inheritance transmitted to them by their ancestors, but none to diminish it, time alone, by means of marriages, legacies and other accidents, brought continual accession of wealth.[45]

The apex for the legal profession and the theologians came with the constitutional settlement of the revolution. The tone was set by William's letter of 7 March 1689. In formulating the new laws the revolution settlement returned to the central tenets of Calvinism and the Presbyterian church;[46] to politics and governance based upon the National Covenant, (with autonomy for society's constituents); to the 'declension of the contingent sovereignty of the kings and magistrates'; and to the certainty that the superiority of the classical syllabus would be the basis for the Scottish professions. Based upon an extensive historical understanding and codification as advanced as any in western Europe – and arguably more so than provided in the theories of John Locke and the English Whigs – the estates took the view that Scotland required a thorough-going rejection of sovereignty as it had been defined by Charles II and James VII, and exercised by privy councils and bishops. Where decisions were seen as having followed the path of tyranny, damaging the true religion, and threatening the security of lands and the people, they were annulled.

The Act of 4 April, and Claim of Right, 11 April, expounded upon Calvinist political theory and the illegality of James' assumption of the throne, and confirmed his removal from the Scots kingship. The surrounding argument was effectively a more thorough removal than James had suffered at Westminster. Parliament restored seized estates, individual rights, due process of law, virtually prohibited torture, and removed the old regime's judges and officials. The economic legislation, the independence for the Court of Session from the Crown, the defence of the Bank of Scotland ('created for the public good'), the unity with England in the War of the League of Augsburg – all followed from this constitutional theory.

The argument of this chapter may be summarised by returning to the views expressed by George Davie in *The Democratic Intellect*.[47] The Presbyterian legacy was extraordinary: 'a complex of social aspirations secular as well as religious, [and] in a fashion perhaps foreign to the Anglo-American world combined metaphysical intellectualism of an anti-empirical sort with a certain measure of democratic sympathies'. This system rested upon four pillars. The first was Calvinism, with

---

[45] William Robertson, *The History of Scotland during the Reigns of Queen Mary and of King James VI*, 2 vols. (Edinburgh, 1791), vol. i, bk 1, 14; E. J. Hobsbawm, 'Scottish reformers of the eighteenth century and capitalist agriculture', in E. J. Hobsbawm (ed.), *Peasants in History: Essays in Honour of David Thorner* (Calcutta, 1980); T. M. Devine, *The Transformation of Rural Scotland Social Change and the Agrarian Economy, 1660–1815* (Edinburgh, 1994), 62–3.

[46] J. Stephen, *Scottish Presbyterians and the Act of Union 1707* (Edinburgh, 2007), chap 1.

[47] G. E. Davie, *The Democratic Intellect: Scotland and her Universities in the Nineteenth Century* (Edinburgh, 1961), xiv.

its extensive secular and religious dimensions and its incorporation of centuries of natural law: this provided the philosophy for the revolution settlement. Second, there was the Scots legal system, resting upon centuries of learning, explained by Lord Stair, Parliament and the Court of Session: this was the legal engine by which the revolution was implemented and sustained. The third pillar was formed by the grammar schools with their diverse sources drawn from the ancient world, and the Universities with their openness to new learning: these provided the key method of instilling in the middle and upper ranks the ways in which the system should work for the national good. Fourth, as a more disparate support for Calvinism, law and the formation of individuals, came the 'metaphysical intellectualism' and the commonsense philosophy adopted by numerous professionals and landowners. The recovery of a constitutional theory associated with Calvinism offered a large space in which the middling ranks could flourish. It is in these areas of thought that historians will continue to uncover more nuances of the country's intellectual life, which will in turn assist in a broader assessment of the Scots intellect in the eighteenth century.

George Davie also raised the question of historical method: 'No doubt' historians [of his time] were 'achieving wonders in the way of pure research, but the pity is that their 'scientific' procedure of studying the religious sector in isolation from the legal and the educational spheres makes nonsense of the Scottish story, by obscuring the sociological background to the prolonged spiritual resistance against being completely assimilated to the South'. While historians agree that a narrow focus is well suited for numerous historical questions, the inference of general conclusions to society as a whole, from particular views of how the church was assumed to operate, is, as Davie noted, untenable. Broad questions about separateness and convergence and the background to the Union require a broad canvas upon which to paint.

This chapter has explored the intellectual strengths available to the middling and upper ranks in the Scottish professions. For a country about to embark on an economic and political union, such strengths offered particular advantages. In the determination to fight the Jacobites and the French, the four pillars of the Scottish system and the new constitutional politics stiffened the revolution in England, and secured Scots their place in British public affairs. The intellectual advantages strengthened the professions in the immense tasks of economic development that faced the country after the Union, and also the social problems associated with early industrialisation.

The Scottish Historical Review, Volume LXXXVII: 2008 (Supplement), 61–77
DOI: 10.3366/E0036924108000486

CLARE JACKSON

Chapter 4
Conceptions of Nationhood in the
Anglo-Scottish Union Debates of 1707*

Following the death of William, duke of Gloucester, in 1700, a dynastic predicament developed in both Scotland and England, as it became evident that William of Orange's sister-in-law, Anne, would die without an heir. To ensure a Protestant successor, the English Act of Settlement, enacted in the following year, entailed the crown of England, after Anne's death, on James VI & I's grand-daughter, the Electress Sophia of Hanover and her descendants. In Scotland, this 'succession crisis' had quickly followed another calamity: the collapse of the colonial venture at Darien that had been conducted by the 'Company of Scotland trading to Africa and the Indies', incorporated under a Scots parliamentary patent in 1695. For the London-based Scots pamphleteer, George Ridpath, the hostile actions of William III's English ministers with regard to the Darien project represented the greatest incursion on Scots 'sovereignty and freedom' since the fourteenth-century Wars of Independence.[1]

I

In the aftermath of these twin crises, the language of Scots nationhood was variously invoked, reworked and deployed to different ends. Hitherto, conceptions of nationhood in early-modern Scotland have been examined from a rich range of historical, cultural, literary, antiquarian and cartographic perspectives but rarely have they been subjected to sustained scrutiny by intellectual historians.[2] This is perhaps unsurprising, as historians of political thought are often inclined to privilege analysis of more abstract ideas such as 'sovereignty' or 'the state'. By contrast, 'nationhood' – together with associated

* I am grateful to Mark Goldie, Colin Kidd, John Robertson, Quentin Skinner and Jenny Wormald for their very helpful comments on an earlier draft of this chapter and to Kenneth Campbell for assistance in its preparation. I also acknowledge the generous support of a Leverhulme Trust Research Fellowship in preparing this chapter.

1 [George Ridpath], *Scotland's Grievances relating to Darien &c., Humbly Offered to the Consideration of the Parliament* ([Edinburgh], 1700), p. 1. Regarding Darien, see Douglas Watt, *The Price of Scotland: Darien, Union and the Wealth of Nations* (Edinburgh, 2007).
2 From a large literature, see, for example, Neal Ascherson, *Stone Voices: the Search for Scotland* (London, 2002); Sally L. Mapstone, 'Scotland's stories', in Jenny Wormald (ed.), *Scotland: A History* (Oxford, 2005), 304–34; Tom Keymer, 'Smollett's Scotland: culture politics and nationhood in "Humphry Clinker" and Defoe's "Tour" ', *History Workshop Journal*, 40 (1995), 118–32; Murray Pittock, *Scottish Nationality* (Basingstoke, 2001) and Charles W. J. Withers, *Geography, Science and National Identity: Scotland since 1520* (Cambridge, 2001).

conceptions of 'national identity', 'national consciousness' and, indeed, 'nationalism' – might be regarded as being overly affective and inimical to rational analysis. After investigating relationships between political power and 'the nation' across early-modern Europe, Len Scales and Oliver Zimmer recently observed that ideas associated with nationhood 'belong to the mostly unexamined, yet highly influential subsoil of commonplace belief and assumption'.[3] In the political lexicon, the term 'nationhood' is a nineteenth-century neologism to which the *Oxford English Dictionary* ascribes three, far from synonymous, meanings: first, 'the fact of being a nation'; second, 'national independence or autonomy' and finally, 'national, ethnic or cultural identity'. Given the potent fusion of Romantic ideals of national identity with post-French revolutionary concepts of popular sovereignty, it might be assumed, from a nineteenth-century perspective, that the aim of nationalist sentiment is invariably political independence: i.e. the creation of a sovereign state co-extensive with the nation. Such a supposition, however, downplays the extent to which ideas of nationhood have, throughout history, served to stimulate group identity and national unity. Since conceptions of 'the nation' eschew fixed meaning, demanding terminological exactitude is perhaps as unfeasible as it is anachronistic. Indeed, in the negotiations surrounding the Anglo-Scottish Union of 1707, considerable overlap subsisted between allusions to the Scots 'nation' and accounts of both the Scots 'kingdom' and the Scots 'people'.

At the same time, modern political theorists have observed that present-day conceptions of nationhood remain equally under-theorised. Political philosophers often appear to take nationhood 'for granted', relying on tacit assumptions about the resilience and ubiquity of national boundaries to underpin theories about, *inter alia*, democracy, social justice and liberalism. In criticising such assumptions, Margaret Canovan has drawn on Benedict Anderson's famous theory of 'imagined communities' to identify the strength of nationhood as lying in its subtle ability to mediate between divergent aspects of historical experience as well as between different members of the same nation. Drawing equally on particularistic forces for internal cohesion within a nation, and on those forces provoked by confronting an external 'other', nations comprise an intricate web of custom, contrivance and fiction that often allows polities to function as if they were much smaller, kin-based communities. Accordingly, even amidst contemporary forces of globalisation and supra-national politics, Canovan has underscored the extent to which nations possess a considerable reservoir of latent power – variously perceived as positive and pernicious – that is capable of rapid and collective mobilisation at moments of political crisis.[4]

---

[3] Len Scales and Oliver Zimmer (eds), *Power and the Nation in Early Modern European History* (Cambridge, 2005), 7.

[4] Margaret Canovan, *Nationhood and Political Theory* (Cheltenham, 1996); see also, by the same author, 'Sleeping dogs, prowling cats and soaring doves: three

Making a similar point, Sheila Croucher has insisted that 'contemporary conditions of globalisation provide the motivation and mechanisms for imagining, and perpetuating already imagined, nations' which ensures that 'nationhood persists as a form of belonging ... because it tends to work'.[5]

More widely, determining the precise chronological trajectory by which 'national consciousness' became sufficiently politicised to constitute 'nationalism' has generated extensive historiographical disagreement. On the one hand, resolute modernists, such as Eric Hobsbawm, Ernest Gellner and John Breuilly, have been primarily interested in post-1789 nationalist movements that aimed to create or dismantle states according to the principle of nationality.[6] Their modernism has, however, been challenged by historians such as Susan Reynolds, Anthony Smith and Adrian Hastings, who have emphasised the importance of pre-existing, 'primordial', ethnic or cultural bonds in shaping national identities.[7] From a different perspective, Leah Greenfeld has suggested that, rather than modernisation creating nations, nationhood has generated most of the sociological features that comprise modernity. Deeming nationhood to be highly particularistic, Greenfeld identified events in early-modern England as transformative in shaping the language of nationhood: as vertical status differences within society were conceptually overcome, the Protestant Reformation conferred notions of an 'elect nation', whilst the mid-seventeenth-century civil wars severely tested all prior forms of allegiance and identity.[8] Within Scotland, Neil Davidson's *The Origins of Scottish Nationhood* (2000) represented a politicised contribution to such debates; Davidson's Marxist perspective led him to conclude that 'a Scottish nation did not exist in 1320, nor in 1560, nor yet in 1707'.[9] By contrast, Bridget MacPhail has argued that 'nationalism was alive and well in early eighteenth century Britain', which not only ensured 'that it was nationalism which to a large degree shaped the respective kingdoms' responses to one another'

4   (*Continued*) paradoxes in the political theory of nationhood', *Political Studies*, 49 (2001), 203–15. Regarding 'imagined communities', see Benedict Anderson, *Imagined Communities: Reflections on the Origin and Spread of Nationalism* (London, 1983).

5   Sheila L. Croucher, 'Perpetual imagining: nationhood in a global era', *International Studies Review*, 5 (2003), 20.

6   See, for example, Eric Hobsbawm, *Nations and Nationalism since 1780* (Cambridge, 1990); Ernest Gellner, *Nations and Nationalism* (Oxford, 1983) and John Breuilly, 'Changes in the political uses of the nation: continuity or discontinuity?' in Scales and Zimmer (eds.), *Power and the Nation*, 371–98 and John Breuilly, 'Nationalism and the history of ideas', *Proceedings of the British Academy*, 105 (2000), 187–223.

7   See, for example, Susan Reynolds, *Kingdoms and Communities in Western Europe, 900–1300*, 2nd edn., (Oxford, 1997); Adrian Hastings, *The Construction of Nationhood: Ethnicity, Religion and Nationalism* (Cambridge, 1997) and Anthony D. Smith, *The Nation History: Historiographical Debates about Ethnicity and Nationalism* (Cambridge, 2000).

8   Leah Greenfeld, *Nationalism: Five Roads to Modernity* (Cambridge MA, 1992), chapter 1; see also Elizabeth Sauer, 'Milton's true religion, Protestant nationhood, and the negotiation of liberty', *Milton Quarterly*, 40 (2006), 1–19.

9   Neil Davidson, *The Origins of Scottish Nationhood* (London, 2000), 3.

during the Anglo-Scottish Union debates, but also that the Union itself should thus be accounted 'an episode in political thought which was capable of both provoking and reconciling nationalist discourses'.[10]

The tercentenary anniversary of the Act of Union offers a propitious time to relate the insights of these broader conceptual discussions of nationhood to the debates surrounding the Anglo-Scottish Union – debates which are now recognised as constituting a significant moment in the intellectual history of early-modern Europe. It was not always thus. Until the 1990s, the historiographical orthodoxy concerning the making of the Union elevated pragmatism and patronage over principle, intimidation over ideology, and economic expediency over political philosophising. Since then, however, John Robertson has convincingly shown how the parameters of debate were formed by the complex connections between conceptions of 'empire' and 'union' current in sixteenth- and seventeenth-century political discourse. Robertson has also subjected conceptions of 'sovereignty' to detailed inspection, emphasising the extent to which the 'elusiveness' of early-modern Scots sovereignty rendered it 'a sovereignty almost impossible to put into a viable constitutional form'.[11] In a similar spirit, Colin Kidd has drawn attention to the centrality of religious realignments during the debates to show how such adjustments created 'an ideological environment in which a multiconfessional state was conceivable'.[12] Christopher Whatley and Derek Patrick have enhanced accounts of the economic rationale for Union with detailed analysis of the key personnel involved to argue that 'principle and patriotism were not the exclusive properties of the anti-unionist opposition'.[13] Meanwhile, Karin Bowie has examined the interaction of grass-roots public opinion with printed publications to claim that 'the politics of opinion shaped and influenced the crisis from beginning to end'.[14]

Directing attention towards conceptions of Scots nationhood, this chapter investigates the politicisation of national sentiment during a short period of acute crisis. In doing so, it emphasises the considerable extent to which conceptions of the nation, as embodied in an ancient free and independent Scots *regnum*, commanded consensus. Furthermore, it argues that the Scots Parliament increasingly came to be regarded as the main institutional focus for national loyalties after

---

[10] Bridget MacPhail, 'The Nations Within. Anglo-Scottish Conflict and the Union of 1707', unpublished Ph.D. thesis (University of Auckland, 2000), 10.

[11] John Robertson, 'Preface', in John Robertson (ed.), *A Union for Empire. Political Thought and the Union of 1707* (Cambridge, 1995), xvii.

[12] Colin Kidd, 'Religious realignment between the Restoration and the union', in Robertson (ed.), *Union for Empire*, 146.

[13] Derek J. Patrick and Christopher A. Whatley, 'Persistence, principle and patriotism in the making of the union of 1707: the revolution, the Scottish parliament and the *squadrone volante*', *History*, 92 (2007), 184; see also, Christopher A. Whatley with Derek J. Patrick, *The Scots and the Union* (Edinburgh, 2006).

[14] Karin Bowie, *Scottish Public Opinion and the Anglo-Scottish Union, 1699–1707* (Woodbridge, 2007), 159.

the Williamite Revolution of 1689. Attachment to nationhood did not, however, necessarily lead to a narrowly 'nationalist' outcome. Instead, the Union debates revolved around whether such a civic identity was compatible with incorporating union with England or, conversely, whether sacrifice of the independent *regnum* entailed a concomitant loss of nationhood. Eschewing binary divisions between 'unionist' and 'nationalist' interpretations, this article illustrates the multifarious ways in which the language of Scots nationhood was appropriated and advanced. Distinguishing modern languages of patriotism from those of nationalism, Maurizio Viroli has argued that the former enables adherents 'to keep both eyes clearly fixed on all the past, present and future' of one's country, inspiring 'a love that does not come from excitement and admiration for the greatness and glory of our country, but from the perception of its weakness and fragility'.[15] In this context, supporters and opponents alike of incorporating Anglo-Scottish Union in 1707 all predicated their positions on calculations of long-term utility and the means by which the *salus patriae* could best be preserved. At the same time, this chapter also suggests that the Union debates constituted a crisis in the political theory of Scots nationhood. For whilst conceptions of Scots nationhood remained characteristically inclusive and capable of accommodating a plurality of 'imagined communities', Robertson's characterisation of early-modern Scots sovereignty as 'elusive' is echoed in a series of contested – and ultimately intangible – attempts to define and locate the embodiment of the Scots 'political nation'.

II

At one level, invocations of nationhood could serve as a focus for consensus. Whilst competing conceptions of nationhood were generated during the Union debates, few, if any, authors questioned the existence of Scotland as a separate nation. Both pro- and anti-unionists regarded attachment to what was widely deemed to be one of the oldest nations in the world with approbation. In the first of his *Two Discourses concerning the Affairs of Scotland* (1698), for example, Andrew Fletcher of Saltoun insisted that 'no inclination is so honourable, nor has anything been so much esteemed in all nations, and ages, as the love of that country and society in which every man is born'; for him, nothing could 'be more powerful in the minds of men' than an instinctive inclination and duty 'to serve the interest of their country.'[16] Likewise, in 1706, the Jacobite antiquary, Patrick Abercromby, eloquently observed that 'so true it is, that love to one's native soil, is ingrafted in the very nature of man, and that our hearts move as naturally backwards to the

---

[15] Maurizio Viroli, *For Love of Country. An Essay on Patriotism and Nationalism* (Oxford, 1995), 164.

[16] Andrew Fletcher, 'Two discourses concerning the affairs of Scotland', in *Political Works: Andrew Fletcher*, John Robertson, ed. (Cambridge, 1997), 34.

origin of our blood, as the waters when they return to the sea'.[17] The extent to which Scotland's existence as a separate nation was widely accepted was not, of course, synonymous with the proposition that such a separate nation must necessarily be an independent sovereign state. The appellation 'patriot', so often now attached to Fletcher and other vociferous opponents of incorporating union, was conspicuously appropriated by partisans on all sides, despite the term's residual connotations of radical opposition against monarch and court.[18] Hence the Presbyterian judge, Sir Francis Grant, Lord Cullen, styled himself 'the patriot resolved' in a pamphlet published in 1707, in which Cullen articulated the reasons behind his recent conversion from committed opponent of incorporating union with England to strong supporter and advocate.[19] At the same time, however, attachment to 'the nation' could also be held to offer a legitimating pretext for disingenuousness. Opposing incorporating union in 1703, for example, Fletcher of Saltoun acknowledged to the assembled commissioners of the Scots Parliament that 'there are many different views among us, and all men pretend the good of the nation',[20] whilst in 1706, Queen Anne's Secretary, and ardent supporter of incorporating union, Sir George Mackenzie, Viscount Tarbat, later first earl of Cromarty, echoed such views, asserting that 'no doubt every opinion in this matter, will pretend to be for the national advantage'.[21]

Strictly speaking, however, the meaning of the term 'nationhood' was primarily ethnic, rather than political. References to 'nation' derived etymologically from the Latin 'natus'; the term conveyed connotations of a separate people or some form of ethnic community. Given, however, that the history of Scotland encompassed a history not only of the Scotic and Pictish peoples, but also of Britons from Strathclyde, Glasgow and Northumbria, together with Dalriadic Gaels, there were few strictly ethnographic conceptions. As Mackenzie of Cromarty insisted in A Second Letter on the British Union (1706), 'Scotland was a name not known to our people; in our true antiquity; for we never had, nor have such a word in our Scotish language; given us indeed it is by other neighbours; but whether for distinction or derision, we are left

---

[17] [Patrick Abercromby], The Advantages of the Act of Security, Compar'd with These of the Intended Act of Union ([Edinburgh], 1706), 19.

[18] Maurizio Viroli has drawn attention to the extent to which royalist versions of patriotism co-existed alongside more 'republican' versions in late seventeenth-century England, citing Sir Robert Filmer's Patriarcha (1680), wherein Filmer had observed, referring to the 1630s, that 'the new coined distinction onto Royalists and Patriots is most unnatural' (Viroli, For Love of Country, 56–7).

[19] Sir Francis Grant, The Patriot Resolved. In a Letter to an Addresser, from his Friend; of the Same Sentiments with Himself; concerning the Union ([Edinburgh], 1707).

[20] Andrew Fletcher, 'Speeches by a member of the Parliament which began at Edinburgh the 6th of May, 1703', in Robertson (ed.), Political Works, 158.

[21] [Sir George Mackenzie, earl of Cromarty], A Second Letter, on the British Union ([Edinburgh], 1706), 17.

to judge with the Guelphs and Gibelins'.[22] Inevitably, not all agreed. Equally as committed in his hostility to union as Mackenzie was in his advocacy, John Hamilton, second Lord Belhaven, had asserted the unique homogeneity of the Scots nation in a speech to the Scots Parliament in 1701, in which he bitterly attacked the conduct of William III's English ministers towards the ill-fated Darien venture. As Belhaven contended, 'the Romans and Danes conquered the Brittons, the Danes and Normans the Saxons, so that by the Providence of God, we are at this day the only Ab-origines of great Brittain.'[23] Indeed, Belhaven's insistence on Scots racial homogeneity echoed claims advanced in print during the 1680s by Mackenzie of Cromarty's first cousin and namesake, Sir George Mackenzie of Rosehaugh, who had become involved in a historiographical dispute with Anglican clerics seeking to challenge traditional Scots' claims to be the oldest monarchy in the world. As Mackenzie of Rosehaugh had observed, it was 'much easier' for the Scots to preserve their national traditions than for the English, 'we being all descended from the same race, and being still the same people living under the uninterrupted succession of the same royal-line', whereas the English had been continually 'oblig'd to suppress the traditions and memorials of the people they had conquer'd'.[24]

Notwithstanding, few contributors to the union debates in 1706–7 asserted Scots nationhood by claiming that the Scots constituted a distinct ethnic group. Much more compelling was a conception of Scots nationhood that derived from an ancient and independent Scots *regnum* which, however fancifully, could trace its dynastic lineage back to the fourth century B.C.E. Appropriation of a Dalriadic independence ensured, as Colin Kidd has shown, that although, for many writers, 'Gaeldom defined the historic essence of nationhood', it also, somewhat ironically, represented 'an alien otherness' for a Lowland Scots political nation that readily affirmed its cultural superiority over perceived Gaelic barbarism.[25] Instead of focusing on ethnic conceptions, a greater premium was placed on emphasising that the kingdom of 'Scotland', thus imagined, had never been subjected to foreign conquest. To this end, the anti-unionist, James Hodges, indicated in his *Rights and Interests of the Two British Monarchies* (1706) that he had often

> considered, with admiration, the extraordinary and wonderful Providence of God, toward the Scots nation, that, tho' a people small in number, and short in wealth, in regard of other nations, yet they have been enabled to maintain, and preserve their fundamental rights of sovereignty, independency, and national freedom, now for above a third part of the

22   *Ibid.*, 2; the Guelphs and Gibelins were two factions that kept medieval Italy divided and devastated by civil wars.

23   John Hamilton, Lord Belhaven, *A Speech in Parliament on the 10th day of January 1701, by the Lord Belhaven &c.* (Edinburgh, 1701), 11.

24   Sir George Mackenzie, *A Defence of the Antiquity of the Royal Lines of Scotland, with a True Account when the Scots were Govern'd by Kings in the Isle of Britain* (London, 1685), 18–19.

25   Colin Kidd, *British Identities before Nationalism* (Cambridge, 1999), 123.

world's age since the Creation, against the most violent, and numerous
assaults of most potent enemies ... by the Romans, Britains, Picts, Irish,
Norwegians, Danes, Saxons, English, and sometimes by the Romans then
conquerors of the world, and the Britains, and Picts all combined, and
confederated against them, and have yet remained the only nation of
Europe, unconquer'd to this day: I confess that upon this reflection,
I cannot give over hope, but that God hath so wonderfully preserved
these their rights for some better end, than that they should be barter'd,
exchang'd, or sold, for a share of the sugar, and tobacco of the English
plantations.[26]

As Hodges's comments suggest, the extent to which Scots nationhood was conceived in terms of political independence assumed
renewed importance during the so-called 'imperial crowns' debate, first
studied in detail by William Ferguson during the 1970s.[27] Following the
publication of evidence by the English historiographer-royal, Thomas
Rymer, purporting to prove that the eleventh-century Scots monarch,
Malcolm Canmore, had performed homage to his English counterpart,
Edward the Confessor, George Ridpath published a translation of
Thomas Craig of Riccarton's early seventeenth-century treatise on
homage, 'De hominio', under the title *Scotland's Sovereignty Asserted*
(1695), denying that Anglo-Scottish relations were to be understood
in terms of medieval feudal precepts of superiority and homage. In
response, a number of tracts were published in the early 1700s by the
English antiquaries, William Atwood and James Drake, among others,
which insisted that, since English monarchs were heir to an ancient pan-
Britannic *imperium*, the kingdom of Scotland was necessarily a feu held
by 'sub-kings' of Scotland who were obliged to perform feudal homage
to their English superiors. Such tracts were not only publicly burned
by order of the Scots Parliament, but were also answered at length
by Scots historians, including James Hodges and James Anderson.
The latter, in particular, reproduced numerous historic documents to
illustrate that the English claims of feudal superiority were, as he put it,
'chiefly founded upon forgeries, vitiated or patcht up laws, fables and
extorted acknowledgements: which are the very shrewd signs of a bad
cause'.[28] Such disagreements were not solely of antiquarian interest. For
if the arguments for English feudal superiority were not challenged, the
English Act of Settlement of 1701, which had entailed descent of the
English Crown to the Protestant Hanoverian dynasty, could be assumed
to apply automatically to the vassal-kingdom of Scotland, irrespective
of whether or not Scots parliamentary acquiescence had been obtained.

---

[26] [James Hodges], *The Rights and Interests of the Two British Monarchies, with Special Respect
to an United or Separate State. Treatise III* (London, 1706), 75.

[27] See William Ferguson, 'Imperial crowns: a neglected facet of the background to
the Treaty of Union of 1707', *Scottish Historical Review*, 53 (1974), 22–44; see also
Ferguson's *The Identity of the Scottish Nation. An Historic Quest* (Edinburgh, 1998).

[28] James Anderson, *An Historical Essay, Shewing that the Crown and Kingdom of Scotland,
is Imperial and Independent* (Edinburgh, 1705), 'Preface'.

Events during the Williamite Revolution of 1689 had also irrevocably undermined the extent to which attachment to the Stuart dynasty stood proxy for Scots nationhood. Ingeniously grafting a Lockean epistemology onto a Hobbesian political philosophy, Sir Archibald Sinclair observed during the Union debates that, following James VII & II's flight to France, 'the original contract was found to be dissolved', meaning that 'we were reduced to what Mr. Hobbs calls a state of nature: the nation was then a blank, capable to receive any impression'.[29] Meanwhile, the English pro-union propagandist, Daniel Defoe, was quick to point out that, since 'the Estates of Scotland were the first and earnest movers of the very manner of the union, as now treated of' in 1689, those who opposed union in 1706–7 were unworthy heirs to their parliamentary predecessors, whom Defoe acclaimed as 'noble patriots'.[30]

Yet although the Convention of Estates had eschewed making the offer of the Scottish crown to William and Mary conditional on renegotiation of the regal union at the Revolution, the national humiliation experienced in relation to the Darien venture had subsequently cast doubt on the extent to which William could be regarded as acting in Scotland's interests. Absentee monarchy itself was not a novel scenario, but a new, post-1689 era of enhanced international engagements revealed the long-term likelihood that an English monarch's priorities would trump those of a Scots monarch, should the two collide. As the anonymous author, 'Philo-Caledon', lamented in 1699, 'the king of England, he is our enemy', whilst 'the king of Scotland is detain'd in England, and not Master of himself, but is forc'd to act thus contrary to the interest of his own antient crown and kingdom'.[31] Denouncing the English administration's actions over Darien as 'a piece of the blackest injustice that one nation can be guilty of towards another', Ridpath targeted members of the English Board of Trade as being 'amongst the chief of those that advise to this way of proceeding against us'. As MacPhail has suggested, although Ridpath did not name names, his attack on those members who 'place all their hopes of heaven upon justice [be]twixt man and man, and yet seem to have no sense of justice betwixt nation and nation' presumably denoted a covert attack on the ironic discrepancy between the radical language of natural rights

---

[29] [Sir Archibald Sinclair], *The State of the Nation Enquir'd into, Shewing the Necessity of Laying Hold of the Present Opportunity to Secure our Laws and Liberties from English Influence, and Procure a Free Trade with that Nation* ([Edinburgh, 1705/6]), 2.

[30] [Daniel Defoe], *A fourth Essay, at Removing National Prejudices; with some Reply to Mr. H—dges and some other Authors &c.* ([Edinburgh], 1706), 21–2. Defoe's point has been underscored by Whatley and Patrick who deem it 'significant that virtually all of the more prominent Scots émigrés (or their descendants) who landed with William at Torbay on 5 November 1688 and who were still in Parliament in 1706 and 1707, voted for incorporation.' Whatley, *Scots and the Union*, 30.

[31] 'Philo-Caledon', *A Defence of the Scots Settlement at Darien with an Answer to the Spanish Memorial against it &c.* (n.p., 1699), 41.

propounded by one of the Board's members, John Locke, and the Board's actions in relation to the Scots colonial project.[32]

III

In this context, the Scots Parliament increasingly came to represent an alternative cynosure for Scots nationhood, confirming the existence of a latent 'non-ethnic conception of nationhood' which Alan MacDonald has observed surfacing at specific junctures, such as 1637–51 or 1688–89, when the actions of particular monarchs 'precipitated strong reactions from the political community'.[33] Moreover, Parliament's status as the institutional embodiment of the political nation was rendered increasingly compelling after 1689, once appeals to dynastic loyalty risked incurring suspicions of Jacobitism and once the Darien experience had rendered the notion of a Scots 'king-in-parliament' potentially hollow. Accordingly, as the early eighteenth-century 'imperial crowns debate' demonstrated, any future dynastic arrangement regarding the crown of Scotland would be a parliamentary matter.

In 1704, the Scots Parliament passed the Act for the Security of the Kingdom, asserting its right to nominate a Protestant successor to Queen Anne as monarch of Scotland, but reserving the option to name a different successor from that of England unless outstanding political, religious and economic grievances were redressed. Unsurprisingly, the 'Security Act' ran into difficulty because of its need to secure royal assent from the queen's parliamentary commissioner, James Douglas, second duke of Queensberry, while it also provoked legislative retaliation from the English Parliament. Nevertheless, for Fletcher of Saltoun, the 'Security Act' represented 'the very being of the nation'. Indeed, Fletcher acclaimed it as 'an act that preserves us from anarchy; an act that arms a defenceless people; an act that has cost the representatives of this kingdom much time and labour to frame, and the nation a very great expense; an act that has passed by a great majority; and, above all, an act that contains a caution of the highest importance for the amendment of our constitution'.[34] Sinclair likewise judged the Security Act to be 'an inestimable treasure and, next to God Almighty's protection, the best Magna Charta we have to depend on, after the queen's decease' whilst another pamphleteer predicted that the Act would 'inspire every citizen with such a love to their country, that every one will respect the publick cause as his own, and be always ready and zealous in its defence'.[35]

---

[32] [Ridpath], *Scotland's Grievances*, 17; quoted in MacPhail, 'The nations within', 138, n.256.

[33] Alan R. MacDonald, 'Statehood, nation and treason in early modern Scotland', in Linas Eriksonas and Leos Müller (eds.), *Statehood before and beyond Ethnicity. Minor States in Northern and Eastern Europe, 1600–2000* (Brussels, 2005), 86.

[34] Fletcher, 'Speeches by a member of parliament', in Robertson (ed.), *Political Works*, 152.

[35] [Sinclair], *State of the Nation Enquir'd into*, 6–7; Anon., *The Act of Security is the only Rational Method of Procuring Scotland a Happy Constitution, Free from the Illegal Invasions*

When a piece of parliamentary legislation could be regarded as 'the very being of a nation', the Scottish Parliament assumed special importance as a bedrock of the ancient Scottish constitution. For although the Scots Parliament never attracted the same degree of national loyalty as the English Parliament had during the civil wars of the 1640s, the 'imperial crowns debate' did ignite a revived interest in its historical origins and jurisdictional competence. In 1703, for example, Ridpath observed that 'the last age, or 17th century, was by some called the age of kings, the meaning of which was, in plain Scots, an age of tyrants', and he added that this period had seen attempts 'to make our estates of parliament mere vassals to our princes'. Addressing the parliamentary commissioners directly, Ridpath insisted that his antiquarian researches had confirmed that political dominion arose from property ownership, and that 'your ancestors were our hereditary sovereigns and legislators, and ... our kings had their power and authority from them as an office of trust, but not of property'.[36] Rather than regarding the abolition in 1689 of the crown-appointed Lords of the Articles committee as heralding a new era of legislative independence, he contended that the power of the eighteenth-century Scottish Estates had actually been emasculated. Ridpath alleged that, in former times, the Scots Parliament had enjoyed the right to nominate its own president and state officers, to meet annually, to challenge the monarch without incurring charges of treason and to enact legislation without royal assent.[37] Indeed, if the latter were indeed the case, the controversial Act of Security would have had no need of royal assent to become law.

Aside from responsibility for resolving the dynastic question, by 1706 responsibility for determining the institutional future of Scots nationhood also lay with the Parliament. That year, Defoe sought to flatter his Scots readers by confirming that the English regarded the entire notion of union 'as a thing which depends wholly upon the parliament in this kingdom' and such was 'this happy disposition ... that if the parliament of Scotland closes with it, and no unreasonable difficulties are raised from hence', its subsequent ratification south of the border would be a mere formality.[38] Despite Defoe's confidence in the attractions of a bilateral treaty, not all commentators were persuaded that the Scots Estates possessed the right to enact parliamentary union, indicating the intractable difficulties provoked by

[35] (*Continued*) *of its Liberties and Laws, and the Base Usurpation of its Ancient Sovereignty* ([Edinburgh?], 1704), 7.

[36] [George Ridpath], *An Historical Account of the Antient Rights and Power of the Parliament of Scotland* ([Edinburgh], 1703), iv, viii.

[37] As Ridpath reminded his readers, Mary, Queen of Scots, and Francis II of France had 'refus'd to give their assent to the acts establishing the Reformation; but being enacted in a Parliament legally assembled, they had the force of a law notwithstanding'. *Ibid.*, 17–18.

[38] [Daniel Defoe], *An Essay, at Removing National Prejudices, against a Union with England. Part III* ([Edinburgh], 1706), 23.

attempts to insist that the Scots Parliament either did, or even should, embody and represent Scots nationhood. Those who disputed the Parliament's right to enact union revived, posthumously, the arguments of two Restoration Lord Advocates, Sir John Nisbet of Dirleton and Mackenzie of Rosehaugh, both of whom had unambiguously denied the right of a parliament to vote itself out of existence. In various works, Nisbet and Mackenzie had insisted that a union of parliaments would not only contradict fundamental law, but also, even were such a union to be negotiated, it would need to be positively sanctioned by all the members of the Scottish Estates. Emphasising the dangerously conditional limits of obedience were political protection to fail, Hodges invoked the earlier arguments of Nisbet and Mackenzie to insist:

> That, whatever power the law hath in a free government, and whatever it may declare, order and enact, and whatever alterations it may make in the publick affairs of a free people for the common benefit of the whole in their independent constitution, it can never reach the foundation of national freedom, and sovereign independency, on which it subsists, so as to do, or endeavour any thing to the prejudice thereof; but at the same time instant, it must annihilate its self, and consequently be render'd incapable of transferring any manner of obligation to obedience, upon a free people, whose freedom it endeavours to betray, instead of being a support and defence to it, wherein its being and power are chiefly grounded.[39]

The complex range of political claims advanced in the union debates thus accentuated the considerable distance between rhetorical polemic and constitutional actualities. For if, as Ridpath had claimed, dominion really did follow property, disagreement arose as to whether or not the right to sit in the Scottish Parliament constituted a form of freehold. For Ridpath, 'that power of legislature and judicature' was 'an entail of a higher nature' than that applied to private estates, 'for they may be extinguish'd, but freeholds can never die.' Hence, with regard to abolishing the Parliament, it was 'not this or that party that ought to be consulted in the matter, but the whole kingdom'. Furthermore, he warned that 'if all the freeholders of Scotland were poll'd upon this account, it would be found that the majority will never agree to it'.[40] Since a language of 'freeholder rights' was relatively rare in Scots law, Ridpath's claims were, presumably, a strategic – if unstable – attempt to accord early eighteenth-century Scots electors with traditional rights claimed by 'free-born' Englishmen. Such constitutional reasoning was endorsed by Presbyterian opponents to union, such as Robert Wylie, who denounced 'sinking our parliament' as treason and insisted that

---

[39] [Hodges], *Rights and Interests … Treatise III*, 63.

[40] [George Ridpath], *Considerations upon the Union of the Two Kingdoms: with an Account of the Methods Taken by Ancient and Modern Governments, to Effect an Union, without Endangering the Fundamental Constitution of the United Countries* ([Edinburgh?], 1706), 61–2.

any treaty which resulted in 'the cutting of us off from being a nation' required approval by 'the whole nation'.[41]

By contrast, those who disagreed with such claims included the author of an anonymous pro-union tract–attributed either to the printer, Andrew Symson, or his father, David–which rejected the notion that abolishing the office of commissioner to the Scots Parliament was equivalent to divesting oneself of one's property. In this author's view, every commissioner bore 'a twofold person, one, natural, his own as a private subject; another politick, the person of those he represents'. Since the commissioners were entrusted, above all, to rescue Scotland from its 'sinking condition', the idea that the nation 'out-of-doors' should be consulted on this matter was thus as foolish as recommending that 'the steersman of a ship in a storm [should] quit the helm and go forsooth and consult with the passengers what is to be done'.[42] Other supporters of union, more quixotically, denied that abolition of the Scots Parliament necessarily denoted a loss of Scottish sovereignty. The Presbyterian judge, Lord Cullen, for example, claimed that 'our sovereignty (taking that word in its full import) is far from being surrendered, or sunk, by the union' since 'a main part of it remains among our selves', including the protection of private legal rights in the Court of Session, discrete trading privileges in the Convention of Royal Burghs and separate ecclesiastical governance by the General Assembly.[43] Ironically, in this context, it proved difficult for pro-unionists to resist appropriating their opponents' arguments for their own purposes. In the same tract in which he had extolled the supreme authority of the Scots Estates to vote for incorporating union, Defoe confirmed that any ecclesiastical arrangements devised for the Church of Scotland would be held sacrosanct by future British Parliaments. As Defoe claimed, 'if a parliament destroys the constitution, by which a nation is form'd, that parliament ceases, and power reverts to its original source to form a new one'.[44]

The politicisation of nationhood that occurred during the union debates of 1706–7 thus reflected a growing distinction between one the one hand, 'the people of Scotland in their civil and politick capacity', whom Defoe had identified as, legally, the subjects of the Treaty of Union, governed by a common monarch and represented in a united parliament and, on the other hand, 'the people of Scotland in their religious capacity' who were entirely separate and subject to the authority of session, presbytery, synod and assembly.[45]

[41] Robert Wylie, *A Letter concerning the Union, with Sir George Mackenzie's Observations and Sir John Nisbet's Opinion upon the Same Subject* ([Edinburgh?], 1706), 4, 7.
[42] [Andrew or David Symson?], *Sir George McKenzie's Arguments against an Incorporating Union, Particularly Considered* (Edinburgh, 1706), 11, 5.
[43] [Grant], *Patriot Resolved*, 10.
[44] [Defoe], *Essay, at Removing National Prejudices ... Part III*, 13.
[45] [Daniel Defoe], *Two Great Questions Considered, I. What is the Obligation of Parliaments to the Addresses or Petitions of the People ... II. Whether the Obligation of the Covenant or other*

Neither 'capacity', however, could be comprehensively equated with nationhood. In constitutional terms, powerful appeals to fundamental law and to the rights of the country's freeholders ultimately proved insufficient obstacles to prevent the commissioners of the Scots Parliament from voting for incorporating union. Moreover, despite rhetorical temptations to equate Scots nationhood with the Scots people at large, distinctions between the 'political nation' and the 'people' (or 'multitude') largely prevailed, and there were few attempts to render Scots sovereignty and Scots nationhood synonymous. Although a copy of the fourteenth-century Declaration of Arbroath had been rediscovered in the late seventeenth century and translated and published by Mackenzie of Rosehaugh, neither the Declaration's assertion on behalf of the *communitas regni*, nor alternative heraldic or iconographic symbols of medieval Scots nationhood, such as 'the Lion', featured prominently in the early eighteenth-century union debates.[46]

Meanwhile, although nationhood could also be defined in religious terms, since effective invocation of an independent Scots nation largely depended on an inclusive 'imagined community', there was little potential for conceptions of Scots nationhood to be accommodated comfortably within the exclusive Covenanting Presbyterian Protestantism that, during the seventeenth-century civil wars at least, had actively promoted a pan-British imperial policy. Moreover, whilst Mackenzie's principled opposition to incorporating union was widely invoked (together with that of his predecessor, Nisbet of Dirleton), the sitting Lord Advocate in 1707, Sir James Steuart of Goodtrees, kept his views to himself, despite having previously penned an anonymous tract, *Jus populi vindicatum, or the People's Right to Defend Themselves, and their Covenanted Religion, Vindicated* (1669), which had fused biblical, natural law and contractual arguments in support of private rights of violent resistance against tyrannical oppression. Only at the margins did extreme Presbyterian apologists support the rights of popular sovereignty. Recalling the Covenanters' opposition to Charles II's administration, the anonymous author of *The Smoaking Flax Unquenchable* (1706), for example, exhorted his readers to follow 'our worthy ancestors … in casting off tyranny, and in abolishing and annulling all acts made against religion and tyranny (in the years 80 and 81)'. Were the people of Scotland 'by the same power [to] annul the present unlawful union betwixt the kingdoms', he was confident that their actions 'shall be approven of God, and ratified in heaven.'[47] Meanwhile, although Steuart of Goodtrees kept his counsel, excerpts from his earlier *Jus populi vindicatum* were reproduced. They

---

45   (*Continued*) *National Engagements is Concern'd in the Treaty of Union? Being a Sixth Essay at Removing National Prejudices against the Union* ([Edinburgh], 1707), 23.

46   Regarding the latter, in 1304, Scots defenders of Stirling Castle against Edward I's English forces had proclaimed national allegiance to 'the Lion', rather than to any individual monarch.

47   Anon., *The Smoaking Flax Unquenchable; Where the Union betwixt the Two Kingdoms is Dissecated* [sic], *Anatomized, Confuted and Annuled* ([Edinburgh], 1706), 11.

appeared, for example, in a tract entitled *The Scotch Echo to the English Legion* (1707), whose anonymous author drew attention to those same rights that had, ironically, been championed by Defoe in 1701 when he had presented his 'Legion's memorial' to the Speaker of the House of Commons, Robert Harley, demanding the release of Kentish freeholders who had petitioned Parliament. Citing Steuart's *Jus populi*, the author observed that

> If parliaments, instead of acting the part of trustees, tutors, curators, delegates and servants, shall turn tyrants, wolves, tygers and enemies to the commonwealth themselves, or conspire, join or enter into a confederacy with a tyrant, and so seek the destruction of the community, the community is allowed to see to the preservation of their own rights and priviledges the best way they can.[48]

IV

Paradoxically, therefore, the consensus attached to conceptions of the 'Scots nation' effectively rendered such notions resistant to exclusive appropriation, definition or circumscription by any particular constituency during the Union debates. Instead, the language of interests comfortably trumped attempts to convert attachment to nationhood into insurmountable constitutional, legal or religious obstacles to union. Affixing a Ciceronian epithet to his title-page, the anonymous author of *A Discourse of Present Importance* (1704), for example, besought the parliamentary commissioners simply to ask themselves whether 'Scotland's interest, that is now low, would be any way bettered' by all proposals laid before them.[49] Even Defoe acknowledged the over-riding priority of self-preservation when he reversed James VI & I's famous metaphor of suffering 'a divided or monstrous body' as joint ruler, or head, of both Scotland and England.[50] Instead, Defoe observed a pair of Siamese twins: 'two nations ... tyed together in all the foundation-parts ... inseparably join'd in those parts which are the support and strength of the body', but 'divided in their upper parts, have two constitutions, two digestures, two wills, and too much opposite inclinations.' In a worst case scenario, were one nation fatally to attack the other, Defoe warned that 'the mortality of the other would descend to the parts that were essential to them both' and 'the whole must die', rendering the aggressor guilty of suicide.[51] In a sermon preached at Edinburgh's Mercat Cross in 1706, John Arbuthnot took as his text, Ecclesiastes 10.27 ('Better is he that laboureth and aboundeth in all things, than he that boasteth himself

---

[48] Anon., *The Scotch Echo to the English Legion: or, Union in Danger, from the Principles of some Old and Modern Whigs, in both Nations, about the Power of Parliaments* (Edinburgh, 1707), 20.

[49] Anon., *A Discourse of Present Importance Humbly Offered to the Consideration of the Right Honourable Members of Parliament &c.* ([Edinburgh?], 1704), 23.

[50] James VI and I, 'Speach ... the XIX day of March 1603', in Johann P. Sommerville (ed.), *Political Writings: King James VI and I* (Cambridge, 1994), 136.

[51] [Defoe], *Fourth Essay*, 43.

and wanteth bread'). Arbuthnot's message was clear: 'in lieu of this titular sovereignty, and imaginary independency, by an union you acquire true and solid power and dominion'.[52] In his later *History of the Union*, Sir John Clerk of Penicuik evocatively accepted that 'after 1603, the glory of Scotland either perished or faded in England's lustre like the stars at sunrise, so that the mere name of a kingdom was all we retained of our majesty and power'. Denying that the pro-unionists had acted unpatriotically, Clerk insisted that it was to prevent Scotland perishing that they 'had reasone to talk so who in their consciences believed the union to be the *summum bonum* of their countrey'.[53] In this context, whilst MacPhail has argued that pro-unionist writings are 'best understood as exercises in conflict resolution rather than nation-building', Robertson has likewise drawn attention to the extent to which both pro- and anti-unionists had 'taken Hobbes's point that sovereignty was justified by its utility'.[54]

Whilst Scots sovereignty risked becoming a casualty of incorporating union, nationhood did not. After 1707, an enduring and separate Scots 'imagined community' continued to co-exist alongside a new British 'imagined community'. Although Defoe's pro-unionist arguments concerning Scots nationhood prevailed when the Articles of Union were ratified, his definition of what such a union would entail proved overly reductionist. For Defoe, parliamentary union with England demanded 'a union of the very soul of the nation, all its constitutions, customs, trade and manners, must be blended together, digested and concocted, for the mutual, united, undistinguish't, good, growth and health of the whole united body, and this I understand by union'.[55] Defoe later endorsed this vision in *The Scots Nation and Union Vindicated* (1714), claiming that 'in fact there is not a Scotsman or an Englishman in the world, the two natures, nationally speaking, being dissolved into one, viz. Britain'.[56] By contrast, the experience of the Anglo-Scottish Union proved to be neither Defoe's characterisation of an entire merger nor, indeed, a wholly English acquisition. Creating a British state was an entirely separate process from building a British nation and events in 1707 bore little resemblance to James VI & I's vaunted aspirations towards a union of Anglo-Scottish 'hearts and minds'. In this context, Leith Davis has contrasted the emotive appeals made during the union debates to an ancient, mythic Scots nationhood with self-consciously

---

52 [John Arbuthnot], *A Sermon Preach'd to the People, at the Mercat Cross of Edinburgh; on the Subject of the Union* ([Edinburgh?], 1706), 13.

53 Sir John Clerk of Penicuik, *History of the Union of Scotland and England*, Douglas Duncan (trans. and ed.), (Edinburgh, 1993), 172, 20.

54 MacPhail, 'The Nations Within', 180; John Robertson, 'The Idea of sovereignty and the act of union', in H. T. Dickinson and Michael Lynch (eds), *The Challenge to Westminster: Sovereignty, Devolution and Independence* (East Linton, 2000), 39.

55 [Defoe], *Essay, at Removing National Prejudices . . . Part III*, 7.

56 [Daniel Defoe], *The Scots Nation and Union Vindicated; From the Reflections Cast on them, in an Infamous Libel, entitl'd, The Publick Spirit of the Whigs &c.* (London, 1714), 14. Hence, even after union had been concluded, John Kerrigan has observed how 'Defoe kept arguing, interpreting, inciting and pushing for integration' (John Kerrigan, *Archipelagic English. Literature, History and Politics 1603–1707* (Oxford, 2008), 348).

mimetic constructions of British nationhood that generated 'an image of Britain not as a stable nation, but as a concept created through dialogue'.[57] Mackenzie of Cromarty's oft-quoted invocation, 'May wee be Britons, and down goe the old ignominious names of Scotland and England', thus pointed towards the eighteenth-century creation of a new British identity, as Linda Colley and Colin Kidd, among others, have illuminated.[58]

Finally, the union debates were not restricted solely to the consideration of arguments for and against incorporating union. A considerable reservoir of support subsisted for forms of so-called 'federal' or 'confederal' union that advocated closer dynastic, economic and military union with England, but still retaining a separate Scots Parliament to preserve the institutional integrity of Scots nationhood.[59] Although such constitutional alternatives are often dismissed as inconsequential amid the *realpolitik* of eighteenth-century negotiations, they reinforced the inclination to regard Parliament as the institutional embodiment of Scots nationhood after 1689. More broadly, appreciating the sheer diversity of national visions articulated in the early eighteenth-century Union debates enhances our historiographical appreciation of why narrow nationalist ideologies remained relatively weak in nineteenth- and twentieth-century Scotland, while it also supplies antecedents for adherence to nineteenth-century forms of 'unionist-nationalism'.[60] For while the popularity of preferred constitutional outcomes may fluctuate over time, the enduring resilience of political and civic conceptions of Scots nationhood restores historic resonance and conceptual continuity to modern debates about nationhood and identity in post-devolutionary Scotland.

---

[57] Leith Davis, 'Writing the nation in 1707: Daniel Defoe, Lord Belhaven and the "vast conjunction" of Britain', in Davis, *Acts of Union, Scotland and the Literary Negotiation of the British Nation, 1707–1830* (Stanford, CA, 1998), 45.

[58] See Linda Colley, *Britons: Forging the Nation, 1707–1837* (New Haven, CT, 1992) and Colin Kidd, 'Eighteenth-century Scotland and the three unions', *Proceedings of the British Academy*, 127 (2005), 171–87 and Colin Kidd, 'North Britishness and the nature of eighteenth-century British patriotisms', *Historical Journal*, 39 (1996), 361–82.

[59] See, for example, Anon., *State of the Controversy betwixt United and separate Parliaments &c.* ([London], 1706) and *A Scheme for Uniting the Two Kingdoms of England and Scotland Different from Any that has been Hitherto Laid Down* ([Edinburgh, 1706] and Peter Paxton, *A Scheme of Union between England and Scotland, with Advantages to both Kingdoms* (London, 1705). More radical was Fletcher of Saltoun's vision of a re-ordered Continental Europe set forth in 'An account of a conversation concerning a right regulation of governments for the common good of mankind', in Robertson (ed.), *Political Works*; see also John Robertson, 'Andrew Fletcher's vision of union', in Roger A. Mason (ed.), *Scotland and England, 1286–1815* (Edinburgh, 1987), 203–25.

[60] See, for example, Graeme Morton, 'What if? The significance of Scotland's missing nationalism in the nineteenth century', in D. Broun, R. Finlay and M. Lynch (eds.), *Image and Identity: the Making and Remaking of Scotland through the Ages* (Edinburgh, 1998), 157–76 and Graeme Morton, *Unionist Nationalism: Governing Urban Scotland, 1830–1860* (East Linton, 1999). Regarding the pre-1707 period, and especially the talismanic significance retrospectively conferred on the 1689 Claim of Right, see Antonia Kearton, 'Imagining the "mongrel nation": political uses of history in the recent Scottish nationalist movement', *National Identities*, 7 (2005), 23–50.

The Scottish Historical Review, Volume LXXXVII: 2008 (Supplement), 78–93
DOI: 10.3366/E0036924108000498

KARIN BOWIE

Chapter 5
Publicity, Parties and Patronage: Parliamentary Management and the Ratification of the Anglo-Scottish Union

Since 1707, observers have asked to what degree the Scottish parliament of 1706–7 was 'managed' into ratifying a treaty of union with England. Given the national spirit evident in the Scottish parliament at its sessions of 1703 and 1704, it has seemed to many that only clandestine activity could explain the members' turn towards accepting an incorporating union. As one contemporary put it, when he considered 'hou opposite the same parliament [in] 1703 wer with thir measures, I incline to think a Scots parliament that sits beyond 2 or 3 years are soe far modelled by English Influence that they are noe longer vox populi'.[1] Leading Scottish historians from George Lockhart of Carnwath in the early eighteenth century to William Ferguson in the later twentieth century have emphasised the role of patronage and secret payments in creating a majority for incorporating union, while the eminent historian of the Union, P. W. J. Riley, has pointed to the harnessing of members into noble-led factions.[2] More recent research, however, has stressed the ideological foundations of these factions and their alignment in a Court-Country party structure influenced by an increasingly activist and public political culture.[3] It is no longer adequate to claim that the Union was 'bought' by means of political jobbery; instead, political management must be placed in a wider context of ideological loyalties and public politics. This is not, however, to downplay management as representing an underlying 'business as usual' in a pre-modern parliamentary system. Of course the crown tried to manage Parliament; but what is interesting is the degree to which

---

[1] National Library of Scotland (NLS), Wodrow quarto xl, item 8 (newsletter), 4 November 1706.

[2] D. Szechi (ed.), *'Scotland's Ruine': Lockhart of Carnwath's Memoirs of the Union* (Aberdeen, 1995); W. Ferguson, 'The making of the treaty of Union of 1707', *Scottish Historical Review*, 43 (1964), pp. 89–110; P. W. J. Riley, *The Union of England and Scotland* (Manchester, 1978).

[3] C. A. Whatley, *The Scots and the Union* (Edinburgh, 2006); D. J. Patrick and C. A. Whatley, 'Persistence, principle and patriotism in the making of the Union of 1707: The Revolution, Scottish Parliament and the *squadrone volante*', *History*, 92 (2007), pp. 162–86; K. M. Brown, 'Party politics and parliament: Scotland's last election and its aftermath, 1702–3', in K. M. Brown and A. J. Mann (eds), *The History of the Scottish Parliament, vol. II: Parliament and Politics in Scotland 1567–1707* (Edinburgh, 2005), pp. 245–86; K. Bowie, *Scottish Public Opinion and the Anglo-Scottish Union, 1699–1707* (Woodbridge, 2007).

its ministers failed to do so between 1700 and 1705. Given this failure, how significant were the well-known management methods deployed in 1706–7?

This chapter will assess the impact of management in the ratification of the Union treaty, not by rehearsing familiar instances of patronage and power-broking, but by demonstrating how these tactics evolved in response to the rise of more public and partisan politics in Scotland. It will argue that from the Darien crisis onwards, the changing nature of Scottish politics challenged the crown's normal methods of management and forced ministers to develop a wider range of practices, including concessions to oppositional opinion expressed in public debate, to rebuild a Court party majority. By tracing the interaction between public and party politics and the crown's management efforts from 1700, the chapter will provide a contextual understanding of the role of management in the passage of the Union treaty in 1706–7.

***

Popular and party politics began to make real trouble for William and his Scottish government in May 1700, when ministers lost control of Parliament in a session lasting just nine days. A volatile combination of economic and political grievances had exploded, fanned by Country party agitations. Economic complaints had been swelling as repeated crop failures, combined with the falling trade and higher taxes associated with William's Nine Years War (1688–1697), produced a severe recession. In a declining economy, the hopes of many had been pinned on the Company of Scotland and its attempt to found a colony at Darien on territory claimed by Spain. The extensive publicity efforts of the Company had created a strong popular perception of the colony as a patriotic enterprise. Further, the Company's allegations of English attempts to wreck capital subscriptions in London and Hamburg, combined with the king's public refusal to back the Company, aroused angry resentment in Scotland. In August 1699, a Scottish correspondent had warned William Carstares, the king's chaplain and adviser in London, that 'you cannot believe how great an edge is upon persons of all degrees and ranks here' for the Darien colony, threatened as it was by Spanish invasion and denied English aid. Though more recent historians have demonstrated the internal weaknesses of the Darien project, the information publicly available at the time had led many Scots to blame the failure on the English and the king they shared with the English.[4]

As the Company and its colony were widely viewed as a Scottish national enterprise, the affairs of the Company became enmeshed in

[4] Whatley, *Scots and the Union*, chap 4; D. Watt, *The Price of Scotland: Darien, Union and the Wealth of Nations* (Edinburgh, 2007), pp. 41–3, 47–63, 79–89; J. McCormick (ed.), *State-Papers and Letters Addressed to William Carstares*, (Edinburgh, 1774), p. 488; *A Selection from the Papers of the Earls of Marchmont, 1685–1750, in the Possession of the Right Hon. Sir George Henry Rose*, 3 vols (London, 1831), vol. iii, pp. 179–81, 184.

parliamentary party politics. The Company had petitioned Parliament for backing in 1698, and had secured an address from the estates to the king. In October 1699, Company directors petitioned the king to ask for a new meeting of Parliament so 'that your Majesty may have the Advice and Assistance of the Great Council of this Nation in such a weighty and general concern'.[5] At the same time, the second marquis of Tweeddale began to work with the duke of Hamilton and the earl of Tullibardine (later first duke of Atholl) to initiate a popular address to the king. When the government attempted to discourage signatures by means of a royal proclamation, public outrage spurred more to sign. With a reported 21,000 signatures, the national address was presented in London to King William by Tweeddale on 25 March 1700. A further eight petitions from certain shires and burghs were presented to Parliament at a session called for 21 May 1700 after repeated delays.[6] Alongside these petitions, printed and manuscript pamphlets also began to circulate in support of the opposition and its demands.[7]

While the national address asked the king to allow Parliament to meet 'to support the Interest and Credit' of the Company of Scotland, the eight petitions to Parliament from shires and burghs outlined a broad set of grievances that went beyond the problems of the Company. Alongside assertions of the rights of the Company of Scotland and its colony, complaints were also made about rising poverty, the decay of trade due to the war with France and the continuing French prohibitions on key Scottish exports, and the king's maintenance of standing armed forces in peacetime Scotland, despite the disbanding of such forces in England. Though respect for conventions meant the petitioners refrained from attacking the king directly, their patriotic rhetoric portrayed the Company's problems as a blow to Scotland's honour, requiring vindication by Parliament.[8]

The Country party's campaign presented a new kind of public challenge to the Scottish ministry – a challenge that it proved unready to meet as Parliament opened in May. At the start of the session, the duke

5 C. Innes and T. Thomson (eds), *Acts of the Parliament of Scotland* (*APS*), 12 vols (Edinburgh, 1814–1875), vol. x, p. 134, appendix at pp. 19–20, 24; *A Full and Exact Collection of... Publick Papers, relating to the Company of Scotland* ([Edinburgh], 1700), pp. 7–26, 87.

6 Edinburgh, National Archives of Scotland (NAS), Papers of the Dukes of Hamilton and Brandon, GD 406/1/444, 4368; *A Full and Exact Collection of... Publick Papers, relating to the Company of Scotland*, pp. 105–7; *Selection from the Papers of the Earls of Marchmont*, pp. 192–8; L. W. Sharp (ed.), *Early Letters of Robert Wodrow, 1698–1709* (Edinburgh, 1937), p. 59; *APS*, vol. x, appendix at pp. 34–41.

7 These included Anon., *The People of Scotland's Groans and Lamentable Complaints* ([Edinburgh, 1700]); [George Ridpath], *Scotland's Grievances relating to Darien* ([Edinburgh], 1700); [William Seton of Pitmedden], *Memorial to the Members of Parliament of the Court Party* ([Edinburgh, 1700]); Anon., *A Short Speech Prepared to be Spoken, by a Worthy Member in Parliament* ([Edinburgh], 1700); Anon., *Heads of Things Fit to be Granted and Done in the Ensuing Session of Parliament* (1700), Edinburgh, National Library of Scotland, Adv. MS. 83.7.6(154). See also Bowie, *Scottish Public Opinion*, pp. 30, 32, 70–3.

8 *APS*, vol. x, appendix at pp. 36–41.

of Queensberry and the earl of Marchmont used their speeches as royal commissioner and chancellor respectively to encourage loyal obedience to the king, emphasising the debt owed to him for the Revolution and for the re-establishment of Presbyterianism within the national Church. But it soon became clear that recent events held more weight for many in the Court party and they deserted to the opposition. The Country party gained an early 'resolve' [formal resolution] intended to wrest control of the session away from the government: 'that all motions and overtures be first made in plain Parliament and that no motion or overture come in from any of the Committees but upon matters first remitted to them by the Parliament'. Overtures from the government in favour of the Presbyterian establishment and against popery and profanity – made to reinforce the fidelity of Presbyterian members – were countered with demands for the rescinding of acts confirming the king's power to call and dissolve the General Assembly. Attention then turned to the Company of Scotland, with the presentation of a new petition from the Company, the eight local petitions and a 'resolve' from the duke of Hamilton 'asserting the Companie's interest and legal title to Caledonia in Darien'. Faced with these challenges, on 30 May Queensberry adjourned Parliament to 20 June to enable him to seek further instructions from the king. On 17 June, a proclamation further postponed the session until 4 July.[9]

This debacle in May demonstrated to the government that, in the present circumstances, they could not maintain a stable Court party majority with their usual methods. The degree of anger felt across Scotland over the king's policies, encouraged by the Country party's public protests, had created rebellion within the estates. William, as usual, refused to come to Scotland to help his ministers woo members and he did not authorise any concessions on the opposition's key complaints. Though the king's letter to Parliament expressed regret for Scotland's recent 'misfortunes and losses' and promised new acts to encourage trade, it offered no explicit support for the Company of Scotland nor any public rationale for William's refusal to defend the Darien colony.[10]

At the time of Queensberry's initial adjournment, the Country party maintained its pressure on the government by organising an immediate address to the king from about ninety members demanding the re-assembly of the estates. On 20 June, party leaders encouraged illuminations in Edinburgh in favour of the Darien colony, triggering

[9] *APS*, vol. x, pp. 190–4, appendix at pp. 34–5; Sir David Hume of Crossrigg, *A Diary of the Proceedings of the Parliament and Privy Council of Scotland, May 21, 1700—March 7, 1707* (Edinburgh, 1823), pp. 1–6; *A Full and Exact Collection of . . . Publick Papers, relating to the Company of Scotland*, p. 127; NAS, PC 13/3/1700 (17 June 1700).

[10] *APS*, vol. x, p. 190. During the summer of 1700, James Hodges proposed himself to viscount Seafield as a pamphleteer in the king's interest for a salary of £300, but though Seafield expressed interest, Hodges' services were not taken up and by 1703 he was writing for the opposition. McCormick (ed.), *State-Papers and Letters addressed to William Carstares*, p. 598.

a major riot in which the homes of government supporters were attacked.[11] By July, 'a great Number' of signatures were being collected for a third address to the king. This address demanded a Parliament not just to support the colony but also to pass acts to assert the freedom of the Scottish kingdom, secure the king from outside influence, and reduce the corrupting power of patronage in the Scottish Parliament. A further call for an act of *habeas corpus* also appeared.[12] These points were echoed in pamphlets, as Country discourse shifted towards a broad critique of English hegemony in the Union of Crowns.[13]

With a nearly-empty Scottish treasury limiting patronage opportunities, ministers began to despair of managing Parliament without the king's presence in Scotland. Fortunately for them, the final collapse of the Darien colony allowed ministers to issue a conciliatory proclamation in William's name in early August. This stated that – although the loss of the colony now made a declaration of support for it unnecessary – the king would seek the release of colonists held captive by Spain and would support parliamentary measures to assist the Company. Aided by this expression of royal empathy, leading ministers and their lieutenants, including the duke of Queensberry, viscount Seafield, and the earls of Argyll and Mar, worked busily to restore relations with their followers.[14]

By the time Parliament reconvened on 29 October 1700, the abandonment of the colony and the blandishments of ministers had started to bring some Court party rebels back to the fold. As royal commissioner, the duke of Queensberry sought to develop good relations with members by inviting them to join him for dinner on the king's birthday. Ministers deployed other patronage carrots and sticks, prompting a parliamentary resolve from Hamilton against anyone 'offering a good deed or office, or threatening Members of Parliament for votes'.[15] Yet alongside these methods, the government also acknowledged oppositional complaints. The king's letter to Parliament offered a justification for his failure to support the Darien colony and promised to approve 'what shall be reasonably proposed' to assist the Company of Scotland.[16] Moreover, economic grievances were dealt with as Parliament devoted three months of deliberations to

---

[11] *Full and Exact Collection of... Publick Papers, relating to the Company of Scotland*, pp. 127–9; J. Grant (ed.), *Seafield Correspondence from 1685 to 1708* (Edinburgh, 1912), p. 290; *Selection from the Papers of the Earls of Marchmont*, pp. 210–11; Bowie, *Scottish Public Opinion*, pp. 34–5; Watt, *Price of Scotland*, pp. 197–9.

[12] *Full and Exact Collection of... Publick Papers, relating to the Company of Scotland*, pp. 133–7; Grant (ed.), *Seafield Correspondence*, p. 304.

[13] See note 7.

[14] Grant (ed.), *Seafield Correspondence*, pp. 299–303; NAS, PC 13/3/1700 (6 August 1700); *Full and Exact Collection of... Publick Papers, relating to the Company of Scotland*, pp. 130–2; McCormick (ed.), *State-Papers and Letters addressed to William Carstares*, pp. 585, 601, 603, 611, 618, 647.

[15] McCormick (ed.), *State-Papers and Letters addressed to William Carstares*, pp. 595, 611; Hume of Crossrigg, *Diary*, pp. 9, 23.

[16] *APS*, vol. x, pp. 201–2.

proposals to improve trade. These led to an act blocking the import of French wine in hopes of persuading France to lift its barriers against Scottish trade. The government also backed acts against popery and profanity and an act 'anent wrongous imprisonment' (*habeas corpus*).[17]

Having made these concessions, the government was better able to manage the debates on the Company of Scotland when these were resumed, although its influence was limited. In mid-December, an observer noted that 'the Country party are much weakened' and that they would 'desist from pressing Caledonia any more', but in January 1701 Hamilton's party offered, and secured unanimous support for, a series of patriotic resolves which attacked the English Parliament for 'undue Intermeddling in the Affairs of this Kingdom' and which characterised the English proclamations of 1699 forbidding aid to the Darien colonists as 'inhumane barbarous and contrare to the law of Nations'. Another petition from the Company and eighteen new addresses from shires and burghs continued the pressure for an act to assert the rights of the Company. Despite this, the Court managed to convince a small majority to support an address to the king rather than an act, in part on the pragmatic grounds that 'an Address without an Act would be better than an Act without the Royal Assent'. Unusually for the royal commissioner, Queensberry offered a speech to Parliament as part of the debate. The final vote split 108 to 84, or 56% to 44%, for the less provocative address.[18]

Ministers retained their fragile hold on Parliament only by means of another compromise, this time on supply for the standing forces. As Country speakers argued for a militia to replace the standing army, government speakers, again including Queensberry, reminded members of the army's importance in maintaining the Revolution. Country opposition succeeded in reducing troop numbers from over 4,000 to 3,000, with a motion to reduce the forces to only 2,000 defeated by just fourteen voices (108 to 94). Ministers secured a six-month cess (land tax) to fund the agreed 3,000-man force, but had to assure members that any troops maintained above this number would be financed from the king's own excise revenues.[19]

In the following year, the Country party escalated its opposition by withdrawing from the new Queen Anne's first meeting of Parliament on the grounds that new elections should have been called according to a 1696 act regulating the succession on William's death. At the opening of Parliament on 9 June 1702, Hamilton led out his party to the cheering of crowds around Parliament House. A petition to the queen

---

[17] *Minuts of the Proceedings in Parliament*, nos. 1–57 (29 October 1700–1 February 1701); *Selection from the Papers of the Earls of Marchmont*, p. 215; Hume of Crossrigg, *Diary*, pp. 23, 36.

[18] Sharp (ed.), *Early Letters of Robert Wodrow*, p. 135; *Minuts*, no. 37 (9 January 1701); no. 38 (10 January 1701); no. 40 (13 January 1701); nos. 46–7 (20–21 January 1701); Hume of Crossrigg, *Diary*, pp. 45–51; *APS*, vol. x, pp. 242–57, appendix at pp. 73–86.

[19] *Minuts*, no. 49 (23 Jan 1701); no. 50 (24 Jan 1701); nos. 52–6 (27–31 Jan 1701).

soon followed, signed by dozens of members, along with supporters in Edinburgh. The Faculty of Advocates also initiated a petition to the queen to protest the illegality of the session. Although Anne refused to accept the Country party petition, and Parliament quashed the Advocates' address as unwarrantable, together these protests cast a shadow over all the acts passed by the rump Parliament. The Country party attempted to raise a boycott of the cess authorised in the 1702 session, but although the boycott worried the government, the Country party's legal challenge to Anne's Parliament was not as effective in motivating support at the grassroots level as the Darien issue had been in 1700–1. As Robert Wylie, minister of Hamilton parish and political adviser to the duke of Hamilton, pointed out in July, the party had failed to publish pamphlets explaining their stance and the issues proved opaque to many.[20]

Besides the cess, Queensberry in 1702 also secured acts confirming Anne's accession and authorising negotiations with England for a closer union. Yet even within a Court-dominated rump Parliament, he faced management problems. Differences emerged between Episcopalian and Presbyterian interests, as Anne's association with high Anglican Tories in England encouraged Episcopalian dissenters in Scotland. On the presentation of an act to confirm the Presbyterian Church settlement, Sir Alexander Bruce (later earl of Kincardine), commissioner for the burgh of Sanquhar, argued that Scottish Presbyterianism was 'inconsistent with the essence of monarchy'. After being expelled from the house by an appalled Presbyterian majority, Bruce subsequently published a version of his inflammatory comments as a pamphlet. Chancellor Marchmont responded by introducing an act for the abjuration of the pretender, which would have blocked any Jacobite Episcopalians from sitting in Parliament or holding office under Anne. Faced with Marchmont's unilateral action, Queensberry was forced to adjourn Parliament.[21]

With her 1702 act for union negotiations, Anne sought to fulfil William's vision for an incorporating union as a means to neutralise an increasingly activist, populist and partisan Scottish political system. Among Country pamphleteers, only the London-based writer, George Ridpath, engaged with this act in 1702, publishing a tract to influence the union negotiations that were held over the winter of 1702–3.[22] In Scotland, party attention remained focused on the domestic scene as Martinmas elections produced a new grouping of Episcopalian and

[20] *APS*, vol. xi, p. 5; *A Selection from the Papers of the Earls of Marchmont*, pp. 239–41; Szechi (ed.), '*Scotland's Ruine*', pp. 13–14; Hume of Crossrigg, *Diary*, pp. 83, 89–90, 93–4; NAS, GD 406/1/4813, 4815, 4830, 5181, 4900; Bowie, *Scottish Public Opinion*, pp. 35–6.

[21] Hume of Crossrigg, *Diary*, pp. 83–95; Szechi (ed.), '*Scotland's Ruine*', pp. 14–17; [Sir Alexander Bruce], *A Speech in the Parliament of Scotland* ([1702]); Riley, *The Union*, pp. 37–9.

[22] [George Ridpath], *A Discourse upon the Union of Scotland and England* (1702).

Jacobite commissioners to Parliament, known as the 'Cavaliers'. This, combined with Anne's favouring of Episcopalians in her ministerial appointments, raised the real possibility of a shift in the Court party away from William's ideological core of mostly Presbyterian Revolution supporters towards Episcopalians and even Jacobites.[23] When Parliament opened in May 1703, the Court party imploded as the Cavaliers backed a public campaign for legal toleration of Episcopalian worship, and Court and Country Presbyterians came together in opposition.

Pamphlets and petitions were deployed, as a heated public debate erupted between Episcopalian and Presbyterian interests. In March, dissenting clergy made a play for royal support with an address asking for the queen's indulgence for the practice of their religion. Other Episcopalians, such as the Jacobite Lord Balcarres in Fife, organised addresses from lay supporters in localities including the counties of Fife, Stirling and Angus and the burghs of Glasgow, Dundee, Aberdeen and Elgin. At the same time, a number of pro-toleration pamphlets began to appear, among them some by Anne's new secretary, the earl of Cromartie (formerly viscount Tarbat). These urged toleration for dissenters and stressed the breadth of popular support for Episcopalian worship.[24] Presbyterians perceived this as an open challenge to the Revolution settlement, in particular the Claim of Right's statement that prelacy was a grievance of the people. Their vigorous responses included a petition to the 1703 Parliament from the Commission of the General Assembly and a number of pamphlets attacking Episcopalian toleration as dangerous to the Revolution interest and Presbyterian Church. As one Presbyterian author put it, 'the Prelatick and Jacobite party aim at no less, than the overthrow of the present Establishment, and the Restauration of Prelacy in this Church in spite of the Claim of Right'. Some writers also linked toleration to the Country issue of English hegemony, seeing the influence of Anglican Tories in the Episcopalian dissenters' campaign.[25] On the ground, crowds in Glasgow demonstrated their concern over Episcopalian ambitions by attacking one of their local congregations that had begun to meet more openly.[26]

Led by Marchmont, Argyll and the marquis of Annandale, Court Presbyterians joined with Country members to brush aside Cavalier

23 Brown, 'Party politics and parliament', pp. 254–68.
24 Anon., *To the Queen's Most Excellent Majestie, the Humble Address and Supplication of the Suffering Episcopal clergy*, (1703); Sharp (ed.), *Early Letters of Robert Wodrow*, p. 255; NAS, GD 406/1/5181; [George Mackenzie, earl of Cromartie], *A Few Brief and Modest Reflexions Perswading a Just Indulgence to be Granted to the Episcopal Clergy and People in Scotland* ([Edinburgh], 1703); [George Mackenzie, earl of Cromartie], *A Continuation of a Few Brief and Modest Reflexions* ([Edinburgh], 1703).
25 *The Humble Representation of the Commission of the late General Assembly* ([Edinburgh, 1703]); [George Ridpath], *An Account of the Proceedings of the Parliament of Scotland*, (1704); [James Hadow], *A Survey of the Case* (Edinburgh, 1703), p. 4; [James Webster], *An Essay upon Toleration* ([Edinburgh], 1703), pp. 19, 24.
26 NLS, Wodrow quarto xxviii, fo. 151; NAS, PC 1/52(520, 524–6).

overtures for toleration and to pass acts confirming the Revolution and the Presbyterian Church. In response to the pro-toleration pamphlets, open criticism of the Claim of Right was now declared treasonous. Stymied, the Cavaliers retreated from the Court party but remained a separate faction, leaving neither the Court nor the Country party in outright control of Parliament.[27]

As the Court party disintegrated, a Country party agenda for constitutional reform came to dominate the session, with the opposition's return to the patriotic, anti-English rhetoric that it had developed in 1700–1. While Andrew Fletcher of Saltoun whipped up resentment of English hegemony and demanded limitations on the royal prerogative, Cavaliers joined the Country party in delaying the settlement of the Scottish succession.[28] For the moment, deep ideological differences between Country Presbyterians and Episcopalian Cavaliers were subsumed in a shared willingness to capitalise on public discontent and claim the mantle of patriotism. The apparently nationalist Parliament of 1703 thus represented a marriage of convenience between two differing oppositional groups, but it was a marriage riven with potential areas of disagreement.[29]

The hallmark of the 1703 Parliament, the Act of Security, emerged from contentious debates launched by a Country resolve from Tweeddale for 'such conditions of government and regulations in the constitution of this Kingdom to take place after the decease of her Majestie . . . as shall be necessary for the preservation of religion and liberty'. Further overtures added the preservation of Scottish trade to this agenda and made radical proposals for limitations on Anne's successor. A broad majority approved a final act that, while it did not place any particular limitations on the prerogative, none the less insisted that 'conditions of government' be enacted to secure Scottish sovereignty, trade and religion before England's Hanoverian successor could be accepted. Reflecting the concerns from 1700–1, this act also demanded that 'a free Communication of Trade, the freedom of Navigation and the liberty of the Plantations' be secured from the English. A clause to arm a Protestant militia satisfied earlier arguments

27 APS, vol. xi, pp. 46–7; [Ridpath], An Account of Proceedings, pp. 28–9, 38–9; Szechi (ed.), 'Scotland's Ruine', pp. 30–1, 33; Hume of Crossrigg, Diary, pp. 98, 102–4.

28 The Scottish succession was open because the death of Queen Anne's last child in 1700 had left the Revolution monarchy without any direct heirs. In 1701 the English parliament had passed an act naming Sophia of Hanover, a descendant of James VI and I, as the Protestant heir. Anne's plan in 1702 for incorporating union would have settled the succession in Scotland, but with the failure of union talks she needed the Scottish parliament to accept the 'Hanoverian succession' through an act of parliament or a fresh attempt at union.

29 P. W. J. Riley has rightly questioned historians who interpret the legislation of the parliament of 1703 as a transparent declaration of Scottish independence, but he goes too far in the opposite direction by arguing that 'the Court was faced, not by a nationalist revolt, but by a problem of parliamentary management which it was unable to solve'. The Court faced both. P. W. J. Riley, 'The Scottish parliament of 1703', Scottish Historical Review, 47 (1968), p. 131.

on the standing army, while a separate Act anent Peace and War responded to complaints made concerning the Nine Years War.[30]

These Parliamentary debates were closely watched as visitors thronged the house and crowds outside cheered votes on popular issues, notably the passage of the clause for a trade on an equal footing with England and its colonies. A wave of printed overtures, speeches and tracts dealing with free trade, limitations on sovereignty, and the union of crowns aroused public interest on these issues, with only a few writers offering a Court point of view.[31] Describing free trade as 'a thing, generally desired by the people of Scotland', George Ridpath attributed this to the 'intollerable Dishonour and Loss in the Affair of Caledonia'. Anne's ministers recognised the strength of public feeling, and Seafield warned London of 'the great resentment there is in this nation because of the act of navigation and the loss of our colony of Caledonia', recommending that 'a communicatione of trade... be obtained either by a concession from England or by a treatty of a federal or intire union'.[32]

Faced with a Country-Cavalier alliance on patriotic reforms, Queensberry proved unable to achieve his primary objective of supply. The Court Presbyterian revolt also continued, as Marchmont unilaterally offered an overture naming Sophia of Hanover as Anne's successor with specific limitations, though not a communication of trade. The abject failure of this overture exposed the queen's weakness on the succession issue. While the Cavaliers opposed the Hanoverian settlement in principle, even Revolution supporters expected to secure significant reforms of the Union of the Crowns before conceding the succession.[33] Queensberry indicated that he would give the royal assent to the Act anent Peace and War in hopes that this would gain him supply; but after three months of uncontrolled debate, during which the Country party twice threatened to address the queen, he was forced to adjourn without giving the royal assent to the Act of Security.[34]

Queensberry responded to the embarrassment of 1703 by attempting to smear his noble rivals as Jacobites in a plot that backfired and cost him his job as royal commissioner. Anne responded by inviting the Presbyterian wing of the Country party into government in

---

30 [Ridpath], *Account of Proceedings*, pp. 134–8, 188–9; *APS*, vol. xi, pp. 41, 63, 69–70, 74–5, 107; Szechi (ed.), '*Scotland's Ruine*', p. 38; Hume of Crossrigg, *Diary*, pp. 100, 109, 112, 115.

31 Sir John Clerk of Penicuik, who published in support of an incorporating union in 1706, started to write for the Court party in 1703. Sir John Clerk of Penicuik, *History of the Union of Scotland and England*, D. Duncan (trans. and ed.), (Edinburgh, 1993), p. 3.

32 [Ridpath], *Account of Proceedings*, pp. 193–8; H. Paton (ed.), *Report on the Laing Manuscripts preserved in the University of Edinburgh*, 2 vols. (London, 1914–1925), vol. ii, p. 36.

33 Hume of Crossrigg, *Diary*, pp. 131–2.

34 Anon., *Overture by Way of Act Concerning the Succession* (1703); [Ridpath], *Account of Proceedings*, pp. 21–3, 328–31; Szechi (ed.), '*Scotland's Ruine*', pp. 37, 39; *APS*, vol. xi, pp. 84, 112; Hume of Crossrigg, *Diary*, p. 118, 133–4.

the hope of creating a Revolution coalition that would vote for the Hanoverian succession with limitations. Led by Tweeddale and including Marchmont, this group became known as the New Party (and, by 1705, as the *squadrone volante*). While the idea of a Revolution coalition for the succession was plausible in theory, in practice the queen could not offer sufficient reforms to win the succession. Meanwhile, factional rivalry ensured that Queensberry's followers moved into the opposition.[35]

As in 1703, the 1704 Parliament took place in an atmosphere of keen public interest. This interest was fuelled by angry resentment over an address of March 1704 by the English House of Lords to the queen concerning Queensberry's plot to smear his rivals; this address had also decried the open Scottish succession and called for a closer union.[36] The Country party continued to capitalise on public anger over English hegemony by demanding reform of the Union of the Crowns, a demand that was supported by the Cavaliers. A resolve from the duke of Hamilton insisted that Parliament should not name a successor before 'we have had a previous treaty with England in relation to Commerce and other Concerns with that Nation'. This became conjoined with a Court resolve for limitations to produce a motion that 'took with the house' and was supported by 'a vast plurality of voices' in the estates as attentive crowds outside cheered the leaders of the opposition. Hamilton then offered the 1703 Act of Security with the clause on communication of trade removed, followed by a separate resolve for a treaty with England. Fletcher backed the latter with an overture for the nomination of treaty commissioners. This was taken up by Parliament almost to the point of naming the commissioners, but when the dukes of Atholl and Hamilton, as rival opposition leaders, could not agree on a slate of candidates, Parliament moved on to consider Queensberry's plot.[37] Despite this slip, the opposition secured another patriotic resolve that condemned the Lords' address as 'an undue Intermeddling with our concerns, and an Incroachment upon the Independency, Honour and Sovereignty of this Nation'. Parliament also voted to address Anne, warning that 'nothing can obstruct more our comeing into... the succession' than 'any more encroachments of that nature'. A final address to the queen closed the session with a protest against the paucity of the papers sent up from London for a parliamentary investigation of the Queensberry plot.[38]

Tweeddale's New Party had promised in Anne's opening letter that the government would introduce acts for 'quieting the minds of all

[35] Szechi (ed.), *'Scotland's Ruine'*, pp. 63–5, 84, 89.

[36] *Journals of the House of Lords*, vol. 17, (London), pp. 505–6, 554.

[37] *APS*, vol. xi, pp. 127–9; *Minuts*, no. 3 (13 July 1704), nos. 5–6 (19, 21 July 1704); Szechi (ed.), *'Scotland's Ruine'*, pp. 72–5, 78–9; Hume of Crossrigg, *Diary*, pp. 138–40, 143–4.

[38] *Minuts*, no. 11 (8 August 1704); *APS*, vol. xi, pp. 152, 204–5; Szechi (ed.), *'Scotland's Ruine'*, pp. 76–7; Hume of Crossrigg, *Diary*, pp. 161–2.

our good subjects', including 'Terms and Conditions of Government'; but they could only guarantee 'whatever can in reason be demanded, and is in our power to grant'.[39] With these restrictions, the New Party could not secure the succession, even though the renewed war with France now allowed Marchmont, and several supporting pamphleteers, to highlight a Franco-Jacobite threat to the Revolution interest. Meanwhile, Tweeddale faced a new level of oppositional aggression as an attempt was made to tack the Act of Security to an act for supply. In order to prevent this and to secure the much-needed cess for a wartime army, Tweeddale gave the royal assent to the reintroduced Act of Security.[40]

Even without the clause on free trade, the price paid by Tweeddale for supply became a political liability for Anne and her ministers in England. In response, a Whig-led English Parliament passed the 1705 Alien Act, designed to force the Scottish Parliament either to settle the succession or to nominate commissioners for union negotiations. This, combined with the concurrent trial in Edinburgh of an English crew suspected of pirating a Company of Scotland ship, produced an explosion of anti-English feeling in Scotland, expressed in angry pamphleteering and riotous crowds. Public animosity ensured that three members of the English crew were hanged for piracy in April as the privy council resisted pressure from London for a reprieve. Though the New Party hoped that the hangings would gain them support in the next parliamentary session, Anne turned to the second duke of Argyll to form a new government. Under immense pressure to resolve the Scottish situation, Argyll brought back the duke of Queensberry and expelled the New Party from office. When his new ministry could not agree on whether to attempt to gain the succession by means of limitations or a treaty, the queen's letter left this up to Parliament.[41]

Despite Queensberry's return to the Court party, Argyll still needed to attract members from the *squadrone volante*, the Cavaliers, or Hamilton's Country party in order to make a parliamentary majority. Country pressure since 1700 for a treaty to reform the Anglo-Scottish union proved to be the key for Argyll as he capitalised on what Lockhart called a 'great inclination in the house to set a treaty on foot'. Both the earl of Mar for the Court party and Hamilton for the Country party proposed resolves for a treaty with England and both Court and Country pamphlets now urged an act for a treaty, though

---

[39] *APS*, vol. xi, pp. 125–6.

[40] Anon., *The Great Danger of Scotland as to All its Sacred and Civil Concerns* ([Edinburgh, 1704]); Anon., *A Watch-word to Scotland in Perilous Times* ([Edinburgh, 1704]); Hume of Crossrigg, *Diary*, pp. 138, 144–8, 151; Szechi (ed.), *'Scotland's Ruine'*, pp. 72, 77–8; *APS*, vol. xi, pp. 130, 133, 136–7.

[41] Bowie, *Scottish Public Opinion*, pp. 41–3, 80; G. E. M. Kynynmond, Earl of Minto (ed.), *Correspondence of George Baillie of Jerviswood, MDCCII-MDCCVIII* (Edinburgh, 1842), pp. 64–6, 104, 107; *APS*, vol. xi, pp. 213–4.

Country writers firmly rejected the notion that incorporating union should be an outcome of treaty talks.[42] After acts had been passed on trade and limitations, momentum increased for a treaty with the defeat of a Country clause demanding the repeal of the Alien Act before negotiations could commence. A majority settled for an address to the queen expressing their resentment of the Alien Act as well as their interest in a 'nearer and more complete union'. There was not, however, any mention of incorporation in the act for a treaty, nor had entire union been mentioned in the queen's letter. Only luck allowed ministers to defeat a clause from Hamilton that the union would not 'derogat any ways from any Fundamental Laws, Ancient Priviledges, Offices, Rights, Dignities, and Liberties of this Kingdom', as the absence of several Country and Cavalier members meant there was a bare majority of two votes against the motion. Other safeguards became necessary to secure votes: the act blocked discussion of alterations in the Presbyterian Church of Scotland and required that Parliament ratify any treaty resulting from the authorised negotiations. These measures, combined with memories of the failed talks of 1702–3, brought some members to see the act for a treaty as an easy way out of the Alien Act impasse.[43]

The passage of the 1705 act for a treaty demonstrated that the Court party could regain control of Parliament only when it engaged with longstanding demands for reform of the Anglo-Scottish union, and particularly for a treaty on trade. Private agreements with factional interests also played a part, as Queensberry brought his followers back to the Court party and as dealings with the duke of Hamilton ensured that the queen would nominate the Scottish negotiators.[44] Yet these arrangements alone could not secure the act for a treaty; the government also had to collect votes by drawing on the public interest in reform of the existing union, without specifying the introduction of an incorporating union. Given the conditional nature of many of these votes, the queen faced a fresh management challenge when it came to ratifying her treaty of incorporation in 1706–7.

The experience of 1705 suggested that ministers might continue to win over elements of the opposition if they could portray the treaty as a patriotic response to public complaints on the union. As Seafield put it in late 1705, 'there is no other way of taking from the opposing party their pretensions of having a country-interest,

---

42 Hume of Crossrigg, *Diary*, pp. 163, 165; Anon., *A Speech Concerning a Treaty of Union with England* ([Edinburgh, 1705]); Anon., *A Speech Intended to have been Spoken in Parliament by a Member who was Necessarily Absent* ([Edinburgh, 1705]).

43 In contrast, the 1702 act for treaty negotiations had been passed with a less restrictive letter to the queen asking her to preserve the Presbyterian Church. *APS*, vol. xi, pp. 26–7, 213–14, 236–8, 295; *Minuts*, no. 29 (31 August 1705); Szechi (ed.), *'Scotland's Ruine'*, pp. 95, 100–3.

44 *Minuts*, no. 19 (14 August 1705); Szechi (ed.), *'Scotland's Ruine'*, pp. 86, 89, 105–6, 108–9.

but by having a treaty'.[45] Recent historians have emphasised that the treaty did respond to Scottish demands by offering free trade and compensation for the Company of Scotland. The treaty also provided an agreement on the Hanoverian succession, which many Revolution supporters desired, provided it was combined with reforms of the union. When parliamentary speeches, pamphlets, petitions and protests expressed manifold objections to incorporating union, especially the threat to the Presbyterian Church, the loss of Scottish sovereignty, and the burden of higher taxes, Scottish ministers ignored advice from London and negotiated further guarantees for the security of the Presbyterian Church, along with articles on the Scottish regalia and on trade and taxation.[46] At the same time, Court party writers offered not just a few pamphlets but extensive printed arguments in support of incorporating union, claiming a patriotic stance for the treaty in direct competition with the Country party.[47] Alongside this new populism, the government also produced its now well-known management incentives, including secret payment of arrears of salary to selected members of the Court party and the allocation of lucrative post-union jobs to key factional leaders.[48] This combination of attractions drew the Presbyterian *squadrone volante* into alliance with the Court party, leaving the Cavaliers and the Countrymen as a minority interest under the leadership of the rival dukes of Atholl and Hamilton.[49]

By late November 1706, it seemed that the government had managed to offer enough concessions and carrots to build a stable parliamentary majority. Fervent and sometimes violent public protests still threatened to disrupt the parliamentary session, but ideological differences between Country and Cavalier interests now began to reduce the effectiveness of the opposition. While in previous years the Country and Cavalier groups would work together to delay the succession, the negotiation of a treaty that included free trade forced Hamilton's Country party to press instead for the Hanoverian succession with limitations. In turn, Cavalier resistance to Hanover undermined attempts to formulate a united Country-Cavalier challenge to the treaty. The two groups did co-operate in a campaign to generate dozens of petitions from burghs, shires and parishes, in part by developing a joint statement that condemned the treaty without mentioning the succession. Their disagreements, however, undermined two potentially significant mass protests: a gathering of petitioners in Edinburgh in December 1706 and a walk-out of the opposition in January, both of which were to be followed by an address to the queen. In December, as hundreds of Jacobites and Presbyterians alike poured into Edinburgh,

[45] McCormick (ed.), *State-Papers and Letters addressed to William Carstares*, p. 738.
[46] Whatley, *Scots and the Union*; Bowie, *Scottish Public Opinion*.
[47] Bowie, *Scottish Public Opinion*, pp. 103–14; K. Bowie, 'Popular resistance, religion and the Union of 1707', in T. M. Devine (ed.), *Scotland and the Union* (Edinburgh, 2008).
[48] Ferguson, 'The making of the treaty', pp. 106–10.
[49] Patrick and Whatley, 'Persistence, principle and patriotism'.

Hamilton insisted that an address to the queen should not only ask for the election of a new Parliament but advocate the Hanoverian succession as well. As the leaders argued over this, the government dispersed their followers with a proclamation forbidding unauthorised meetings. In January, some Cavalier members agreed to join a last-ditch walkout even though the protest statement drafted by the Country party promoted the Hanoverian succession. Atholl, however, would not support the statement, leaving the planned exodus leaderless – as Hamilton refused to act for fear of being blamed by the queen for wrecking the treaty.[50] The collapse of this final oppositional manoeuvre allowed ministers to confirm the ratification of the treaty on 16 January 1707.

***

Those who focus on the contrast between the parliamentary sessions of 1703–4 and 1706–7 usually struggle to explain the ratification of the treaty of union in terms other than corruption and management. This chapter has suggested that by taking a longer perspective of 1700 to 1707, the ratification of union can be seen as resulting from an extended crisis during which the Court party collapsed under the pressure of pervasive grievances brought to parliamentary politics by a populist Country party. From 1703, the election of a Cavalier faction further disrupted the Court party and reinforced the patriotic opposition fronted by the Country party. Over time, the government learned that to rebuild a Court party majority it would have to acknowledge at least some popular grievances, offer public rationale for its policies, and deploy augmented patronage resources. In 1706–7, ministers reconstructed a Court party based on Revolution interests by accommodating the ideological and personal interests of a former Country faction, the *squadrone volante*, and by reinforcing the loyalties of Court party followers. This was done through a combination of private incentives and extensively advertised claims for the public benefits of incorporation. At the same time, the terms of the treaty exposed differences between the Country and Cavalier factions and reduced their ability to concert effective resistance, despite their pursuit of aggressively populist strategies drawing on fervent objections to incorporating union.

Was the Scottish Parliament of 1706–7 'managed' into accepting a treaty of union? The answer to this depends on the definition of management. For historians like Ferguson and Riley, management has meant patronage and other private accommodations, used to secure the compliance of factional leaders. Yet the evidence of 1700–5 shows that many members of Parliament did not simply follow their leaders; instead, they could be swayed by public debate and Country party

---

[50]   Szechi (ed.), *'Scotland's Ruine'*, pp. 184–96; Bowie, 'Popular resistance', pp. 49–50.

leadership to rebel against the Court party when crown policy was inconsistent with their ideologies and interests. In 1706–7, ministers made greater efforts to manage not just leaders but followers by offering real concessions on grievances and substantive contributions to public debates. Though intended to 'manage' Parliament, these activities differed from patronage in relying on open dialogue rather than private conversations. The use of patronage in personal negotiations continued to be important, particularly in securing the acquiescence of party leaders on both sides, but the dynamic political culture of the early 1700s also required the deployment of public persuasion to ensure the co-operation of followers. We might call this management, but it was not business as usual.

The Scottish Historical Review, Volume LXXXVII: 2008 (Supplement), 94–115
DOI: 10.3366/E0036924108000504

DEREK J. PATRICK

Chapter 6
The Kirk, Parliament and the Union, 1706–7

On the eve of its recent tercentenary, histories of the Union could, in most instances, be categorised as belonging to one of two contrasting schools. In the first of these schools, the Union has been portrayed as marking the end of Scotland's independence and thus as inconsistent with the 'honour, fundamentall Laws and Constitution of [the] Kingdom'[1], in the second, the Union has been viewed as a calculated measure borne out of economic necessity. The first school, epitomised by the works of William Ferguson and Paul H. Scott, has focused on corruption, English intimidation and the venality of Scots Members of Parliament, the infamous 'parcel of rogues'.[2] In contrast, the second school, represented by the work of T. C. Smout and Christopher A. Whatley, has emphasised the economic implications, including free trade and the long-term benefits that an impoverished Scotland stood to gain from closer union with her English neighbour.[3]

Religion and concerns over the future of the Presbyterian government of the Church of Scotland – live issues that polarised opinion, influenced debate and excited contemporaries – have received less scrutiny by historians; for the most part, the notion that Scottish members of Parliament supported (or opposed) incorporating union on account of their religious beliefs has been all but ignored. In his account of the Revolution of 1688–90 in Scotland, the historian P. W. J. Riley went so far as to contend that many Scottish politicians had no real interest in religion and that religious 'affiliation could be modified'; it was personal ambition, not religion, that determined political alignment.[4] For a number of leading historians,

---

[1] National Archives of Scotland [NAS], Supplementary Warrants and Parliamentary Papers, PA 7/28/1.

[2] W. Ferguson, *Scotland's Relations with England: A Survey to 1707* (Edinburgh, 1994); P. H. Scott, *Andrew Fletcher and the Treaty of Union* (Edinburgh, 1994).

[3] T. C. Smout, 'The road to union', in G. Holmes (ed.), *Britain after the Glorious Revolution* (London, 1969), 176–96; C. A. Whatley, 'Economic causes and consequences of the union of 1707: A survey', *Scottish Historical Review*, 63 (1989), 150–81; C. A. Whatley, *The Scots and the Union* (Edinburgh, 2006).

[4] P. W. J. Riley, *King William and the Scottish Politicians* (Edinburgh, 1979), 7; P. W. J. Riley, *The Union of England and Scotland* (Manchester, 1978), 224, 314. In Riley's opinion, religion did little to shape the behaviour of Scots MPs. In his opinion the Scottish political system was inherently flawed and had 'no future but anarchy, civil war and English conquest'. Consequently, management and 'frictionless administration' were the most pressing demands of Scots courtiers who had first-hand experience of Anglo-Scots politics since the collapse of Darien.

the 'Act for Securing the Protestant Religion and Presbyterian Church Government', agreed on 12 November 1706, was little more than a 'successful strategy', calculated to 'draw the teeth of the opposition of the Kirk', rather than an undertaking born out of genuine conviction on the part of many members of the Scottish Parliament.[5] Not all Scots politicians were committed to the Presbyterian Church settlement. On 11 November 1706, the chancellor, James Ogilvie, first earl of Seafield, mentioned a 'difficultie with some of our [the court's] friends to perswad them to vot for a perpetual securitie to Presbiterian government'.[6] However, this is inconsistent with the attitudes of most members of the Scottish Estates.

Our knowledge of the Church of Scotland's role in the events that shaped the Union has been greatly enhanced by the recent work of Jeffrey Stephen.[7] He has demonstrated that the act securing Presbyterianism was not a 'master stroke' on the part of the Scots government; rather, the original draft act was necessarily (and reluctantly) amended to ensure it would be acceptable to the majority of churchmen. In Stephen's view, the act was 'exacted out of the government'.[8] While government ministers were careful to avoid too many amendments, fearful that these might provoke the English Parliament and jeopardise the achievement of the Union, voting on the Church act suggests that most Scots MPs were receptive to the Kirk's demands. The act, in short, was not simply a matter of political expediency. In his recent study of the Union, Christopher Whatley has challenged much of the established historiography associated with 1706-7.[9] Rather than simply rehash the tried and tested arguments that influenced the debates over the Union, Whatley's longer-term approach has identified considerable continuity during the period 1688 to 1707; from the Glorious Revolution to the Union, Scots politics were shaped by a similar set of considerations and by many of the same people. The majority of these people were committed to the Revolution settlement and Protestant succession, while they were increasingly concerned over Scotland's deteriorating economy, worsening Anglo-Scottish relations, Catholicism, France, and James Francis Edward Stuart (the Jacobite James VIII); in 1706-7 the Estates were faced with the real prospect that what had been restored in 1689-90 (a Protestant king and Presbyterian Church government) would be undermined. Members of the Scottish

---

[5] T. M. Devine, *The Scottish Nation 1700-2000* (London, 1999), 12; Scott, *Andrew Fletcher*, 194; D. Daiches, *Scotland and the Union* (London, 1977), 151; P. H. Scott, *Defoe in Edinburgh* (East Linton, 1995) 23.

[6] P. Hume Brown (ed.), *Letters Relating to Scotland in the Reign of Queen Anne by James Ogilvy, First Earl of Seafield and Others*, Scottish History Society (Edinburgh, 1915), 103.

[7] J. Stephen, 'The Kirk and the union, 1706-07: a reappraisal', *Records of the Scottish Church History Society*, 31 (2001), 68-96.

[8] *Ibid.*, 68, 91.

[9] Whatley, *Scots and the Union*.

Parliament were aware of this bigger picture, which had a clear impact on their attitudes towards incorporating union.

This chapter will build upon Whatley's seminal study by examining the demands of the Kirk. It will explore how these were addressed in the Scottish Parliament and it will consider the wider significance of the church act. Was this act essentially political, designed to appease Presbyterian churchmen and weaken popular opposition, or is there evidence that Presbyterianism was as significant to the majority of members of Parliament as it was to the Kirk and the Scots people in general?

The Kirk has been accurately described as the only institution with the potential to have mobilised national opposition to incorporating union.[10] Most Presbyterian churchmen were at first suspicious, if not actually opposed to a closer union with Scotland's Anglican neighbour; England, they knew, would be the senior partner in any agreement and ministers were concerned over the implications for the Church of Scotland. Their anxieties were increased by the fact that the commissioners appointed to negotiate the terms of the Treaty were instructed to forbear any discussion of the religious settlement.[11] Officers of state were aware that this could have a devastating (perhaps fatal) impact on the union negotiations and they regretted the influence of the Church ministers, who were condemned by John Erskine, sixth earl of Mar, Principal Secretary of State, for 'preaching up fear and danger'.[12] Mar later confessed the Kirk was 'the great rock wee [the court] were most afraid to spleet on'.[13] Similar sentiments were expressed by the English pro-union propagandist Daniel Defoe, who on 29 October 1706 (some few days before the crucial vote on the first article of Union) described the Presbyterian ministry as 'goeing Mad', adding that the 'parsons are out of their wits... I fear the Church will Joyn the Worst of their Enemies against the Union'.[14] However, Stephen has suggested that these and similar accounts may have been exaggerated, and he has further observed that the tendency of historians to concentrate on the more extreme religious elements in and around Edinburgh, Glasgow and the south west can give a false impression of Kirk activities.[15] But, irrespective of the level and spread of active opposition, the content of ministers' sermons and influence over their congregations, many (if not all) Presbyterian churchmen

---

[10] K. M. Brown, *Kingdom or Province? Scotland and the Regal Union* (London, 1992), 190.

[11] Stephen, 'The Kirk and the union', 77–81.

[12] Historical Manuscripts Commission [HMC], *Report on the Manuscripts of the Earl of Mar and Kellie* (London, 1904), 308; P. Hume Brown (ed.), *Letters Relating to Scotland in the Reign of Queen Anne by James Ogilvy, First Earl of Seafield and Others* (Scottish History Society, Edinburgh, 1915), 99, 103.

[13] *Ibid.*, 318.

[14] G. H. Healey (ed.), *The Letters of Daniel Defoe* (Oxford, 1955), 137.

[15] Stephen, 'The Kirk and the union', 83; NAS, Hamilton Muniments, GD 406/1/8032, James, fourth duke of Hamilton to [Anne, duchess of Hamilton], Holyroodhouse, 17 December 1706.

were anxious about the unwelcome changes that could come about as a consequence of closer union with England.

The Kirk's immediate reaction was understandable. In Scotland, Presbyterian Church government had by 1706 made only limited progress in many parishes located above the River Tay, where Episcopalian clergymen retained their churches and stipends by legal or, in some cases, illegal means. This was central to the Church of Scotland's opposition to the union treaty, as most Presbyterians believed a closer union with England could lead to the eventual restoration of the episcopate in the Church of Scotland.[16] Further, the activities of the Covenanting remnant, particularly in the south west, added to the Kirk's insecurities. But the Church's reaction to union was also influenced by international concerns. Roman Catholicism was a constant source of alarm and was perceived as a real threat to the Revolution Church settlement.[17] Amid the doubts over the succession to the British Crown after Queen Anne, Scottish churchmen became increasingly preoccupied by the enemy without – a resurgent France committed to placing a Catholic Stuart on the British throne. To some extent this concern explains why the Commission of the General Assembly of the Church of Scotland never wholeheartedly opposed a treaty of union, especially as that union did eventually promise to secure Presbyterian Church government. But as there was no explicit provision for the Church of Scotland in the initial treaty articles, it was clear that religion would be a matter of considerable interest to both MPs and church ministers when the Scottish Parliament assembled to debate an incorporating union.

The fourth and final session of Queen Anne's Scottish Parliament began on 3 October 1706. In her letter to the Estates the queen recommended that an 'entire and perfect Union [would be the] solid foundation of lasting Peace [and] will secure your Religion, Liberty and property', repeating former assurances 'to maintain the government of the Church as by Law established in Scotland'.[18] The latter point was a priority for the Commission of the General Assembly which was then sitting in Edinburgh. On 9 October 1706, it appointed a committee that included the moderator, William Wishart[19], the reverend William Carstares (William of Orange's former chaplain and now principal of the University of Edinburgh)[20] and several members of Parliament, to consider what would be most expedient for 'the preservation of the puritie of the doctrine, worship and of the discipline and government

---

[16] Stephen, 'The Kirk and the union', 72.

[17] Scottish Catholic Archives (SCA), Scottish Mission, SM 3/12/15; SCA, SM 3/2/15.

[18] T. Thomson (ed.), *The Acts of the Parliaments of Scotland (APS), Vol. XI* (Edinburgh, 1824), 306.

[19] J. Warwick, *The Moderators of the Church of Scotland from 1690–1740* (Edinburgh, 1913), 185. Wishart was described as a 'man of calm judgement and ripe wisdom'.

[20] A. I. Dunlop, *William Carstares and the Kirk by Law Established* (Edinburgh, 1964), 113.

of this church according to our Confession of Faith'.[21] To this end, the committee set about drafting an address to Parliament outlining the Kirk's concerns.

However, progress was disrupted by John Bannatyne and Thomas Linning, ministers from the Synod of Glasgow and Ayr, who proposed that the Commission of the General Assembly should petition the Estates for a national fast soliciting God's guidance 'in so weightie affairs as [were] now befor them'.[22] The Synod had organised a fast 'for the interest of the church and nation' at the beginning of October, and now recommended the same to the Commission; however, conscious that this could cause friction between church and state, the question of a national fast was referred to a committee while the Kirk's address was amended.[23] The address was approved by the Commission on 11 October and delivered to the Queen's high commissioner, James Douglas, second duke of Queensberry, and also to chancellor Seafield, on Monday 14. Both men were said to have received the address 'very kindlie' and expressed no doubt that the Kirk would be successful.[24] The address was straightforward, expressed in general terms, and neither opposed or condemned union.[25] It asked that Parliament 'establish and confirm the treu Protestant Religion and all [the Kirk's] sacred and Religious concerns in the most effectual manner for their unalterable security', and confirm legislation that would safeguard the Presbyterian government, worship and discipline of the Church of Scotland.[26]

But, in the meantime (the Commission's first address was received by Parliament on 17 October), the Estates were occupied debating the question of a national fast. On 12 October 1706, in anticipation of the Kirk's resolve, Walter Stewart of Pardovan, the member from Linlithgow, a member of the Commission of the General Assembly and a former émigré, moved that Parliament sanction a national fast.[27] He was seconded by several members of the confederated opposition, including James, fourth duke of Hamilton; John Murray, first duke of Atholl and John Hamilton, second lord Belhaven, who hoped to exploit the Kirk's concerns, delay progress of the articles of union, and cause an irreparable breach between the Church and Parliament.[28] Sir David Home of Crossrig reported that the question of the national

[21] NAS, Commission of the General Assembly, Scroll Minutes, CH 1/4/2, 9 October 1706.

[22] *Ibid*.

[23] NAS, Synod of Glasgow and Ayr 1705–15, CH 2/464/2, fol. 104–5.

[24] NAS, CH 1/4/2, 14 October 1706.

[25] Stephen, 'The Kirk and the union', 88.

[26] NLS, Wod.Qu.XL, fol. 57–8.

[27] HMC, *Manuscripts of the Earl of Mar and Kellie*, 290; A. L. Drummond, *The Kirk and the Continent* (Edinburgh, 1956), 106. The secretary, John Erskine, sixth earl of Mar, considered Pardovan a 'foolish fellow'.

[28] HMC, *Manuscripts of the Earl of Mar and Kellie*, 290, 298. On 26 October 1706, Mar informed Sir David Nairn that he had been 'credibly inform'd [that] my Lord Bellhaven said, that he wou'd make the Kirk and State knock hard heads'.

fast 'occasioned a long jangle', which was only brought to a conclusion when William Johnstone, first marquis of Annandale (a member of the opposition), recommended that the matter would be best served if Parliament left it to the Commission.[29]

On 14 October, the day its address was offered to Queensberry and Seafield, the Commission issued instructions appointing a day of 'publick humiliation and prayer to God for Direction to the Parliament in the great affair before them'. A special service would be conducted in the New Kirk, Edinburgh, on 18 October, and copies of the instructions were ordered to be transmitted to all Presbyteries recommending 'their concurrance'.[30] But this was not enough to satisfy members who wanted a national fast. On 21 October, following protracted debates in committee, it was proposed that a circular letter should be sent to every Presbytery, recommending that they each decide on whether to appoint a 'day of solemn fasting' within their own bounds.[31] The resolve was unanimously approved by the Commission; a clear signal that the Kirk was not prepared to join the coordinated opposition to union that Hamilton and his supporters had hoped to organise.

Mar was particularly satisfied with this outcome and attributed the success to Carstares, describing him as 'the principall man in managding this affair'.[32] Carstares was aware that this was a sensitive and potentially hazardous issue. Had the Commission applied to Parliament for civil sanction for a national fast, the Estates' refusal could have resulted in a complete break between Kirk and Parliament.[33] While Carstares and other moderate churchmen wished to avoid such a break, this was exactly the scenario that members of the opposition had hoped to contrive. Consequently, the Commission's rejection of the national fast in favour of local action by presbyteries dealt a critical blow to the aspirations of Hamilton's coalition. Hamilton condemned the Kirk's resolution in a letter to his mother (the formidable Anne, duchess of Hamilton), declaring 'My heart's Broke for I see noe good to bee done. The Comition have triefled with the [national] fast and tho they fancy they have Gott what's as good, they [the Commission] have falen into the Court's Trap'.[34]

On the whole, opposition efforts to win the support of the Kirk were ineffective. Only three presbyteries, Lanark, Hamilton and Dunblane, addressed Parliament to protest that an incorporating union, as offered in the treaty, would be dangerous to both church and state. The Dunblane address referred to 'the Fatal Consequences... [for] our

[29] Sir David Home of Crossrig, *A Diary of the Proceedings in the Parliament and Privy Council of Scotland 1700–1707* (Bannatyne Club, Edinburgh, 1820), 173.

[30] NAS, CH 1/4/2, 14 October 1706.

[31] *Ibid.*, 21 October 1706; NAS, Presbytery of Dunfermline 1704–17, CH 2//105/4, fol. 92; NAS, CH 1/4/2, 21 October 1706; Stephen, 'The Kirk and the union', 87.

[32] HMC, *Manuscripts of the Earl of Mar and Kellie*, 297.

[33] R. H. Story, *William Carstares: A Character and Career* (London, 1874), 295–96.

[34] NAS, GD 406/1/5294, James fourth duke of Hamilton to [Anne, duchess of Hamilton], Holyroodhouse, 22 October 1706.

Sacred and Religious Concerns', and described the treaty as 'a manifest Breach of our Solemn Covenants'.[35] The opposition's attempts to secure addresses from presbyteries in Dumbarton, Stirling, Irvine, Ayr and Paisley proved unsuccessful.[36] In any event, the presbyterial (and the majority of the kirk session) addresses to Parliament were not strictly anti-union. The Kirk was concerned over the terms of the treaty and the lack of any explicit safeguard for Presbyterian Church government. But should the ministers' fears be addressed and the Kirk be offered protection from Anglican and Episcopal influence, Scots Presbyterians were not opposed to the concept of closer union.[37]

Although their hopes of having Parliament appoint a national fast were disappointed, Hamilton and his allies knew that the religious settlement would be far from straightforward and could still disrupt the treaty negotiations. On 28 October, John Murray, first duke of Atholl, proposed that the Reverends George Meldrum and George Hamilton should be appointed to preach in Parliament House on 7 November, the same day the Presbytery of Edinburgh had chosen for its fast (held in accordance with the Commission's instructions of 21 October). Conscious that this could be interpreted as Parliament giving tacit approval to the Presbytery's fast and that the occasion could be hijacked by the opposition, the motion was rejected on the grounds that it encroached on the authority of the Queen's high commissioner.[38] An exasperated Andrew Fletcher of Saltoun chastised those members of Parliament who were also members of the Commission of the General Assembly, declaring 'if it were not to rip up a sore he cou'd make them blush'.[39] However, this provocative and ill-advised remark prompted an angry response from those whose integrity he had questioned, obliging Saltoun's supporters to withdraw their backing from Atholl's proposal. Church affairs were contentious and apt to excite even the most judicious member of Parliament.

Meanwhile, the members of the committee appointed by the Commission of the General Assembly on 9 October, had identified several heads requiring Parliament's attention if the Presbyterian settlement were to be secured. Concentrating on the structural problems associated with incorporating union, the Commission asked that the Estates consider some means of regulating the plantation

[35] NLS, Dunblane Address, 1.301(42); Stephen, 'The Kirk and the union', 76. The Hamilton and Lanark addresses conveyed similar concerns (although Hamilton's made no mention of the Covenants, obligations that many members of the post Revolution church no longer considered binding), beseeching Parliament to listen to the Kirk's 'dying groans', looking on union 'as destructive to the true interest of the nation, as well as the church'. While all three addresses were opposed to closer union with England based on the articles then under negotiation, they did not condemn the project.

[36] NLS, Wod.Qu.LXXIII, fol. 277.

[37] Stephen, 'The Kirk and the union', 72.

[38] Crossrig, *Diary*, 177.

[39] HMC, *Manuscripts of the Earl of Mar and Kellie*, 304.

of churches and the valuation of teinds [the Church of Scotland's equivalent of tithes], of making adequate provision for visiting schools and universities, and of creating a suitable body for redressing Church grievances if, as expected, the Privy Council were to be abolished.[40] The Commission, anticipating the imminent appearance of a draft act for the security of the Church, appointed several of its number to lobby members of Parliament and ascertain whether or not the issues highlighted by the Church's committee had been or were due to be discussed.

On 29 October, the Commission considered a second paper prepared by its committee for public affairs, emphasising difficulties pertaining to various oaths that would be introduced as a consequence of the Union. One of these concerned the coronation oath by which the sovereign of Great Britain would only be sworn to maintain the rights and privileges of the Church of England. Likewise, it was observed that the English abjuration oath excluded from the succession all 'who are not of the communion of the Church of England as now by law established there'.[41] The committee raised the question of whether the British Parliament should be excluded from imposing oaths in Scotland that were incompatible with the principles of the Kirk. In addition, the committee recommended that Scots be exempt from the sacramental test, which 'secludes all from any office in Brittain or benefite from the Crown thereof, that are of the Communion of the Church of Scotland'.[42]

Hamilton raised the matter of the sacramental test in Parliament the next day. Immediately after the Estates had heard the twenty-fifth article, 'That all Laws and Statutes in either Kingdom, so far as they are contrary to, or inconsistent with the Terms of these Articles ... become void',[43] Hamilton enquired whether the sacramental test would also be cancelled 'for if not, then this union was very unequal'. He added 'there is nothing to hinder any Englishman to come here and enjoy a place in Scotland. They [the English] may enjoy our places, be Governors of our Castles, Collonels of our Regiments, but we cannot enjoy so much as an Ensign's Commission in England until this oath be taken'.[44] The Duke considered his conscience 'not so strait, but raither than want a good place he cou'd take it', but he knew many Presbyterians 'whos consciences were so very strict, that rather than take this oath wou'd want a place'.[45] Following some spirited sparring between Hamilton, Patrick Home, first earl of Marchmont, and John Dalrymple, first earl of Stair, further consideration of the sacramental test was referred to a future sederunt.

[40] NAS, CH 1/4/2, 28 October 1706.
[41] *Ibid.*, 29 October 1706.
[42] *Ibid.*
[43] C. A. Whatley, *Bought and Sold for English Gold?* (East Linton, 2001), 117.
[44] NAS, GD 406/M9/266, 30 October 1706, fol. 23.
[45] *Ibid.*

On 1 November, the Commission set about drafting an additional grievance. This was prompted by the composition of the Westminster Parliament, 'where twenty-six bishops do sit as members ... inconsistent both with the principles of Presbyterians and the Covenants and engagements of this Church and Nation'.[46] Having 'discoursed at some length', the Commission agreed on a second address for Parliament incorporating the first, third and fourth heads, as identified by its committee on 29 October (the three clauses dealing with the coronation oath, an exemption from incompatible English obligations and the sacramental test).[47] The Kirk's decisions on the second and fifth clauses, reflecting on the abjuration oath and membership of a British Parliament, were delayed for several days.

On 2 November, after weeks spent in examining the articles, Parliament moved to determine the order in which they would be discussed and voted. Some argued that debate should begin with the first article, 'that the two Kingdoms of Scotland and England, shall ... be united into one Kingdom by the Name of Great-Britain'.[48] Others proposed that Parliament should first consider the fourth article, 'that all the Subjects of the united Kingdom of Great-Britain shall ... have full Freedom and Intercourse of Trade and Navigation'.[49] Still others recommended that Parliament settle the security of the Kirk before considering any of the articles. However, as one observer noted, 'twas out of the road to consider the security of the church, until it was once known what progress the house wou'd make in [the first] article, for unless an Incorporating union were agreed to, the Church needs no other security then what it has'.[50] In an attempt to reach an agreement, the Clerk Register, Sir James Murray of Philiphaugh, suggested that Parliament begin with the first article, with the added proviso that unless all other articles were approved, the first would be of no consequence.[51] Then, once article one was agreed, the Estates could consider the 'act for [the] security of the Doctrine, Discipline, worship and government of the Church, as nou by Lau establish'd'.[52] Stewart of Pardovan (who had staunchly supported the national fast) contended that Parliament should first confirm the Presbyterian government of the Kirk before it discussed any of the articles.[53] Being put to a vote, Philiphaugh's proposal was approved by a majority of 36 votes.[54]

Parliament made no further progress with the act of security until 4 November, when a draft was introduced by the Lord Justice

[46] NAS, CH 1/4/2, 1 November 1706.
[47] Ibid.
[48] Whatley, Bought and Sold, 100.
[49] Ibid., 102.
[50] NAS, GD 406/M9/266, 2 November 1706, fol. 29.
[51] Ibid., fol. 29; Crossrig, Diary, 178–9.
[52] NAS, GD 406/M9/266, 2 November 1706, fol. 29.
[53] Ibid., fol. 29; Crossrig, Diary, 179.
[54] Crossrig, Diary, 179.

Clerk, Adam Cockburn of Ormiston.[55] In the interim, the Estates' attention was focused on the protracted debates and theatrical speeches concerning the first article. This was eventually passed by 116 votes to 83; in the opinion of John Erskine, sixth earl of Mar, 'a good plurality (thirty-three), but fewer than we expected'. When Parliament turned to the draft of the church act, the Commission was finalising its second address. On 7 November, 'after much reasoning', the Commission agreed to add the two heads dealing with the abjuration oath and English bishops in the House of Lords. These were added to the three clauses agreed on 1 November and another detailing the structural problems identified on 28 October.[56] However, before voting, several Kirk elders, including Marchmont; John Leslie, ninth earl of Rothes; Lord Polwarth; Sir Alexander Ogilvie of Forglen; Sir James Campbell of Auchinbreck; James Campbell of Ardkinglas and George Baillie of Jerviswood – all but one members of Parliament – dissented from the Commission's second address and protested against a decision they deemed 'tactless and rash'.[57] These elders argued that 'since the ministers had already won parliament's assurance that any union treaty would confirm the church's established status and legislate for its future security, they had little to gain by bringing these specific concerns to parliament's attention, and could be suspected of disaffection and mistrust'.[58]

On 8 November, Parliament received the 'Humble Representation of the Commission of the General Assembly' comprising six sections. The address described the sacramental test to be 'of most dangerous consequence to this Church'. It asked that Scotland not enter into closer union 'unless it be provided that no oath, bond or Test of any kind shall be required... which are Inconsistent with the known principles of this Church'.[59] The coronation oath was to be adjusted so the British monarch would also 'be engaged to maintain the doctrine, worship, Discipline and Government of this Church'.[60] The address proposed that, in the event of union, Parliament should find some suitable means to facilitate the plantation of churches and valuation of teinds, and appoint an administrative body to hear Church grievances and correspond with the Church 'anent ffasts and Thanksgivings'.[61] The oath of abjuration should be revised so as to be compatible with the principles of the Kirk. Finally, the Commission questioned the English

---

[55] *Ibid.*
[56] NAS, CH 1/4/2, 7 November 1706.
[57] D. Duncan (ed.), *History of the Union of Scotland and England by Sir John Clerk of Penicuik* (Edinburgh, 1993), 119; HMC, *Manuscripts of the Earl of Mar and Kellie*, 315.
[58] Duncan (ed.), *History of the Union of Scotland and England by Sir John Clerk of Penicuik*, 119.
[59] NLS, Wod.Qu.XL, fol. 59.
[60] *Ibid.*
[61] *Ibid.*

bishops' seats in a British Parliament, 'contrary to our known principles and Covenants'.[62]

It was moved that the Estates proceed to consider the church act but Atholl proposed that the Commission's second address should be printed and any consideration of the act be delayed until members of Parliament had had an opportunity to reflect on the address. He recommended that as an alternative Parliament should discuss the cess act which was agreed with little opposition. The Estates offered eight months' supply 'in consideration [of] the danger that still threatens this Kingdom by reason of the continuance of the present war'.[63] The Earl of Mar considered this 'a verie good daye's work … [as] it pleases the troops so makes them sure to us'.[64] There may have been truth in the rumour that the opposition mistakenly believed that Parliament would be adjourned after the court had secured sufficient funds.[65] This was a relatively common tactic employed by government ministers when securing adequate supply was crucial and the Parliament was difficult to manage. Nonetheless, Queensberry had no intention of bringing this session to a premature close. Parliament resumed consideration of the act of security on 9 November. Once the act had been read, Belhaven proposed that the section referring in a general way to existing legislation securing the Presbyterian establishment should be expanded to list all major acts in support of the Kirk.[66] This was opposed by several members, including Leven; Marchmont; Atholl; John Campbell, second duke of Argyll; John, fifteenth earl of Sutherland; and Thomas Hamilton, sixth earl of Haddington; who together maintained that 'a general clause was as good, and in case a particular enumeration were made, some might be left out and by that thought to be laid aside'.[67] The long-term security of the Scots universities occasioned a 'long debate', but the disputed clauses were resolved to Mar's satisfaction.[68] The opposition proposed several additional amendments,[69] although, in the opinion of one observer, 'none of any importance', and Parliament was adjourned until 12 November.[70]

The Earl of Mar was optimistic that the act of security would be passed but he was concerned the opposition would attempt to add

[62] *Ibid.*

[63] *APS, Vol. XI*, 317.

[64] HMC, *Manuscripts of the Earl of Mar and Kellie*, 317.

[65] Duncan (ed.), *History of the Union of Scotland and England by Sir John Clerk of Penicuik*, 120.

[66] NAS, GD 406/M9/266, 9 November 1706, fol. 41; Crossrig, *Diary*, 181.

[67] *Ibid.*

[68] HMC, *Manuscripts of the Earl of Mar and Kellie*, 317; Crossrig, *Diary*, 181. Both the day's votes were carried by the pro-union parties.

[69] Duncan (ed.), *History of the Union of Scotland and England by Sir John Clerk of Penicuik*, 120. Penicuik considered the proposed amendments as either 'additional safeguards [or] from others the raising of captious questions and difficulties designed to sink union under a great show of care for the kirk'.

[70] NAS, GD 406/M9/266, 9 November 1706, fol. 41.

a number of clauses that would make it abhorrent in England.[71] His worries were not misplaced. Hamilton's coalition made a last-ditch effort to load the act with conditions that would appeal to the Kirk and cause offence in Westminster. Reflecting on the sacramental test, Belhaven proposed (not unreasonably) that Scots should be 'capable of [holding] any office, civil or military, and [be eligible] to receive any grant, gift or right, and to have command or place of trust from and under the Sovereign within any part of Great Brittain'.[72] The test act was described as unjust to Presbyterians, while the English practise of kneeling to take the sacrament was condemned as 'adoration and heretical'.[73] Lord Belhaven maintained that the test would limit the opportunities for Scots and would consequently 'deprive this church of their greatest supporters, which will end certainly in their ruine'.[74] In response, representatives of the pro-union parties argued that the Scottish Parliament should not meddle in the government of the Church of England: 'we ought do whatever was in our [the Scots] pouer relative to our Church' without 'pull[ing] doun that which the English thinks the greatest hedge to theirs'.[75] This was 'long and stronglie debeat', but in the end Belhaven's amendment was rejected by 39 votes.[76]

One of the anti-union commissioners from Lanarkshire, William Baillie of Lamington, seemingly influenced by the Kirk's second address, recommended that in any future British Parliament, bishops should be excluded from voting on matters pertaining to the Church of Scotland. He was seconded by Sir John Lauder of Fountainhall, who, in describing the origins of the spiritual estate in Scotland claimed that it had 'as much if not more pretence to purity as any church in Europe, for tho Bishops became temporal Lords in other places about the second or third century, yet we had none here till the twelfth, in Malcolm Canmore's time'. Further, Fountainhall recalled the claims of the Archbishop of York to superiority over the Scottish Church in the early twelfth century, adding that 'we don't knou, but this or something else may be trumped up against us'.[77] The opposition offered several additional clauses, including an oath, to be taken by all future office holders in Scotland, acknowledging Presbyterian Church government as unalterable and 'truly apostolic'. However, the opposition did not insist on any of these clauses.[78] Parts of the church act were amended before the final draft was presented to the Estates, but the opposition's

---

[71] HMC, *Manuscripts of the Earl of Mar and Kellie*, 318.
[72] NAS, GD 406/M9/266, 12 November 1706, fol. 41; Scott, *Andrew Fletcher*, 193.
[73] *Ibid.*
[74] *Ibid.*
[75] *Ibid.*, fol. 42.
[76] HMC, *Manuscripts of the Earl of Mar and Kellie*, 318.
[77] NAS, GD 406/M9/266, 12 November 1706, fol. 42.
[78] Duncan (ed.), *History of the Union of Scotland and England by Sir John Clerk of Penicuik*, 121.

best efforts to derail it proved unsuccessful. Overall there were fewer changes than had been anticipated by the Earl of Mar.[79]

Before voting on the act commenced, Lord Belhaven protested that the act '[was] no valid security to the Church of Scotland ... in case of an Union, and that the Church of Scotland can have no real and solid security by any manner of Union by which our Claim of Right is unhinged and our distinct Sovereignty and Independency intirely abolished'.[80] Twenty-three members adhered to Belhaven's protest, including several who contemporaries considered to be at odds with both Presbyterian Church government and the Revolution settlement. This perception was not lost on Daniel Defoe who proceeded to class all the 'protestors and adherers' as 'known Enemies of the Church'.[81] However, Belhaven's protest had no real impact on the final vote which approved the act securing the Kirk by an overwhelming majority of 112 votes to 38 (a majority of 74) on 12 November.

While some have viewed the act as simply a concession 'calculated to calm the anxiety of those who felt that the Union would put the Kirk at the mercy of the overwhelming majority in the British Parliament', closer analysis of the church vote and division lists suggests that support for the act was not solely a matter of political expediency.[82] Many members of Parliament had both a commitment to the Revolution settlement (which was inextricably linked with the re-establishment of Presbyterian Church government in 1690) and a more general concern for the future of Protestantism across Europe, that helped shape their attitudes to England and incorporating union; for them, the legislation guaranteeing the Kirk's status was a crucial component of the union package.

Calculating the overall voting strengths of the principal parties in the last session of the Scottish Parliament is not straightforward. On average the pro-union parties enjoyed more consistent support, achieving a maximum of 154 votes on the fourth article of union (21 November 1706). However, the combined court and *squadrone volante* vote of 116 on article one (4 November 1706) is a more accurate reflection of their total strength. This remained constant throughout the session, only dropping below 110 on twelve out of thirty occasions. Likewise, the 83 opposition votes on article one or the 84 votes against proceeding to article two (14 November 1706) are a reasonable reflection on the overall size of the country party.[83] But, in fact, the opposition vote was rather more erratic. Hamilton's coalition (the old country and cavalier

---

[79] HMC, *Manuscripts of the Earl of Mar and Kellie*, 319.

[80] *APS, Vol. XI*, 320.

[81] Healey (ed.), *Letters of Daniel Defoe*, 148; *APS, Vol. XI*, 320.

[82] Scott, *Andrew Fletcher*, 194.

[83] Statistics are based on the thirty division lists recorded in *APS*. These cover the votes on the first article of union on 4 November 1706 to ratification on 16 January 1707. The opposition vote exceeded 84 on only three occasions: 6 December (89 votes), 20 December (93 votes) and 24 December 1706 (86 votes).

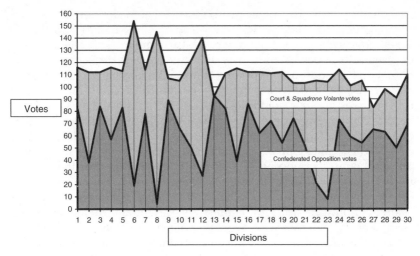

Figure 1: Pro-Union and Opposition Votes, 4 November 1706–16 January 1707.

parties) polled in excess of 80 votes on only seven of thirty occasions. Nevertheless, throughout November and most of December 1706 opposition votes were relatively consistent even if prone to fluctuation. Disregarding Parliament's proclamation against 'unlawful convocations' on 29 November (which was supported by both sides of the House), the opposition vote was markedly reduced on only three occasions. These dealt with what contemporaries considered some of the most fundamental components of incorporating union: the security of the Church of Scotland (12 November 1706), the Protestant succession (15 November) and free trade with England (21 November). In the first instance, opposition votes fell by more than 50 per cent from 83 on the first article to 38. Likewise, on 15 November, country votes dropped from a previous high of 84 to only 57. Finally, on article four, the confederated opposition polled only 19 votes in comparison with 83 on the third article only three days earlier. The unionist parties secured majorities of 74, 59 and 135 respectively. This last was comparatively unusual as any significant decline in opposition support was seldom simultaneous with an increase in court votes. The above graph (Figure 1), plotting pro-union and country party votes across the thirty recorded parliamentary divisions (4 November 1706 to 16 January 1707), shows that this occurred on only three occasions – the votes on article four, clauses of article fifteen (the Equivalent) and Parliament's popular proclamation against illegal meetings.[84]

On the matter of the Kirk's act of security, the slump in the opposition numbers was not accompanied by a corresponding increase

[84] Divisions 6 (article four, 15 Nov. 1706), 11, 12 (article fifteen, 7 Dec. 1706) and 8 ('tumultuary meetings', 29 Nov. 1706).

in court votes.[85] In some respects this could be interpreted as contradicting the notion that Presbyterian Church government was a key concern for most members of Parliament. The fact that the opposition vote decreased by over 40 would suggest that a considerable number of Hamilton's supporters were either absent or abstained. If this can be explained by a general reluctance to vote against an act that secured the Kirk, would this not have been reflected by an increase in the court's share of the vote? Conversely, it could be surmised that several members of the old country party were unwilling to vote against their allies but were equally loath to vote against the church act. This is, alas, impossible to determine: the division lists that appear in the *Acts of the Parliaments of Scotland* include only bare facts (pro or con) but are none the less the most detailed source available. Closer examination of the lists and members of Parliament, their careers and often shared experience of Scottish politics since the Revolution of 1689–90, is crucial in explaining the broader significance of the Kirk and Presbyterianism in 1706–7.

Recent analysis of the membership of the Union Parliament has identified significant continuity running from the Revolution in 1689–90 in terms of both politics and personnel. Previous parliamentary experience had a considerable impact on an individual's voting behaviour; the longer an MP had sat in Parliament, the more likely they were to vote for incorporating union.[86] A total of 226 members sat in the last session of the old Scottish Parliament.[87] Of these, 36 (16 per cent) had been members of the largely Presbyterian Convention of Estates in 1689 that had crafted the Revolution settlement, restored the Kirk, and offered the Scottish throne to William and Mary. In addition, some 73 MPs (32 per cent) had been members of King William's Estates, entering Parliament at some point between 1689 and 1702. Overall, 48 per cent of MPs in 1706–7 had also been members of the previous Revolution Parliament. The significance of these statistics becomes more apparent when viewed together with each commissioner's votes on the articles of union. No fewer than 24 (67 per cent) of those who had sat in the Convention, alongside 45 (62 per cent) of the men who had served in the last Parliament, cast all or the majority of their votes with the pro-union parties. In short, some 55 per cent of Scots MPs who can be categorized as supporters of closer union with England (or be associated with the court or *squadrone volante* parties) had been active in politics for at least part of King William's reign.[88]

---

[85] Division 2 (12 November 1706).

[86] Whatley, *Scots and the Union*, chap 3.

[87] In total, 227 men sat in the final session including Sir Archibald Hope of Rankeillour (one of the commissioners from Fife) who died before voting began and was replaced by his son Thomas.

[88] In Parliament 1706–7, 126 MPs cast all or the majority of their votes with the court or *squadrone volante*. Where evidence of voting is limited attempts to categorize an individual can be problematic. However, in most instances, the voting patterns of this

These statistics are consistent when the same criteria are applied to those who voted for the act securing Presbyterian Church government. Twenty-one (58 per cent) of the members of Parliament (1706–7) who had sat in the Convention of Estates supported the act, as did 40 MPs, representing some 55 per cent of members who had served in the Revolution Parliament. Overall, 54 per cent of those who supported the act had been members of King William's Estates. This group included some of the staunchest supporters of the Revolution and most consistent advocates of closer union. No less than 12 had been part of the Scots émigré community in the Netherlands. Most, if not all, had joined the Prince of Orange's expedition to Britain in November 1688. In addition, at least 9 members of Parliament were the sons of exiles, while several others had strong links with émigré families.

Some 15 commissioners can be identified as attending a meeting of Scots lords and landed gentlemen convened at Whitehall on 1 January 1689 at Whitehall.[89] It was during this series of meetings that the Scots first considered their preferred settlement in church and state, with incorporating union proposed as a popular means of securing the Revolution. Three MPs who were present at these meetings and who voted for the church act and union in 1706–7 – William, twelfth lord Ross, Adam Cockburn of Ormiston and Sir William Anstruther of that ilk – have also been classified as leaders of the 'Presbyterian and discontented' opposition to King James VII and his catholicizing policies.[90] The greater part of those who voted for the act securing Presbyterian Church government were constant supporters of incorporating union with, in many (if not most) cases, a direct link to the Revolution and commitment to its ideals. The act can be described as a means of appeasing the Kirk but there is no reason to doubt that those who voted in its favour were anything other than committed to the Revolution settlement, Protestant succession and moderate Presbyterianism. Perhaps more than 70 members of Parliament (almost exclusively pro-unionists) held posts or were in receipt of pensions in 1706–7.[91] However, it is impossible to ignore the enduring ideological commitments of men such as Marchmont; Archibald Douglas, third earl of Forfar; Leven; Jerviswood; Ormiston; David Boyle, first earl of Glasgow, and John Dalrymple, first earl of Stair – courtiers, Revolutioners and émigrés – that shaped their attitudes to incorporating union and the Scots demands.

[88] (*Continued*) group are fairly consistent. Some 82 per cent (103 of the commissioners who can be associated with either of the pro-union parties) participated in at least two-thirds of recorded divisions; 89 MPs (70 per cent) took part in at least twenty-five of the thirty recorded votes.

[89] D. J. Patrick, 'Unconventional Procedure: Scottish Electoral Politics after the Revolution' in K. M. Brown and A. J. Mann (eds), *Parliament and Politics in Scotland, 1567–1707* (Edinburgh, 2005), 242–44.

[90] Colin Lindsay, third earl of Balcarres, *Memoirs Touching the Revolution in Scotland 1688–1690*, Bannatyne Club (Edinburgh, 1841), 12.

[91] NAS, GD 406/M1/208/21.

Several members of the country opposition joined with the court and voted against their party colleagues on the Kirk resolution. Some of those who opposed closer union were none the less convinced that an act offering further security to the Church of Scotland was essential. These included David Erskine, ninth earl of Buchan, eldest son of an émigré, Henry Erskine, third lord Cardross (a union commissioner in 1689). Buchan voted against ratifying the treaty but voted in favour of the Kirk act and Protestant succession.[92] Likewise, one of the commissioners from Roxburghshire, Sir Gilbert Elliot of Minto and Headshaw, an émigré and one of those zealous for the Commission's second address, opposed parliamentary union but supported article two (the Hanoverian succession) and the church act.[93] His vote on the last is consistent with that of the Lanarkshire MP, John Sinclair of Stevenson. Like Buchan, Stevenson was the son of an émigré, Sir Robert Sinclair (a member of the Convention Parliament and King William's Privy Council).[94] Stevenson voted with the court in only one recorded division, the act securing the government of the Church. In all, no fewer than 11 members of the confederated opposition aligned themselves with the court and voted in favour of the act. As was the case with Minto and Buchan, William Maxwell of Cardoness, a commissioner from the Stewartry of Kirkcudbright, voted against Parliament's ratification of the articles but in favour of the Kirk act and Protestant succession. He was the son of the Reverend William Maxwell, minister of Minnigaff in the Presbytery of Wigtown, who had been deprived of his church as a result of King Charles II's restoration of Episcopal Church Government in 1662.[95] These experiences may well have influenced Cardoness and shaped his vote on the church act. Similar concerns may also explain the temporary defection of John Forbes of Culloden, one of the commissioners from Nairnshire. His father, Duncan Forbes, had been a committed Whig who advocated the reintroduction of Presbyterianism in Scotland after the Revolution.[96] John Forbes cast only four of his twenty-one votes with the court. It is no coincidence that these votes concerned Presbyterian Church Government and trade. The long-term security of both was vitally important and most Scots sought additional safeguards to guarantee the Kirk's independence, concessions for Scottish trade goods and free access to English markets. Not all members of Parliament considered an incorporating union a suitable means of achieving these ends, but irrespective of the MPs' votes for and against the treaty, the selective

---

[92] Buchan did vote with the opposition on Belhaven's preceding clause concerning the sacramental test.

[93] Whatley, Scots and the Union, 82; HMC, Manuscripts of the Earl of Mar and Kellie, 336.

[94] G. Gardner, The Scottish Exile Community in the Netherlands, 1660–1690 (East Linton, 2004), 197.

[95] H. Scott, Fasti Ecclesiae Scoticane, 11 vols. (Edinburgh, 1917), ii, 372; M. D. Young (ed.), The Parliaments of Scotland: Burgh and Shire Commissioners, 2 vols. (Edinburgh, 1992, 1993), ii, 478.

[96] Young, Parliaments of Scotland: Burgh and Shire Commissioners (Edinburgh, 1992), i, 246.

voting on the security of the Kirk, Scots trade, and economic interests reflects a level of genuine conviction born out of deep-seated beliefs, rather than simple political expediency.[97]

Similar opinions may account for the fact that opposition votes on the act securing Presbyterian Church government fell by more than half. Several members of Hamilton's confederated opposition supported the court's initiative. It is possible that even more approved the act but, on this occasion, were reluctant to vote alongside their political enemies. Some commissioners, whether opposed to union or not, were probably uncomfortable voting against an act that secured the Kirk, while still others may have surmised that the act did not offer the Church enough security. While the reasons why the opposition vote decreased (with no corresponding upsurge in court support) are speculative, there is less doubt over what motivated the 38 members of Parliament who voted against the act. These included some of the most committed members of the country party, with over 80 per cent of them participating in at least two-thirds of the recorded votes. Five had been members of the Convention of Estates and another 34 per cent (13 commissioners) had sat in the Revolution Parliament. However, several were cavaliers (Jacobites or Episcopalians) suspected of disaffection and no allies of the Kirk. David Murray, fifth viscount Stormont, had made a brief appearance in the Convention of Estates in March 1689, but opposed the Revolution settlement and withdrew from politics until the accession of Queen Anne. Alexander Bruce, fourth earl of Kincardine, had been expelled from Parliament in 1702 for claiming that Presbyterian Church government was inconsistent with the essence of monarchy.[98]

Likewise, William Keith, ninth earl Marischal; Charles Hay, thirteenth earl of Erroll; John Fleming, sixth earl of Wigtown; John Lyon, fourth earl of Strathmore; William Livingstone, third viscount Kilsyth; James Ogilvie of Boyne, and Patrick Lyon of Auchterhouse were all implicated in, involved with, or confined as a result of the Jacobites' activities in either 1708 or 1715. Perhaps the best known Jacobite member of Parliament, George Lockhart of Carnwath, was absent on the day of the vote.[99] The several opposition leaders (and a number of their supporters) also voted against the church act. These included Hamilton, Belhaven, Atholl, Annandale (who had served as a Union commissioner in 1702-03 and voted for the Protestant succession on 15 November 1706) and Andrew Fletcher of Saltoun, a former émigré. However, on this occasion the cavaliers accounted for a greater proportion of opposition votes than was usual. The act for the security of the Kirk exposed a crucial weakness in the confederated opposition. The old country party rank-and-file (with their origins

---

[97] In this instance, members of the opposition are defined as either those who voted for more country than pro-unionist divisions, or irrespective of other votes, opposed the ratification of the Union on 16 January 1707.

[98] Young, *Parliaments of Scotland: Burgh and Shire Commissioners*, i, 76.

[99] HMC, *Manuscripts of the Earl of Mar and Kellie*, 318.

in the Parliament of 1698–1702) had little in common with the cavaliers, whose ultimate objective was the restoration of the Pretender, James Francis Edward Stuart.[100]

The shortfall in country (and to some extent court) votes can be attributed to absence or abstention. Michael Fry has suggested that when the church act was approved on 12 November 1706, 'more members abstained than voted at all', an observation that clearly exaggerates the number of Scots parliamentary commissioners who did not participate.[101] It is impossible to calculate the exact number of MPs who abstained on each division, but bearing in mind that 226 names appear in the sederunt of the fourth session of Anne's Parliament, 150 voted for or against the church act, and 199 on article one, while it is unlikely that more than 50 MPs abstained (at most seventy-five). The duke of Queensberry (Anne's commissioner) did not vote due to his office. Neither did the Lord Advocate, Sir James Stewart of Goodtrees, the only officer of state who opposed the Union.[102] In addition, James Stewart, first earl of Bute, had gone home by 9 November, accompanied by John Stewart of Kilwhinleck, one of the commissioners from Bute.[103] Several MPs were absent on 12 November or, based on analysis of their voting behavior, had still to arrive in Edinburgh. For example, Thomas Hay, first viscount Dupplin, who voted in favour of article one, had gone to visit his critically ill second son and made no further contribution until 24 December. Mar mentioned that William Ker, second marquis of Lothian was also absent, as well as 'severall others of our people'. He added that besides court absentees, 'severalls of the opposers were out of the House too'.[104] Considering Mar's observations, it is likely that, in this instance, the number of members of Parliament who abstained was significantly less than the maximum 75 members whose activities (and attendance) are unaccounted for.[105] Of these, 44 cast all or the majority of their votes with the confederated opposition, 25 with the court, 5 did not vote in any of the recorded divisions, while Alexander Montgomerie, ninth earl of Eglinton distributed his 20 votes equally between both sides. Focusing on the 25 absents or abstainers associated with either of the pro-union parties, 18 supported the ratification of the articles and 13 voted in favour of the Protestant succession; for

---

[100] In part this explains the *squadrone volante's* break with the country party in 1702–03.

[101] M. Fry, *The Union, England, Scotland and the Treaty of Union* (Edinburgh, 2006), 273. Fry does acknowledge that the far wider margin for the act of security than article one (incorporation) suggests that the Kirk meant more to many Scots MPs than an independent state.

[102] Whatley, *Scots and the Union*, 258; HMC, *Manuscripts of the Earl of Mar and Kellie*, 280. Goodtrees made no secret of the fact that he was opposed to incorporating union but as an Officer of State, chose not to vote against it.

[103] SCA, BL 2/125/17; NAS, GD 406/1/5360, James Stewart, first earl of Bute to James, fourth duke of Hamilton, Rothesay, 14 December 1706.

[104] HMC, *Manuscripts of the Earl of Mar and Kellie*, 318–19. Mar also acknowledged that some of the pro-union MPs 'who were in [Parliament] did not vote'.

[105] 226 members of Parliament less the Commissioner and 150 MPs who voted on the act.

many this was crucial and inextricably linked to the lasting security of the Church of Scotland. For the 44 opposition members who were either absent or abstained on 12 November 1706, some 27 voted against the ratification of the treaty and 23 against article two; only one MP, Hugh Montgomerie of Busbie, the staunchly Whig commissioner from Glasgow, voted for the Hanoverian succession. Considering that around 45 per cent of those opposition members of Parliament who did not vote on the church act had adopted a similar approach on article two, this may be an indication of their broad religious preferences; they were Protestant, typically Presbyterian, but opposed to closer union and not prepared to vote with the court (or their cavalier allies) on issues that could have a lasting or detrimental impact on the Kirk.[106]

This should not imply that all MPs who voted against the second article or the act securing Presbyterian Church government were opposed to the existing church settlement. Likewise, not all opposition commissioners who were absent or abstained on either issue were indicating their tacit approval of Presbyterianism. But this would seem the most probable explanation for the voting records of such MPs as William Baillie of Lamington or Stewart of Pardovan. Lamington, a commissioner from Lanarkshire, had been chosen as a member of the Convention in March 1689, and had subscribed the Estates' letter of congratulation addressed to William of Orange.[107] Likewise, Walter Stewart, an MP since May 1700, was a member of the Commission of the General Assembly and zealous for Presbyterian Church government. Both were opposed to union and voted with the opposition in over two-thirds of the recorded divisions, but neither voted on article two or the Kirk act. To vote against either would have been inconsistent with their beliefs.

That religion was a divisive issue is reflected both in the large number of pamphlets concerned with the Kirk published in 1706–7 and in the popular (and vocal) opposition outside Parliament House.[108] About half the Scottish Parliament (even more than half if adjustments are made for known absentees) were in favour of the act securing the Presbyterian government of the Kirk. In contrast, the opposition vote was substantially reduced. This is explained by a number of commissioners who were either absent or decided to abstain (at most just over 30 per cent) which had a serious impact on the country and, to a lesser extent, the court vote. While this shift does not necessarily signify implicit approval of the church act, it does suggest that the lasting security of the Kirk was a dilemma for several MPs (especially opposition members), who had reservations over the strength of the

---

[106] Cross voting in Parliament 1706–7 was not unusual but in most instances would appear more common with regard to trade and economic considerations. It was perhaps easier for opposition members to vote on articles where there had been significant amendments and concessions.

[107] Patrick, 'Unconventional Procedure', 239.

[108] Whatley, *Scots and the Union*, 245–46; NAS, GD 406/M 9/208/6.

act or over voting with the court and *squadrone volante*. Consequently, silence was the more appropriate (and diplomatic) response.

Nevertheless, a small number of opposition members were prepared to overlook party classifications and vote with the government on legislation that they considered essential. The evidence surrounding the church act also supports the notion that continuity, in several instances a shared experience of politics since the Restoration and an enduring commitment to the Revolution settlement (or in some cases the House of Stuart), shaped MPs' attitudes to incorporating union. Considering the 109 MPs who had sat in the Convention of Estates or the previous Parliament, 61 (56 per cent) supported the church act, and 18 (circa 17 per cent) voted against. Parliament's act offering security to the Kirk was a vital part of the union package. It was necessary that the Estates were seen to appreciate the concerns of the Commission of the General Assembly, but members of Parliament also held religious convictions. Presbyterianism clearly influenced Scots MPs' votes.[109]

Parliament's Act for Securing the Protestant Religion and Presbyterian Church Government 'Establish[ed] and Confirm[ed] the said true Protestant Religion and the Worship, Discipline and Government of the Church, to continue without any alteration to the people of this land in all succeeding generations'. This lasting guarantee would 'remain and continue unalterable [as] a fundamental and essential condition of any Treaty or Union'.[110] The act had a clear impact on Presbyterian attitudes to the union negotiations. John Clerk of Penicuik observed that the act calmed churchmen's immediate concerns, adding 'the trumpets of sedition began to fall silent'.[111] Daniel Defoe was of the same opinion, informing Robert Harley that the 'Ministers are quieter here now than before'.[112] However, the Church's Commission was not wholly satisfied, as several issues raised in its addresses had not been (and would not be) resolved.[113] By 14 January 1707, the Commission was contemplating preparing an additional address, as its second (8 November 1706) 'hade not had that

---

[109] See also D. J. Patrick and C. A. Whatley, 'Persistence, principle and patriotism in the making of the Union of 1707: The Revolution, Scottish Parliament and the *squadrone volante*', *History*, 92 (April, 2007), 184. The members of the much maligned *squadrone volante*, described by Carnwath as 'never scrupl[ing] to serve their own interest, though at their country's cost', were, in most instances, fully committed to the notion that a Presbyterian Scotland would form an integral part of a secure Protestant British state.

[110] *APS, Vol. IX*, 413–14.

[111] Duncan (ed.), *History of the Union of Scotland and England by Sir John Clerk of Penicuik*, 121.

[112] Healey (ed.), *Letters of Daniel Defoe*, 152.

[113] NAS, CH 1/4/2, 12 December 1706. The Commission sought clarification on the Privy Council or an alternative court for ecclesiastical causes; a resolution on the future method of planting Kirks; an explanation of the abjuration oath and sacramental test, (which 'by degrees [may] bring in corruption to this church'); and lastly some assurance over the royal supremacy, which was considered 'ane incroachment on the prerogative of the Lord Jesus Christ', that 'all possible security [would] be provided against the ressuming of it'.

success that might have been expected'. But, after discussion, a further address was deemed 'unnecessary and highlie inconvenient'.[114] There would be no third address until 16 January, when the Commission became aware that the English Parliament had been authorised to do all it considered expedient for the security of its own church, the Scottish Parliament agreeing to ratify beforehand whatever the English considered necessary.[115]

The Kirk's anxieties were not settled by the act of security, but it did guarantee Presbyterianism which was enough to appease the more negative elements within the established Church. This was a necessity required of Parliament. The act conciliated mainstream Church opposition by securing Presbyterianism. None the less, the act should not be seen as simply a matter of management and political expediency. For the majority of Scots MPs the act was also a matter of principle. Considering the number of commissioners who had sat in the Convention or King William's Parliament 1689–1702 (some 48 per cent of MPs in 1706–7) and their votes on the Treaty, it is apparent that Revolution politics had a greater impact on incorporating union than has been previously appreciated. Continuity was a factor in terms of both personnel and policy. The future of Scotland's Church was more than a passing concern for most members of Parliament; the Kirk was not only of interest to ministers and the mob. What shaped the Estates' response to the various representations of the Commission was a degree of pragmatism (a realisation that an additional act for the further security of the Church of Scotland was unavoidable) combined with no small measure of genuine conviction and commitment.

[114] *Ibid.*, 15 January 1707.
[115] NAS, CH 1/4/2, 16 January 1707. This was described as 'inconsistent with the principalls and engagements of [the] Church'.

The Scottish Historical Review, Volume LXXXVII: 2008 (Supplement), 116–134
DOI: 10.3366/E0036924108000516

ANDREW MACKILLOP

Chapter 7
A Union for Empire?
Scotland, the English East India
Company and the British Union

On 18 December 1707, in the first session of the newly created British Parliament, a customs bill received royal assent. Innocuously entitled an 'Act for better Securing the Duties of East India Goods', the legislation has never once merited attention in any of the major historical works on the Anglo-Scottish Union. It should do. For this act ensured that the monopoly of the English East India Company was extended across Scotland to encompass the whole of the new United Kingdom.[1] In this way a corporation of the City of London was confirmed in a set of privileges which enabled it, rather than private British subjects, to dominate trade in half of the emerging British empire.[2]

This act, and the neglect of the East Indies in the historiography of the union that it symbolises, is a useful starting point for a re-evaluation of the relationship between the British Union and British empire. Such a re-examination might seem unnecessary given the shift away from interpretations that link Scotland's acceptance of the treaty to the influence of England's overseas trade. Unlike the celebratory, pro-unionist tradition of writing that dominated the subject for much of the twentieth century, few if any historians now believe that Scotland exchanged its sovereignty for imperial prosperity.[3] The historiography of the 1960s and 1970s placed far greater emphasis on politics, with free trade relegated to a rhetorical device that facilitated the management of Parliament.[4] At the same time, a more nuanced understanding of the economics of union further undermined assumptions that the Scots had

---

[1] *Journals of the House of Commons, 25ᵗʰ October 1705 to 1ˢᵗ April 1708* (London, 1803), 451 & 474; *The Statues at Large from the Tenth Year of King William III to the End of the Reign of Queen Anne* (London, 1763), 268–9: 6 A. c 3.

[2] Holden Furber, *Rival Empires of Trade in the Orient, 1600–1800* (Oxford, 1976), 128; P. Lawson, *The East India Company: A History* (Harlow, 1993), 56.

[3] William Law Mathieson, *Scotland and the Union: A History of Scotland from 1695–1747* (Glasgow, 1905), 120–1, 146; P. Hume Brown, *The Legislative Union of England and Scotland* (Oxford, 1914), 87, 154–5; A. V. Dicey and R. S. Rait, *Thoughts on the Union between England and Scotland* (London, 1920), 136–7; G. S. Pryde, *The Treaty of Union of Scotland and England* (London, 1950), 75–9.

[4] William Ferguson, 'The making of the Treaty of Union of 1707', *Scottish Historical Review*, 43 (1964), 90–1; William Ferguson, *Scotland's Relations with England: A Survey to 1707* (Edinburgh, 1977), 181–5; P. W. J. Riley, *The Union of England & Scotland: A Study in Anglo-Scottish Politics of the Eighteenth Century* (Manchester, 1978), passim; P. H. Scott, *1707: The Union of Scotland and England* (Edinburgh, 1979), 27–8.

agreed to incorporation in return for access to the colonies. Scottish mercantile weakness formed the basis of this new interpretation. The loss of European markets and growing commercial dependence on England left the country with little option when in 1705–6 English politicians suddenly deemed union to be a necessity.[5]

The impact of these changing perspectives on the Union has been a marked reduction in the perceived importance of empire. This is reflected in the prevailing orthodoxy that, far from being attracted to colonial commerce, many Scots were fearful of free trade. The country in 1707 was simply not in a position to fully exploit imperial markets – either in the Americas or Asia. The most convincing assessment of the economic dimension of union is that the Scottish Parliament embraced the principle of free trade while seeking to protect a range of domestic manufacturers from English competition.[6] Even those who argue that the Empire was to become a formative influence on Scottish society accept that 'the imperial factor seems to have played little direct part in the union debates'.[7]

It is therefore unsurprising that little attention has been paid to the impact of the Asian sector of English imperialism on the Union. The only parts of the empire closely associated with the treaty were the Atlantic colonies. During the 1680s and early 1690s Scottish enterprise had prospered in North America and the West Indies, albeit illegally.[8] Pro-unionist arguments at the time stressed that if Union came to pass Scotland might again succeed in the Americas.[9] Yet this Atlantic emphasis, while understandable, has marginalised the role played by the Asia question in shaping the 1707 settlement. The East Indies appeared to impinge on the events of 1706–7 in one respect only. Article XV of the treaty gave Scotland an 'Equivalent' of £398,085 as compensation for, among other things, the dissolution of the Company of Scotland trading to Africa and the Indies.[10] A striking feature of the historiography of the Union is the lack of debate over this aspect of the treaty. It is as if, after Darien, the Company's demise can be taken

---

[5] T. C. Smout, *Scottish Trade on the Eve of Union, 1660–1707* (Edinburgh, 1963), 233–8, 249; T. C. Smout, 'The Anglo-Scottish Union of 1707, I: The economic background', *Economic History Review*, 16 (1964), 455–66.

[6] T. M. Devine, 'The Union of 1707 & Scottish development', *Scottish Economic & Social History*, 5 (1985), 27–8; Christopher A. Whatley, 'Economic causes and consequences of the Union of 1707: a survey', *Scottish Historical Review*, 68 (1989), 158–63; Christopher A. Whatley, *Bought and Sold for English Gold? Explaining the Union of 1707* (East Linton, 2001), 63–4, 69, 72–9, 162–4.

[7] T. M. Devine, *Scotland's Empire, 1600–1815* (London, 2003), 62.

[8] T. Keith, 'Scottish trade with the plantations before 1707', *Scottish Historical Review*, 6 (1909), 43–7.

[9] George Mackenzie [earl of Cromarty], *Parainesis Pacifica; or a Perswasive to the Union of Britain by a Person of Quality* (London, 1702), 7; W. Seton, *Scotland's Great Advantages by a Union with England: Shown in a Letter from the Country to a Member of Parliament* (Edinburgh, 1706), 7.

[10] *Statutes at Large from the Tenth Year of King William to the End of the Reign of Queen Anne*, 223–35: 5 A. c 8.

as a given.[11] By comparison, far greater attention has focused on the dispute over whether or not the Scots were bribed into the Union by means of the Equivalent.[12]

There is, however, much to be gained by integrating the East Indies trade into an analysis of the Anglo-Scottish treaty. Some of the least contentious aspects of the Union look significantly, and even radically, different when viewed from the eastern half of the empire. The English East India Company's defence of its monopoly of trade with Asia runs counter to the suggestion that England was driven solely by political concerns while the Scots were obsessed only with economics.[13] Commerce mattered to the East India Company, and its interests defined a key aspect of England's negotiating position. The role of the English company also complicates the idea of a direct, causal link between empire and the Union. Moving attention away from the principle of free trade established by article IV to the victory of the English company's monopoly in article XV, for example, highlights the treaty's considerable internal contradictions. Nowhere are these tensions more clearly evident than in the markedly different arrangements made for Britain's trade with the component parts of the Empire.

Highlighting the way in which the East Indies trade was to be conducted by the new United Kingdom challenges the historiography of the Union in other ways. While historians have attached importance to the survival of many of Scotland's civic institutions, the Company of Scotland was a conspicuous exception.[14] The Scottish political nation was either unwilling or unable to defend one of the kingdom's major corporate entities. Similarly, abandoning the aspiration to a free trade in the East Indies entailed the loss of a key principle of national sovereignty. While the political significance of compensation for Darien has rightly determined scholarly assessments of article XV, a greater effort is needed to understand what the Scottish company's dissolution reveals about the nature of the emerging British Union and empire.

It is important, too, to remember that the removal of Scotland's right to trade with Asia was at the behest of a 'general society' of

---

[11] A. Mackillop, 'Accessing empire: Scotland, Europe, Britain, and the Asia trade', 1695–c.1750', *Itinerario*, 23 (2005), 11–15; Michael Fry, *The Union: England, Scotland and the Treaty of 1707* (Edinburgh, 2006), 282–3; Douglas Watt, *The Price of Scotland: Darien, Union and the Wealth of Nations* (Edinburgh, 2007), 230–1; Karin Bowie, *Scottish Public Opinion and the Anglo-Scottish Union, 1699–1707* (Woodbridge, 2007), 97.

[12] *The Anatomy of an Equivalent, by the Marquess of Halifax, Adapted to the Equivalent in the Present Articles, 1706* (Edinburgh, 1706), 1–2; Pryde, *Treaty of Union*, 42; P. H. Scott, *Andrew Fletcher and the Treaty of Union* (Edinburgh, 1992), 158–61; John Stuart Shaw, *The Political History of Eighteenth-Century Scotland* (Basingstoke, 1999), 1–11; Whatley, *Bought and Sold for English Gold?*, 48–50; Scott, *1707*, 39–44; Christopher A. Whatley, *The Scots and the Union* (Edinburgh, 2006), 244.

[13] Smout, *Scottish Trade*, 275.

[14] Ferguson, *Scotland's Relations with England*, 237; Bruce P. Lenman, 'A client society: Scotland between the '15 and the '45', in Jeremy Black (ed.), *Britain in the Age of Walpole* (Basingstoke, 1984), 70–4.

London merchants and financiers.[15] The pre-1707 Scottish state is judged by some to have been a mere carapace for cliques of aristocrats, clergymen and burgh elites.[16] Yet the influence of the London monied interest in shaping the union suggests that the English state, for all its new 'fiscal-military' power, was susceptible to similar special pleading.[17] The English East India lobby ensured the Union settlement was a mixture of monopoly and free trade arrangements. Indeed, the principles underpinning British commerce with Asia directly challenge the orthodoxy that Scotland won a 'communication' of 'full freedom of trade and navigation' rights through union with England.[18]

Nor is it simply the specifics of the treaty that can be revised by paying greater attention to the East Indies. The English company's defence of its privileges underline the need for a greater awareness of the range of English institutions, other than the monarchy and Parliament, which defined the Anglo-Scottish Union.[19] And finally, the East Indies perspective highlights the profound differences in constitutional and commercial ethos that characterised the eastern and western halves of the empire.[20] 'Empire' can be a beguilingly simple concept, suggestive of a single, unified political and commercial arena made accessible to the Scots by virtue of article IV.[21] But by unpicking the multiple meanings of imperialism, as well as the variegated structure of England's colonial system, historians have shown the link between the Anglo-Scottish Union and empire to be far more problematical.[22] The structural and ideological diversity of England's pre-union imperialism raise serious questions about what kind of empire Scotland joined in 1707.

---

[15] *Statutes at Large from the Tenth Year of King William*, 724–40: 9–10 Wm. III, c. 44.

[16] K. M. Brown, *Kingdom or Province? Scotland and the Regal Union, 1603–1715* (Basingstoke, 1992), 33–59, 189–90; T. M. Devine, *The Scottish Nation, 1700–2000* (London, 1999), 12.

[17] John Brewer, *The Sinews of Power: War, Money and the English State, 1688–1783* (London, 1989), 29–69, 119–20; P. G. M. Dickson, *The Financial Revolution in England: A Study in the Development of Public Credit, 1688–1756* (London, 1967), 288–97.

[18] The phrase is taken from article IV, *Statutes at Large from the Tenth Year of King William*, 223–34.

[19] P. W. J. Riley, 'The Union of 1707 as an episode in English politics', *English Historical Review*, 84 (1969), 498–527; Geoffrey Holmes, *British Politics in the Age of Anne* (London, 1987), 84–92.

[20] P. J. Marshall, 'The eighteenth-century empire', in P. J. Marshall (ed.), '*A Free though Conquering People': Eighteenth-Century Britain and its Empire* (Aldershot, 2003), 181–2.

[21] Brian P. Levack, *The Formation of the British State: England, Scotland and the Union, 1603–1707* (Oxford, 1987), 138–42.

[22] Richard Koebner, *Empire* (Cambridge, 1965), 77–80; John Robertson, 'Empire and union: two concepts of the early modern European political order', in John Robertson (ed.), *A Union for Empire: Political Thought and the Union of 1707* (Cambridge, 1995), 3–6, 29–36; David Armitage, *The Ideological Origins of the British Empire* (Cambridge, 2000), 163–7.

I

As union re-emerged between 1702 and 1706 as a possible solution
to the crisis in Anglo-Scottish relations, the question of commercial
contact with Asia had a much greater significance than historians
have commonly allowed. John Clerk of Penicuik claimed that the
1702–3 negotiations had failed because the Scots would not give up the
Company of Scotland without sufficient compensation.[23] The theme of
recompense draws attention to the disaster at Darien rather than to the
issue of future Scottish trade with the East Indies. Yet the controversy
over the Company of Scotland which be-devilled the earlier set of
Anglo-Scottish talks was inextricably bound up with arguments over
the Company's post-union existence.[24] Scotland's ability to trade in the
East was all but non-existent. At stake was not the short-term desire
or capacity to profit from the Asia trades, but rather the country's
sovereign right to do so. Such thinking influenced the legislation passed
by the Scottish Parliament on 30 August 1703. The 'Act in Favor
of the Company tradeing to Africa and the Indies' confirmed the
corporation's privileges and authorised it to seek capital from foreign
sources.[25]

Parliamentary support for the Company of Scotland served two
purposes. First, by entrenching the Company's charter rights the
Scottish Parliament confirmed its value as a potential bargaining chip
in any further Anglo-Scottish negotiations. However, by 1703 any union
with England which would encompass free trade and thus the demise of
the Scottish company seemed a dim and distant prospect. So secondly,
the legislation was designed to encourage some limited trading by
subcontracting the Company's rights to interested parties with sufficient
finances.[26] The 1702–3 talks had, however, established the basis of a
possible compromise. For the Scottish commissioners conceded that if
England offered suitable compensation at a future date, the Company
of Scotland might be dissolved.[27]

The potential for just such an agreement emerged quickly during
the renewed Anglo-Scottish talks from April to July 1706. What had
changed since 1703 was the willingness of the English commissioners to
grant compensation for Darien. In stressing the Equivalent rather than
the issue of Scottish access to Asia within the new British framework,
historians have mirrored the pro-unionist arguments used at the
time. Both Clerk and William Seton of Pitmedden maintained that
the Scottish company had no long-term financial prospects; it was
bankrupt, its leadership was discredited, while ongoing English hostility

---

[23] D. Duncan (ed.), *History of the Union of Scotland and England by Sir John Clerk of Penicuik*
(Edinburgh, 1993), 83; Riley, *Union of England and Scotland*, 181–2.

[24] G. Ridpath, *A Discourse upon the Union of Scotland and England* (Edinburgh, 1702), 110.

[25] *The Acts of the Parliament of Scotland*, xi (Edinburgh, 1824), 77 & 109.

[26] Mackillop, 'Accessing empire', 11.

[27] James Hodges, *The Rights and Interests of the Two British Monarchies Inquired into and
Clear'd; with a Special Respect to a United or Separate State* (Edinburgh, 1703), 78.

stymied any hope of investment from abroad. More persuasive still was Clerk's contention that the Equivalent represented a tangible gain that would inject desperately needed capital into the domestic economy.[28]

The financial boon offered by the Equivalent is now widely acknowledged to have played a key role in securing the Union, if only because it persuaded the *squadrone* to support the court party.[29] But among contemporaries, article XV was never viewed purely in terms of the Equivalent. While the destruction of the Company of Scotland has drawn little comment by later historians, it sparked an intense debate at the time on the commercial principles that shaped the fifteenth article. The court party's response to the controversy was to formulate a political strategy which stressed that the Scottish Parliament could either take the Equivalent or keep the Company. The intention was to scare those wishing to debate the corporation's survival into accepting article XV or else risk losing one of the few practical concessions gained from the London negotiations.[30] This tactic was deployed by the Lord President of the Court of Session, Hew Dalrymple, during a series of meetings with Company directors and shareholders in late 1706. On 6 November, at one such stormy gathering attended by 46 stockholders, Dalrymple dismissed the possibility of debating the Scottish Company's long-term existence. When he was outvoted, the Lord President resorted to a tried and tested method of managerial politics; he proposed that a committee of senior politicians frame the petition to Parliament.[31]

Although the court party failed in its initial attempt to avoid any consideration of the Company of Scotland, subsequent developments seemed to vindicate Dalrymple's line of reasoning. Parliamentary consideration of article XV commenced on 7 December but was delayed by amendments to other parts of the treaty. After a further brief debate on 26 December, the article was approved four days later by 112 votes to 54, thereby ensuring the liquidation of the Company of Scotland.[32]

II

The healthy majority in support of article XV implied that the Scottish Parliament was determined to secure a realistic financial settlement

28 William Seton, *A Speech in the Parliament of Scotland. The Second Day of November 1706 on the first article of Union* (London, 1706), 4; John Clerk, *An Essay upon the XV Article of the Treaty of Union, Wherein the Difficulties that Arise upon the Equivalents, Are fully Cleared and Explained* (Edinburgh, 1706), 6.

29 G. Lockhart, *Memoirs concerning the Affairs of Scotland, from Queen Anne's Accession to the Throne, to the Commencement of the Union of the Two Kingdoms of Scotland and England, in May 1707* (London, 1714), 212–13; Scott, *Andrew Fletcher*, 158; Devine, *Scottish Nation*, 13; Whatley, *The Scots and the Union*, 16, 255–6, 298, 303, 330.

30 Historical Manuscripts Commission, [HMC], *The MSS of His Grace the Duke of Portland Preserved at Welbeck Abbey*, 10 vols (London, 1897), iv, 354–5.

31 Watt, *The Price of Scotland*, 230–1; Roderick Mackenzie, *A Full and Exact Account of the Proceedings of the Court of Directors and Council-General of the Company of Scotland Trading to Africa and the Indies, with relation to the Treaty of Union* (Edinburgh, 1706), 9–11.

32 *Acts of the Parliament of Scotland*, xi, 350–5, 369, 375–6.

from the treaty rather than concern itself with esoteric questions about a branch of trade that was beyond the country's commercial and financial resources. Yet the Company's destruction raised fundamental questions about the subordination of Scottish sovereignty to sectional English interests. In late 1706 opposition politicians sought to highlight the negative commercial (as opposed to venal) consequences of accepting the Equivalent. The opposition knew that it faced an up-hill struggle. As early as April 1706 Robert Blackwood, president of the Company's council, and Roderick Mackenzie, the Company's secretary, were alarmed that the precedent established during the 1702–3 negotiations would be uncritically adopted by the Scottish commissioners. Having been authorised to write to each commissioner asking them to defend the Company's existence as well as its financial affairs, they grew apprehensive at the lack of any response from London.[33] The fear grew that the commissioners were not prepared to stand their ground and protect the Company's post-union existence.[34]

In the event, this is exactly what happened. Much like the proposals for a federal union, the Scottish representatives made only a token effort to discuss the Company of Scotland's status.[35] On 9 May the Scots suggested that the Company be kept intact: crucially, however, they added that if this was 'inconvenient for the trade of the rest of the United Kingdom... the private rights of the said Company of Scotland shall be purchased from the proprietors.' Scottish historians have interpreted the Equivalent as compensation for Darien. There has, however, been little thought given as to how the sum was viewed south of the border. To English eyes the Equivalent did not constitute an acceptance of any liability for events in Central America. Rather, it was a financial transaction whereby the Westminster Parliament, acting on behalf of the English East India lobby, purchased Scotland's theoretical right to trade with Asia. Having been handed exactly what they wanted, the English commissioners had the decency to go through a period of apparent reflection before, on 25 June, deciding that the 'continuance of that Company is inconsistent with the good of trade in the United Kingdom.'[36]

When the provisional articles were published in October 1706, in preparation for debate in the Scottish Parliament, there was a reaction against the perceived abandonment of the Company of Scotland. It was at this point that elements of the corporation's directorate and shareholders fought to have a petition for its survival presented to Parliament. The objections raised on behalf of the Company at this

[33] Huntington Library, Pasadena, California, [HL], Loudoun (Scottish) Collection, LO7171: 20 April 1706, Sir Robert Blackwood to Hugh Campbell, earl of Loudoun; Mackenzie, *A Full and Exact Account*, 9.
[34] Mackenzie, *A Full and Exact Account*, 36.
[35] Whatley, *The Scots and the Union*, 252.
[36] *The Articles of the Treaty for a Union between England and Scotland, agreed on by the Commissioners of both Kingdoms* (London, 1707), 45–6, 49.

crucial juncture have never been fully integrated into assessments of the commercial benefits of union. As was the case with Scottish society in general, opinion within the Company was deeply divided. Understandably, many shareholders felt that the arguments of Clerk, Seton and the lord president were the only realistic way forward; they simply wanted their money back.[37]

There were also political considerations at work which hampered a strong defence of the corporation. Numerous shareholders and parliamentarians felt that the Company had been badly treated by English interests and the negligent indifference of the Scottish commissioners; however, they also feared that Jacobites would use the controversy to their own ends.[38] The corporation could not be left, Clerk argued, 'to serve for a little nurcerie of dissension between us and our neighbours'.[39] Given that Jacobites like William Keith, ninth earl Marischal, were at the forefront of demands for the Company's retention, these political anxieties had some basis in fact.[40]

Others, however, argued that the proposed arrangements for the East Indies trade were unfair both in practice and in principle. In response to court party claims that the Equivalent was a well-negotiated windfall, the Company's petition of 27 November argued that the interest on Company stock was only 5% – while government repayments to English Company shareholders ran at 8%. Attention was also drawn to the fact that the interest rate on the remainder of the Equivalent was 6%.[41] The most damning objection was that Scotland was destroying its own East India Company, and with it any hope of direct involvement in the East Indies trade, while paying England for the privilege.[42] Furthermore, any compensation for Company stock would dissipate rapidly through increases in taxation. Unlike the later historiography, many of these contemporary objections to the Equivalent did not dwell on the issue of bribery; the key criticism was that the commissioners had sold the Company cheap. As one sarcastic commentator noted, it 'may seem to some, a very odd Equivalent'.[43]

No one at the time, or since, doubted the importance of article XV and the Equivalent.[44] What has slipped out of historical analysis is the fact that much of the controversy was not just about whether the Equivalent was a good or bad financial bargain. A powerful criticism of the fifteenth article was that the Scots were not gaining full free

---

[37] HMC, *Portland MSS*, (London, 1907), viii, 275; Mackenzie, *A Full and Exact Account*, 36.

[38] Whatley, *The Scots and the Union*, 305–6.

[39] Clerk, *An Essay upon the XV Article*, 20.

[40] Mackenzie, *A Full and Exact Account*, 26; Clerk, *An Essay upon the XV Article*, 20.

[41] Anon. *An Essay upon the Equivalent, in a Letter to a Friend* (Edinburgh, 1706), 5; Mackenzie, *A Full and Exact Account*, 28.

[42] Riley, *Union of England and Scotland*, 187–8.

[43] Anon., *An Essay upon the Equivalent*, 7.

[44] Lockhart, *Memoirs*, 212–13; Duncan, *History of the Union of Scotland*, 148; Clerk, *An Essay upon the XV Article*, 3; HMC, *Portland MSS*, viii, 274–5.

trade rights to the empire. Its provisions were understood to constitute a negative parallel to article IV. It is this facet of the debate over the Company's existence that casts new light on the clear limits to the free trade liberties seemingly granted to the Scots by the famous fourth article. Few of those espousing the Company's rights were arguing that the country was in a position to profit immediately from the Asia trades. The point at issue was the creation of a level playing field where Scotland's potential overseas trade – which should in theory have increased rapidly in the aftermath of the Union – would not be subordinated to England's powerful mercantile lobby.[45]

Contemporaries grasped the fact that key provisions within the fifteenth article represented the English East India Company's imprint upon the proposed settlement. This may seem surprising given that the English Company is never once mentioned in the treaty. But the English corporation's conspicuous absence did not denote a lack of influence; rather, the opposite in fact. Again and again when the fifteenth article was debated so, too, was the role of the English East India Company.[46] Defoe openly accepted that the Company of Scotland was to be dissolved because there were 'companies in England already embarked on that trade'.[47] The obvious parallel is the subordination of Scotland's struggling woollen industry to England's wool lobby.[48] Less well appreciated is the fact that a similar process occurred in relation to the maritime empire in Asia.

John Murray, first duke of Atholl, sought to exploit the idea that the Equivalent was a perverse bargain whereby Scotland taxed itself in return for liquidating its only means of direct access to a crucial sphere of world trade. On 23 October 1706 he argued that the English Company should be made to pay the Equivalent due to the Darien investors.[49] Even after the implementation of the Union, Scottish and English MPs persisted in their calls for the English East India interest rather than the British taxpayer to pay the Equivalent.[50]

Article XV undoubtedly provided recompense for Darien; but the *quid pro quo* was an entrenchment of English mercantile privilege. The treaty of Union thus promoted monopoly and protectionism on both sides of the border, and not just in Scotland. The concessions that

---

[45] Hodges, *The Rights and Interests of the two British Monarchies*, 78 and 87. For the influx of 'old' and 'new' East India Company influence into the English Commons in 1700, see, Robert Walcott, 'The East India Interest in the General Election of 1700–1701', *English Historical Review*, 71 (1956), pp. 238–7.

[46] Anon. *A Letter Concerning the Consequences of an Incorporating Union in Relation to Trade* (Edinburgh, 1706), 18; William Black. *Answer to a letter concerning trade, sent from several Scots gentlemen, that are merchants in England, to their countrymen that are merchants in . . .* (Edinburgh, 1706), p. 6; Lockhart, *Memoirs*, 244; HMC, *Portland MSS*, viii, 271.

[47] D. Defoe, *An Enquiry into the Disposal of the Equivalent* (Edinburgh, 1706), 2.

[48] Whatley, *The Scots and the Union*, 124, 160, 335, 337.

[49] HMC, *Portland MSS*, viii, 254–5.

[50] Anon., *Reasons why the East-India Company Ought to Pay the Equivalent Agreed to be Paid the Scots Company by the Articles of Union* (London, 1708), 1–4.

shielded Scottish salt, coal, paper and malt producers from English competition are rightly seen to have eased the legislation through the Scottish Parliament.[51] What has not been sufficiently acknowledged is the other side of the protectionist coin, and in particular the easy success with which English economic interests guaranteed their rights and liberties within the British union and empire. The real difference between the defence of commercial privilege north and south of the border lay in the incomparably greater mercantile monopoly secured by the English East India Company. These rights did, after all, encompass England's commercial empire in Asia and a rapidly expanding import trade worth £775,000 per annum.[52]

The scale of the English company's victory was captured brilliantly by the Company of Scotland's intended submission to Parliament, drafted on 13 November. It held that article XV constituted the easy surrender of key national rights and gifted one half of Britain's world trade to a group of London merchants. It proclaimed:

> ... that upon the supposition of our Company being so dissolved the whole nation is thereby barred from trading whereby beyond the Cape of Good Hope; that vast trade being already, by Act of Parliament in England, circumscribed for perpetuity to the English East India Company... [and] considering the great power and interest of that Company ... it is hard to tell, when, if ever, that trade shall be open to the rest of Britain.[53]

This is a radically different image of the commercial benefits of union when compared to the usual emphasis on article IV and free trade. Far from creating a genuinely 'British' empire, the treaty cemented a neo-English commercial system in Asia. In a pro-union pamphlet, London-Scots merchants openly proposed that Scotland should concentrate on the export of its domestic product. They asserted the primacy of the English Company's interests over any attempt by Scotland to involve itself in the East Indies trade; the trafficking of highly profitable luxuries was best left in the hands of the metropole's commercial elite.[54] It is hardly surprising that resistance to the economic and commercial implications of article XV was intense and prolonged. Having defied the court party over the question of a petition, Company of Scotland shareholders met again on 20 November to consider the draft submission to Parliament. Lord President Dalrymple had failed during the interim committee

---

[51] Whatley, *Bought and Sold for English Gold?*, 74–7; Whatley, *The Scots and the Union*, 307–11.

[52] J. M. Price, 'The imperial economy', in Marshall (ed.), *Oxford History of the British Empire, II*, 101; K. N. Chaudhuri, *The Trading World of Asia and the English East India Company, 1660–1760* (Cambridge, 1978), pp. 13–14, 43–4.

[53] Mackenzie, *A Full and Exact Account*, 20.

[54] *A letter concerning trade, from several Scots-gentlemen that are merchants in England, to their country-men that are merchants in Scotland* (Edinburgh, 1706), pp. 8–9.

stage to prevent the address from broaching the matter of the Company's survival. The shareholders' draft petition now envisaged the corporation as an extension of Scottish sovereignty; its dissolution was described as the destruction of 'a national constitution'.[55] The amalgam of national grievance and commercial frustration gave the draft petition of 13 November a raw, indignant tone. Its opening statement proclaimed that 'our Company is invested with as legal a right to subsist as any Company or corporation in Great Britain'.[56]

Dalrymple was incandescent over the draft petition, fearing that its aggressive rhetoric would endanger the principle of compensation enshrined in the Equivalent. He asked for a shareholders' vote to amend the petition's language and the order of priority given to the Company's grievances. The draft document's six major complaints were initially headed by demands that the Company of Scotland be retained after the union. The adroit management skills of the Lord President now began to pay dividends among the committee members who finalised the petition on 22 and 23 November. They produced an entirely new running order of clauses that placed the Equivalent first and a watered-down plea for the Company's survival as the last of the six requests. This radically amended petition was finally approved at a meeting of shareholders on 27 November, although only by a margin of one vote.[57] That the controversy over the Company of Scotland's destruction produced one of the closest results of any political debate sparked by the Union underscores the significance of the East Indies question. Nor should the fact that this narrowest of court party victories occurred at a shareholder's meeting, rather than in Parliament, detract from its importance. The finalised petition was far less militant and undermined any realistic hope that Parliament might move to protect the corporation.

Never the less, opposition to the Company's dissolution persisted. When the delayed vote on article XV came before the Scottish estates on the penultimate day of 1706, a motion was put that the Company could not be dissolved without the full authority of its shareholders. It was, the opposition argued, a matter of property upon which Parliament was bound to consult those concerned. Earlier in October, William Johnstone, first marquis of Annandale, had advanced the same argument but had received only derisory support. By December, however, the political climate had changed. The motion to maintain the Company was lost by 111 votes to 72, a significantly closer margin than the later vote on the same day which finally secured article XV.[58]

55 W. Douglas Jones, 'The Bold Adventurers': a quantitative analysis of the Darien subscription list (1696)', *Scottish Economic and Social History*, 21 (2001), 22; G. Ridpath, *Scotland's Grievances relating to Darien* (Edinburgh, 1700), 15; Mackenzie, *A Full and Exact Account*, 37.

56 Mackenzie, *A Full and Exact Account*, 19.

57 HMC, *Report on the MSS of the Earl of Mar and Kellie* (London, 1904), 336. The two petitions can be compared at Mackenzie, *A Full and Exact Account*, 16–22 & 28–31.

58 HMC, *Portland MSS*, viii, 254–5; *Acts of the Parliament of Scotland*, xi, 369 & 372.

If this division is compared with other important aspects of the treaty, the strength of feeling over the Company's liquidation becomes clear. On 4 November 1706 article I, which enshrined the Union of the two kingdoms, was approved by 116 to 83 – a majority of 33. The attempt on 30 December to debate the Company of Scotland's future was lost by a similar margin of 39 votes.[59]

John Erskine, sixth earl of Mar, was well aware of what was at stake during these debates. He believed that if the question of the Company's retention were left in the hands of the shareholders it 'wou'd indeed be ane effectual stop of the Union'. His relief at the final outcome was clear. Writing to Sir David Nairne on 31 December, after the vote on the fifteenth article, he noted:

> There was a great struggle made against the Company being taken away without first hearing from the proprietors, but the article was approved by a great majoritie, and the oppoasers were so kine on the standing of the Company that they forgot to debeat on the rest of the article.[60]

The effort to protect the Company of Scotland, and with it any prospect that the country might in the future trade to the East Indies, had been one of the defining aspects of the intense controversy over article XV.

The parliamentary opposition did manage one significant amendment to the article. Known in contemporary parlance as 'explanations', the modifications made to the provisional treaty by the Scottish Parliament have been increasingly emphasised by historians of the Union. No longer dismissed as the symbolic posturing of a doomed institution, the explanations constituted an important adjustment of the settlement to better suit political and economic realities in Scotland.[61] One of the least studied explanations was the clause added to article XV regarding the Equivalent. It stated that:

> if the said Stock and Interest shall not be paid in twelve months after the Commencement of the Union, that then the said Company [of Scotland] may from thence forward trade, or give Licence to trade, until the said whole capital ... be paid.[62]

The prospect of a reconstituted Scottish company granting licenses for freelance enterprise to Asia was supposed to guarantee that the largest single financial aspect of the Union was honoured.

III

The controversy over the Company of Scotland was intense enough to force the proponents of union into reassurances that Scots would still

---

[59] *Acts of the Parliament of Scotland*, xi, 372 & 374.
[60] HMC, *Mar and Kellie*, 364–5.
[61] Riley, *Union of Scotland and England*, 290–1; Whatley, *The Scots and the Union*, 307–8.
[62] *Acts of the Parliament of Scotland*, xi, 372.

benefit from the East Indies trade once the treaty took effect. Defoe and
Clerk refuted the charge that 'to capitulate to the English companies
would be a national disgrace' by emphasising that:

> at present we Scots are barred from them as foreigners, but from the
> date of the Union nothing stops us from joining them, since all British
> companies will be open to Scots as to English.[63]

Both writers were either mendacious or were in manifest ignorance of
how the English Company functioned. Since the charter of 1698 the
'new' English East India Company was open to 'all and every person,
natives and foreigners' who had £100 to invest.[64] In other words,
although the Union conceded free trade in the English Atlantic, the
treaty gave absolutely no concessions in relation to Asia that the Scots
did not already possess.

The court party's ill-informed efforts to talk up the opportunities
in Asia afforded by union show that it was not only anti-unionists who
peddled unrealistic economic solutions to Scotland's ills.[65] Some of the
court party's arguments were not only weak – they were deliberately
misleading. The lord president's assertion in November 1706 that the
monopoly of the English company would only last another five years
was dismissed out of hand as blatant political misrepresentation. The
Company of Scotland shareholders who angrily opposed Dalrymple
were perfectly aware of the East India lobby's influence; indeed, the
English Company's monopoly survived for another 107 years until
1813.[66]

In contrast to the court managers' dubious proclamations, some
of those espousing the Scottish Company's continuation had a sound
understanding of the disadvantages for Scotland inherent in the
proposed structure of Britain's East Indies trade. Many feared that
the financial and mercantile dynasties of the City of London which
controlled England's East India trade would stem any meaningful
Scottish involvement in the Company's affairs. Equally worrying was
the realisation that Scotland would remain completely dependent on
London for its imports of Asian commodities. East Indian textiles alone
cost Scottish consumers £18,000 per annum, and were a major cause
of the kingdom's balance of payment deficits.[67] Pamphlets opposing
the Union posited that a direct trade with the East, however difficult,

---

[63] Duncan, *History of the Union*, 153–4; Defoe, *An Enquiry into the Disposal of the Equivalent*, 2.

[64] *Statutes at Large from the Tenth Year of King William*, p. 730: 9–10 Wm. III, c. 44, Articles 48–9.

[65] Smout, *Scottish Trade*, 167–8, 268.

[66] Mackenzie, *A Full and Exact Account*, 11; A. Webster, 'The political economy of trade liberalization: the East India Company Charter Act of 1813', *Economic History Review*, 2nd series, 43 (1990), 404–19.

[67] Black, *Answer to a letter concerning trade, sent from several Scots gentlemen, that are merchants in England*, pp. 6–7; Smout, *Scottish Trade*, 267–8; Whatley, *The Scots and the Union*, 194.

would reduce Scotland's politically and morally damaging reliance on London. If this mercantile connection were not established, any short-term benefits arising from the Equivalent would be dwarfed by decades of spending on metropolitan luxuries.[68]

There were also positive reasons for espousing the Company of Scotland's survival within the new British settlement. It was widely known that England's Asia trade was in the process of fundamental reconstruction as the 'old' and 'new' English East India companies finalised a complex process of corporate unification. It seemed the ideal time to realign the Company of Scotland in a new and radical way. Roderick Mackenzie and Robert Blackwood both felt that the Scottish commissioners should make full use of the sudden English enthusiasm for union by arguing for a genuinely British East India Company. This would be possible by amalgamating the purely nominal stock of the Scots Company (£400,000) with that of the two English corporations. In this way, a small-scale trade with Asia might still be possible out of Leith and Glasgow.[69]

The Company of Scotland's chronic state of bankruptcy is such a well-known aspect of the 1707 Union that it is tempting to dismiss these ideas as yet another example of anti-unionists indulging in fantasy economics. But it is important that Blackwood and Mackenzie's ideas receive proper attention. There is evidence to suggest that their proposals for re-establishing the Company of Scotland's liquidity were not entirely unrealistic. Given the right conditions, the Company's stock could and did become attractive again. The moment the Equivalent was announced, the shares jumped in value.[70] It was of course the grant of £219,000 from Westminster that made the previously worthless stock suddenly valuable again. The importance of Blackwood and Mackenzie's ideas lie in the fact that they proposed an entirely different kind of Equivalent to re-float the Company. Instead of a politically motivated state-subsidy from the English Parliament, they envisaged a 'commercial' Equivalent, supplied by venture capitalists seeking a legitimate avenue of trade to Asia. Subsequent events lend support to the proposition that a political settlement of Anglo-Scottish differences which left the Company of Scotland intact, might have drawn large reserves of enterprise capital north of the border. In the months immediately prior to the Union several hundred thousand pounds was invested by London Scots and their associates in the Leith wine trade. Taking advantage of pre-Union Scotland's lower rate of customs to

---

[68] P. Abercromby, *The Advantages of the Act of Security Compar'd with these of the Intended Union* (Edinburgh, 1706), p. 3; Anon., A *Letter Concerning the Consequences of an Incorporating Union*, 8.

[69] Lockhart, *Memoirs*, 246; Mackenzie, *A Full and Exact Account*, 7 & 38; Mackillop, 'Accessing empire', 13.

[70] Whatley, *The Scots and the Union*, 313.

stockpile wine for the London market, the rush of activity was such that in April 1707 over fifty ships arrived in the Forth.[71]

Along with Mackenzie, Blackwood and the commentator John Bannatyne, a number of London-Scots hoped that the Scottish company would survive, if only to licence independent trading ventures to the East. In 1703 and in early 1707, John Drummond of Quarrel, a London merchant, and Robert Douglas, later twelfth earl of Morton, were ready to invest in East India voyages from Scotland, should the political climate prove favourable.[72] It is surely telling that in the 1710s and again in the 1730s large amounts of capital, drawn from London and across Europe, poured into Ostend and Gothenburg the moment these ports gained an officially sanctioned East India Company.[73] The 1707 union was a real missed opportunity to use the Company of Scotland to generate exactly the sort of capital inflow which later transformed these two European ports. It was this potential transfer of venture finance from London to a Scottish-based East Indies trade that the English Company was determined to prevent. Highlighting the Company of Scotland's post-Union potential is neither to deny its wretched financial state nor the understandable attitude of the shareholders who preferred the immediate security of the 'political' Equivalent. Equally, however, historians of the Union need to ask why, if the Scottish Company were such an irredeemable economic failure, did the English East India Company mark it out for non-negotiable destruction?

In the event, of course, the idea for a commercially motivated Equivalent never received serious consideration. The English East India interest was simply far too powerful. Indeed, if article XV defined the eastern half of the new British empire it also reflected the central importance of the East India Company within the English fiscal-military state.[74] It is remarkable that assessments of the Anglo-Scottish Union have never acknowledged the fact that England's two East India companies were amalgamating at precisely the same moment as the Union. Known to contemporaries as the 'old' and 'new' East India companies, England's competing firms began a complex merger in 1702.[75] Although the processes of corporate and national unification

---

[71] HL, Stowe Collection, ST 57/vol. 1, pp. 84, 94–6, 110; ST 58/vol. 1, p. 150; Whatley, *The Scots and the Union*, 313.

[72] John Bannatyne *Some queries proposed to consideration, relative to the union now intended* (Edinburgh, 1706), p. 3; Mackillop, 'Accessing empire', 11; Watt, *The Price of Scotland*, 216.

[73] Furber, *Rival Empires*, 217–22; J. Parmentier, 'Irish mercantile builders in Ostend, 1690–1790', in T. O' Connor and M. A. Lyons (eds), *Irish Communities in Early-Modern Europe* (Dublin, 2006), 367–78; S.T. Kjellberg, *Svenska Ostindiska Compagnierna, 1731–1813* (Malmö, 1974), 311–13.

[74] Holmes, *British Politics in the Age of Anne*, 153–4; Michael J. Braddick, *The Nerves of State: Taxation and the Financing of the English State, 1558–1714* (Manchester, 1996), 43–4.

[75] Oriental & India Office Collections, British Library [OIOC], B/43, p. 228; B/45, pp. 149–50, 169; Lawson, *The East India Company*, 54–6.

have never been compared, the parallels are striking. Not only did Sidney Godolphin, first earl of Godolphin, manage key aspects of the British Union, but he also arbitrated the fusion of two of England's greatest chartered companies. After a number of disagreements over capital assets, the two sets of company directors finalised a working agreement on 23 September 1706, barely a couple of weeks before the Scottish Parliament met to debate the Union.[76] In language that mirrored exactly the rhetoric of the Anglo-Scottish settlement, a 1708 act of Parliament authorised 'a speedy and compleat union' of the two companies, to take effect from March 1709.[77]

Major issues of political union and company amalgamation were thus debated and implemented within English society in ways that had little or nothing to do with the crisis in Anglo-Scottish relations.[78] Indeed, Union was already a reality in England by September 1706, a development which calls into question the idea that the Scots were far more pro-unionist than their sceptical and unenthusiastic southern neighbours.[79] While the Scots had certainly developed a distinctive tradition of unionism during the seventeenth century, the merger of the English companies shows that political culture south of the border had evolved its own powerful ideology of union.[80] Set against this growing interest in unifying its own bickering civic institutions, England's acceptance of a unionist solution to its Scottish problems suddenly seems far less dramatic or unprecedented.

To the mercantile and financial elites of London's East India lobby, the union of companies mattered as much as, if not more than, the union of nations. In the minutes of the old and new East India companies the British union does not warrant a single comment.[81] The only indication that the directors engaged with wider constitutional developments was their decision in 1706 to halt legal proceedings against the owners of the *Annandale*, one of the last ships freighted under the Company of Scotland's charter. The English company's resolution in January 1704 to seize the vessel had driven anti-English sentiment in Scotland to new heights and resulted in the judicial

---

[76] OIOC, B/46, p. 145; HMC, *MSS of J.B. Fortescue*, 10 vols (London, 1892), i, 28–30; HL, Stowe Collection, ST 57/vol. 1, p. 151.

[77] *Statutes at Large from the Tenth Year of King William*, 291–7, 6 Anne c. 17.

[78] Defoe wrote in 1704 of the need for a 'General Union of Protestants in this [English] Nation' to lessen tensions between English dissenters and the established Anglican church. Daniel Defoe, *The shortest way to peace and union, by the author of the True Born Englishman* (London, 1704), pp. 4 & 8.

[79] Roger A. Mason, 'Introduction', in Roger A. Mason (ed.), *Scotland and England, 1286–1815* (Edinburgh, 1987), 4; T. C. Smout, 'Introduction', in T. C. Smout (ed.), *Anglo-Scottish Relations from 1603–1900* (Oxford, 2005), 3.

[80] P. Auber, *An Analysis of the Constitution of the East India Company* (London, 1826), x–xi, 720; John Toland, *Propositions for Uniting the Two East-India Companies: in a Letter to a Man of Quality,...* (London, 1701), 1–10; E. Settle, *Carmen Irenicum. The Happy Union of the Two East-India Companies. An Heroick Poem* (London, 1702), 1–11.

[81] The relevant directors' minutes for the old and new companies are covered by OIOC, B/45–48.

murder of an English merchant captain and several of his crew.[82] By the beginning of 1706 it was common knowledge in London that the provisional articles of Anglo-Scottish union would be negotiated over the spring and summer. In order to avoid further inflaming national animosities at this delicate stage the directors delayed the legal case against the *Annandale*. But the English East India Company's willingness to pander to aggrieved sentiment north of the border was limited. On 14 August 1706, once the provisional treaty was agreed, but well before the Scottish Parliament had met to debate the articles, the directors ordered that the case be prosecuted. Defence of the Company's monopoly was far more important than smoothing the passage of the British union.[83]

The successful implementation of the 1707 agreement did not end the anger felt among certain Scots at the ease with which the English company had successfully defended its commercial monopoly. Once they arrived at the Westminster Parliament Scots continued to oppose the Asian dimension of the British Union. When the 'Act for better Securing the Duties of East India Goods' came before the Commons on 11 December 1707, Scottish and Tory MPs sought to revisit the new constitutional settlement and in the process to embarrass the incumbent administration. It was proposed that Parliament refuse to 'give unto the English East India Company any right of privilege of trade within that part of Great Britain called Scotland'. The motion also called for alternatives to the established monopoly, and insisted that the Commons 'otherwise dispose of the trade of the East Indies within that part of Great Britain called Scotland'. Remarkably, this amendment, which would have had fundamental implications for the future structure of the new British empire, was defeated by only seven votes.[84]

Such opposition notwithstanding, the British Union heralded a major retrenchment of monopolistic privilege. In March 1709 the union of the old and new English companies finally came to pass. The new corporation's name and nature raises serious questions over the extent to which the Anglo-Scottish settlement inaugurated a truly British empire. Despite the treaty's creation of a new United Kingdom twenty months earlier, the 1709 organisation was formally titled as 'The United Company of Merchants of England trading to the East Indies' – a name it would retain until 1858.[85] The name betrays the fact that in its constitutional and structural ethos England's empire in the East was renewed after the Union.[86] The fears that had been

[82] OIOC, B/47, pp. 250–1; G. P. Insh, *The Company of Scotland Trading to Africa and the Indies* (London, 1932), 283–5.

[83] OIOC, B/47, p. 234; B/48, p. 284; Graham, *A Maritime History of Scotland*, 95–6.

[84] *Statutes at Large from the Tenth Year of King William*, 268–9; *Journal of the House of Commons, 25th October 1705 to 1st April 1708*, 461.

[85] *Statutes at Large from the Tenth Year of King William*, 291–7: 6 Anne c. 17, Article 13.

[86] The pronounced 'English' ethos of the corporation is captured on the crest of the United Company, shown on the map of the East Indies in Herman Moll's, *The World*

voiced by Company of Scotland shareholders that Scots would struggle to penetrate the charmed circle of East India interests in London now proved remarkably prescient. The English company's records show that of the 547 merchants and factors appointed to its bases in Asia between 1700 and 1730, only 17 were Scots.[87] It would take until the 1760s, over half a century after the union, before the Scots secured a meaningful share of East India employment and profits.[88]

IV

Focusing upon the eastern half of the British empire offers a number of fresh perspectives on the Anglo-Scottish Union. In particular, it delineates more clearly the precise structure of English commercial interests and the significant role these played in shaping the final Union settlement. Among Scottish historians the treaty is generally understood in terms of diverse political, social and economic groupings moving to secure their own privileges and liberties. As is well known, the Scottish aristocracy retained control of the landed economy and the legal system required to regulate its social and commercial systems of production. The Kirk, the lawyers, the burghs, the universities, and a number of other specialised economic constituents also managed to guard their particular interests.

Yet when they deal with England, historians of Scotland tend to generalise and summarise the kingdom's political priorities as if the country were one undifferentiated monolith. England was certainly more centralised than Scotland. But the southern kingdom was nonetheless still a pre-modern society made up of a complex mosaic of social groupings and corporations, ranging from the Church of England, the guilds of London, the civic and commercial orders of the provincial towns, to financial giants like the United English East India Company.[89] If it is possible for historians to be sensitive to Scotland's internal intricacies, should there not be an equal regard for England's heterogeneity? A heightened awareness of early eighteenth-century England's internal complexity, and how this diversity shaped the 1707 settlement, is one significant lesson to be learnt by placing the East Indies question at the centre of historical study of the Union.

---

[86] (Continued) Described or, a New and Correct Sett of Maps: Shewing the Several Empires, Kingdoms, Republics . . . in All the Known Parts of the Earth (London, 1709–20).

[87] OIOC, B/43-B/60.

[88] G. J. Bryant, 'Scots in India in the eighteenth century', Scottish Historical Review, 64 (1985), 22–41; J. Riddy, 'Warren Hastings: Scotland's benefactor?', in G. Carnall and C. Nicolson (eds.), The Impeachment of Warren Hastings (Edinburgh, 1989), 30–57; A. Mackillop, 'Europeans, Britons and Scots: Scottish sojourning networks and identities in Asia, c. 1700–1815', in A. McCarthy (ed.), A Global Clan: Scottish Migrant Networks and Identities since the Eighteenth Century (London, 2006), 19–47.

[89] Keith Wrightson, English Society, 1580–1680 (London, 1990), 18–44, 150–5; Phil Withington, The Politics of Commonwealth: Citizens and Freemen in Early Modern England (Cambridge, 2005), 16–48.

Finally, the creation in 1709 of an explicitly 'English' institution as the controlling mechanism for the eastern half of the empire highlights the neglected theme of ongoing English, as opposed to Scottish, distinctiveness within the British Union. There are implications, too, for the empire's impact on Britishness. If the emphasis in historical scholarship is now upon the extent to which the treaty did not fully assimilate Scotland to England, the empire is generally believed to have exerted a major centripetal influence. The domestic Anglo-Scottish Union may have been partial, messy and even contradictory, but the empire is usually held to have been genuinely British in its manpower, its trade, profits and ideologies.[90]

Yet the distinctive structure of the British eastern empire calls this well-established orthodoxy into question. The later decades of the eighteenth century did, eventually, produce an English East India Company replete with Scots, just as Clerk and Defoe predicted. But highlighting the undoubted success of Scots after the 1750s risks underestimating the extent to which the Union failed initially to open up all of England's colonial commerce. Precisely because the incorporation of their monarchy and Parliament forced the Scots to accept English preponderance within the domestic union, the empire came to seen within later eighteenth-century Scotland as a more equitable arena, indeed, as a form of compensation.[91] Yet in the eastern half of the empire, Scots faced a situation where even this semblance of equality was stripped away. Scots participated in the Asian empire as employees of an English corporation, not as Britons. As honorary Englishmen they had no more, or less, formal rights than Irishmen or any other European who acquired an East India Company post. It may not have mattered in material terms that Scotland did not trade directly and autonomously with Asia – she had not done so in the past. The political realism exhibited by the Scottish Parliament at the time of union ensured that the East Indies were never a significant commercial priority. But such pragmatic economic conservatism should not disguise the victory of the English East India Company. The inconsistent ways in which the union reshaped the empire sent a series of mixed messages to the Scots: on the one hand, the treaty opened up the Atlantic economic system while, on the other, it consolidated a neo-English commercial empire in the East. If viewed from the East Indies, the Anglo-Scottish settlement was not an event which inaugurated a uniformly British empire. It was a partial and contradictory union that gave the Scots unrestricted and automatic access to only half an empire.

---

90 David Allan, *Scotland in the Eighteenth Century* (London, 2002), 164–85; Devine, *Scottish Empire*, xxv–xxvi; J. M. Mackenzie, 'Empire and national identities: The case of Scotland', *Transactions of the Royal Historical Society*, sixth series, 8 (1998), 217.

91 John Knox, *A View of the British Empire, more especially Scotland; with some Proposals for the Improvement of that Country, the Extension of its Fisheries* (London, 1784), xliii.

Index